W9-CRK-765

The Young Douglas Hyde

Dominic Daly

THE YOUNG DOUGLAS HYDE

The Dawn of
the Irish Revolution and Renaissance
1874-1893

Foreword by Erskine Childers
President of Ireland

IRISH UNIVERSITY PRESS

© 1974 Dominic Daly

ISBN 0 7165 2205 5

Published by Irish University Press Ltd.
81 Merrion Square, Dublin 2

Printed in the Republic of Ireland
by Cahill & Co. Limited, Dublin

Contents

Foreword

Dubhglas de hÍde, Douglas Hyde, more familiarly called 'An Craoibhín Aoibhinn', was the first to bear the title Uachtarán na hÉireann, President of Ireland, chosen by agreement as the first guardian of the Constitution and, in that office, the first occupant of Áras an Uachtaráin. Eighty years ago, he became the first President of the Gaelic League, the movement which inspired and gave strength to the effort through which Irish nationality survived, Irish industries were founded and Irish independence and statehood grew. He has been called the founder of the Gaelic League, an appellation the real founders did not begrudge him, for he was its precursor, the philosopher and herald who gave this great cultural movement its infant nourishment and growth vitality, its leadership.

His memory has other claims on our veneration. He deserves our gratitude especially for collecting and storing for posterity, and for interpreting in his own inimitable translations, songs and tales in Irish, making one our own day and the centuries past, with links richly adorning our literature and culture in both Irish and English.

One could continue to list his contributions to a country and a people he loved—Ireland and the Irish, their creeds and their classes. Yet, there has been no biography, no complete word-portrait of the man, in any language. Notes and essays—yes—with some sketchy records by himself and by others, but his work for Ireland has claim on more and a knowledge of his aims should be familiar especially to our youth.

One writes in the hope that this contribution, originally composed for a doctorate of Cambridge University, and written around the diaries of the young Douglas Hyde, the youth of fourteen to the leader of fifty-two, will renew our interest in the genius and character, and above all in the achievements of this unique personality. Perhaps indeed the Rev. Fr. Daly, O.S.A., to whom we are here deeply indebted, will himself prepare the full biography and that, at least first, in the language which Dubhglas de hÍde so closely cherished.

Erskine Childers

Áras an Uachtaráin
October 1973

Acknowledgements

Many people have helped me in the preparation of this book. It is impossible, within the space allowed me here, to name them all; I hope I have thanked them individually as the occasion arose. However, there are certain people whom, I believe, I must name. Foremost among these is Dr John Holloway of Queen's College, Cambridge. Anything I might say about his guidance and encouragement would be inadequate. Perhaps I might sum it all up by saying that our initial relationship of supervisor to research student developed into a mutual friendship which I regard as the most enriching experience of my years of apprenticeship in research.

The latter part of my work was done under the supervision of Professor David Greene, Director of the Dublin Institute for Advanced Studies. Professor Greene's thorough familiarity with Gaelic literature in general and with Hyde's work in particular lightened my burden and smoothed my path, while his genial personality enlivened our working sessions. Needless to say, neither of these scholars must be held responsible for the defects or shortcomings of this work; rather, without their guidance the defects would have been more numerous and more serious.

For three happy years at St Edmund's House, Cambridge, I express my gratitude to the Master, Very Rev. Garrett Canon Sweeney, and all his household. Among my Augustinian confrères, too, I have debts to acknowledge: to Very Rev. Killian O'Mahony, provincial, for allowing me time off to do the work and for his friendly interest in it; to Professor F. X. Martin, of University College, Dublin, for his scholarly advice; and to Nicholas Duffner, provincial archivist, who created order out of the initial chaos of my notes and papers. In common with most researchers in Anglo-Irish studies I owe a debt of gratitude to the staffs of the National Library, Dublin, and the British

Museum; in this case a similiar debt is due to the staff of the University Library, Cambridge. I acknowledge my immense debt to Captain Tadhg MacGlinchey, who provided the original material.

Finally, my thanks to Mrs W. Power, our school secretary, to Father Raymond O'Keeffe, for proof-reading and for providing the index, and to Mrs Mary Una Sealy for supplying two photographs of Douglas Hyde for the jacket.

Dominic P. Daly

St Augustine's College
Dungarvan
County Waterford

Introduction

In a talk on the Gaelic League in the Radio Éireann 'Thomas
Davis Lectures' series Professor David Greene spoke of
Douglas Hyde as 'that strange and complex man'. To many of
his listeners the phrase must have sounded surprising. At first
sight Hyde seems anything but complex: he was warm-
hearted, jovial, with a zest for life, a flair for making friends
and a talent for leadership which made him 'the cajoler of
crowds, and of individual men and women' (W. B. Yeats,
Autobiographies, p. 219). And yet, as Professor Greene suggests, there is much that is enigmatic about Hyde. A parson's
son from a typically Anglo-Irish background, he became the
great apostle of Gaelic culture; yet, despite his intense identifica-
tion with everything Gaelic, he retained much of the image of
the country squire, and socially there was always a wide gulf
between him and the peasants whose lore he treasured. The
friend and fellow-worker of Yeats, Lady Gregory, John Synge
and Edward Martyn, and author of one of the acknowledged
source-books of the literary revival, he is virtually unknown to
many researchers in the well-ploughed field of Anglo-Irish
literature. An ardent advocate of Fenianism and physical force
in his youth, he suddenly retired at the height of his fame when
political and militaristic influences invaded the Gaelic League
whose president and guiding star he had been for twenty-two
years. Finally, summoned from seclusion more than twenty
years later to be first President of Ireland, he lay, after his death
in 1949 until very recently, in a grave 'completely overgrown
with grass . . . a profusion of weeds and briars',[1] a forgotten
man.

Hitherto it has not been easy to know much about Hyde.
There is a biography but it is a very brief one, written during
his lifetime. There are articles in abundance on his life and work,
but these are mostly scattered through back numbers of journals

and reviews to be found only in major libraries. Hyde's two fragments of autobiography, *Mise agus an Connradh* and *Mo Thuras go hAmerica* ('Myself and the League' and 'My Journey to America'), are factual chronicles revealing little of Hyde the man except indirectly in his style and in his references to colleagues and contemporaries.

The diaries on which the present work is chiefly based provide an important new source of information not only on Hyde himself but on the interesting times in which he lived, especially his student years in Dublin when he was a member of such nationalist and literary groups as the Young Ireland Society, the Contemporary Club and the lesser-known Society for the Preservation of the Irish Language and the Gaelic Union. Throughout these same years he was a friend of John O'Leary, Maud Gonne, W. B. Yeats, Katherine Tynan, Standish O'Grady, George Sigerson, and a regular guest at the soirées and conversaziones which were such a feature of the period. For the use of this material I gladly acknowledge my indebtedness to Captain T. M. MacGlinchey. It is through his interest in Anglo-Irish literature, and through his firm belief in Hyde's greatness as a scholar and a patriot, that these documents have been collected and preserved.

Hyde began keeping a diary in 1874, shortly after his fourteenth birthday. This fact is established by a note at the beginning of a later volume:

Today, July 25 1878, I bought this book in London because the old book I had before was finished and I had to get another one. This is the fourth book in which I have written the things that happened to me from day to day. The first book in which I wrote my daily life began in March 1874. When that was finished Cecily Hyde gave me another book, a large one, for 1877, and I wrote in it for six or seven months, after which I gave up. Then I got a plain notebook and kept my life in it for eleven months and more. When that was finished I bought this book.

Captain MacGlinchey's collection corresponds exactly with this description except that the third book to which Hyde refers is missing. The first is an old cash-book with mottled cardboard covers in which there are regular entries from 9 March 1874 to 31 December 1876. Next is a Letts desk diary for 1877, on the fly-leaf of which is written

Fuair me an leabhar so o Sissilla ua Heide
Bronntanus a bhi se ag Nollag

which is ungrammatical Irish for

I got this book from Cecily Hyde[2]
It was a present at Christmas

Apart from the missing third book, the sequence is complete from March 1874 to September 1912:

Volume 1	9 March 1874 to 31 December 1876
Volume 2	1 January 1877 to 4 September 1877
Volume 3	25 July 1878 to 9 September 1880
Volume 4	9 September 1880 to 26 October 1882
Volume 5	27 October 1882 to 30 June 1885
Volume 6	19 July 1885 to 18 April 1887
Volume 7	6 May 1887 to 2 March 1890
Volume 8	14 March 1890 to 20 January 1893
Volume 9	21 January 1893 to 31 December 1895
Volume 10	1 January 1896 to 30 November 1899
Volume 11	1 December 1899 to 31 December 1903
Volume 12	1 January 1904 to 7 June 1908
Volume 13	4 July 1908 to 5 September 1912

Volumes 3 to 13 are leather-bound notebooks, not exactly uniform but of roughly the same size, about seven inches by four.

By and large, Hyde was a remarkably regular diarist. There are few breaks in the sequence of thirty-eight years. Such breaks of a week or so as do occur are usually covered by a synopsis and an explanation for the lapse, such as pressure of work, travel, illness or mere forgetfulness. From 1879 onwards at the end of each year he writes a review of the preceding twelve months.

He began writing in English, but within a month the first faltering effort at Irish is found. The second volume has Irish and English in roughly equal proportions. The third and succeeding volumes are all in Irish, except for a few very rare occasions when for a week or so at a time he writes in German, and a few instances when he uses English to record, for example, the debates at the Contemporary Club. In quoting from the diary I use my own English translation; limitations of space make it impossible to set down the Irish text as well.

Douglas Hyde was born on 17 January 1860. He was the third son of the Reverend Arthur Hyde, Protestant Rector of Tibohine, Frenchpark, County Roscommon, and his wife Elizabeth, daughter of the Venerable John Orson Oldfield, Archdeacon of Elphin. His two older brothers were Arthur and Oldfield, and he had one sister, the youngest of the family, Annette.

At the age of thirteen he was sent to a boarding school in Dublin but in his first couple of weeks there he got measles. He was brought home to convalesce and never returned to school. This chance happening had a profound effect on his future. His formal education did not suffer, as his highly successful performance at the Trinity College entrance examination proved. On the other hand, it was during these years that he came to know and be known by the country people around his home; it was then that he became aware of the Irish language, met the last generation of native Irish speakers, and began collecting the fragments of oral tradition which he was just in time to rescue from oblivion.

In 1880 he entered Trinity College, Dublin, and graduated with a large gold medal in modern literature in 1884. He was awarded a first in the final divinity examination in 1885 and won a special theology prize the following year. However, he still could not bring himself to accept a career in holy orders. In a long passage written in German on Sunday, 7 October 1883, he describes 'the awful uncertainty about my future.' He finally reduced the choice to either law or medicine. If he were certain that his health would stand up to the work of the medical school he would not hesitate a moment about setting out to be a doctor, but he was worried, especially about his eyes which had been giving him trouble for some years. The strain of indecision was so intense that life was a hell. Finally he decided on law, and went on to gain the LL.D. in 1888. In the meantime he won the Vice-Chancellor's Prize for English verse in 1885, for prose in 1886, and both prizes in 1887.

In 1891 he went to Canada for a year as interim professor of modern languages in the university of New Brunswick. Apart from that year the whole of his later life was devoted in one way or another to the Irish language and culture. In 1893 he was one of the seven founder members of the Gaelic League, of which he was president for the following twenty-two years. In 1912 he was appointed professor of Modern Irish at the newly established University College, Dublin, a post he held until his retirement in 1932. Six years later he was a unanimous choice as first President of Ireland. Although illness and old age limited his activity in that office, he completed the statutory seven years from 1938 to 1945, but did not seek re-election. He died on 13 July 1949.

I have restricted my study to what may be regarded as Hyde's years of apprenticeship. Even within such limitations there was need for severe pruning. I have sought to trace distinctly formative influences, leaving much interesting material on his personal and social life for the definitive biography which is so long overdue but which must surely be undertaken some day.

Hyde's discovery of the Irish language and his determination to learn it viva voce was, of course, the decisive element in his life and work. Next comes his early acquaintance with the native literature, and therefore I have examined in detail his first book-lists, the foundation of his Gaelic scholarship. This is an important aspect of his background not hitherto known.

In dealing with his years at Trinity College I have been concerned not so much with his academic career as with his relationship with the literary nationalists of the *Dublin University Review,* the Contemporary Club and the Young Ireland Society. There is a striking contrast between the apparent dilettantism of his formal studies, the putting in of his time with courses in divinity and law which he never seriously intended to practise, between these and the solid reading in Gaelic literature and the immensely varied personal contacts which uniquely fitted him for his future role as leader of the Gaelic League.

As a Gaelic scholar Hyde was almost entirely a self-made man.

While his knowledge of the language was still very imperfect he set out to save what he could of the rapidly vanishing traditional culture. He was an amateur, but he was first in the field. By the time trained collectors got to work with recording equipment and expertise much of what they were seeking had disappeared. For instance, the exquisite ' Mo bhrón ar an bhfarraige' ('My grief on the sea') which Hyde first jotted down at the age of seventeen occurs nowhere in the thousands of pages which have since been stored away on the shelves of the Irish Folklore Commission.

Although his *Love Songs of Connacht* is rightly regarded as a source-book of the Anglo-Irish literary revival, Hyde himself was never really one with Yeats, Synge, Lady Gregory and the others in their aim to create a national literature in English. Hyde's interest first and last was the preservation of the Gaelic language and culture; his translation of the Love Songs was made only because

> the exigencies of publication in a weekly newspaper necessitated the translation of it into English. This I do not wholly regret; for a literal translation of these songs will, I hope, be of some advantage to that at present increasing class of Irishmen who take a just pride in their native language. . . . My English prose translation only aims at being literal, and has courageously, though no doubt ruggedly, reproduced the Irish idioms of the original.
>
> *Love Songs of Connacht,* 1893, Preface.

These rugged translations were the model for Lady Gregory's ' Kiltartanese' and Synge's peasant speech.

However, though not sharing the aim of Yeats and his group, Hyde was not hostile to them as other Gaelic enthusiasts such as D. P. Moran of the Dublin *Leader* were. Insofar as the Anglo-Irish writers were reflecting some aspect of the native culture Hyde was in sympathy with them, and as President of the Gaelic League he expressly directed the editor of *An Claidheamh Soluis* (The Sword of Light), the League's official journal, not to attack their work as Moran did in the *Leader*.[3]

Hyde's *Literary History of Ireland* is a landmark in Gaelic scholarship, the fruit of thousands of hours spent in the libraries of Trinity College and the Royal Irish Academy. It is an extraordinary achievement when one takes into account his lack of training in manuscript work and the lack, at the time, of even an adequate Irish-English dictionary. It is arguable that Hyde, the self-made scholar, was the only man of his time capable of such a task.

By 1899 when the *Literary History* was published the Gaelic League was gathering momentum, and Hyde gave all his time and energy to the office of president. By 1915, when he retired from the League, he had burned himself out. Nothing much came from his pen from then on. As Professor of Irish at University College he was liked by everyone[4] but his professorship was academically undistinguished.

Yeats wrote of him in 1902:

> I find myself . . . grudging to propaganda, to scholarship, to oratory, however necessary, a genius which might in modern Irish or in that idiom of the English-speaking country-people discover a new region for the mind to wander in. . . . I wish too that he could put away from himself some of the interruptions of that ceaseless propaganda, and find time for the making of translations, loving and leisurely, like those in *Beside the Fire* and the *Love Songs of Connacht.*
>
> *Samhain,* 1902, reprinted in *Explorations*, pp. 93, 94.

But Hyde himself had no regrets. In a letter to Horace Reynolds he wrote:

> My aim was to save the Irish language from death—it was dying then as fast as ever it could die—and that ambition did not lend itself to English writing except for propagandist purposes. . . .
>
> *The Dublin Magazine,* vol. 13, 1938, p.29.

Hyde's diaries and notebooks reveal an important aspect of his political thinking which has not hitherto been known. As a young man he was fiercely anti-English and altogether in favour of violence to rid the country of English rule. This is borne out not only in his youthful verses but in various passing references in the text of the diaries:

B

8 March 1879 I usually read the papers to him.[5] They are full of news of the Kaffirs, and of the battle in which they killed nine hundred English. Victory and strength to them, and health and success for ever.

He had frequent sessions with his neighbour John Lavin, a Fenian, and the conversation usually came round to politics:

25 November 1879 John Lavin came up this evening and we were playing cards and drinking until after midnight. . . . I got a lot of news from him about the Fenians, etc.
5 March 1881 I read a good deal of ' The Last Conquest of Ireland (Perhaps)' by John Mitchel. I cannot sufficiently praise the author and his work. He is the best prose writer I read for a long time; his style is forceful, and he would make a rebel of me if I weren't one already.
14 October 1881 Dillon and Kelly put in prison today as Parnell was yesterday. My hundred thousand curses on England and on her rule.

As time went on, however, Hyde became more and more convinced that cultural regeneration was more important than political autonomy. He wanted Ireland to regain possession of her soul before she attempted to achieve mere territorial independence. For this reason he jealously guarded the Gaelic League from any political partisanship. He failed in his purpose; his disciples, inspired by his vision of a Gaelic Ireland, determined to make it ' not only Gaelic but free as well '.

In his historic speech ' On the Necessity for de-Anglicizing the Irish Nation ' Hyde urged the Irish race to develop upon Irish lines ' even at the risk of encouraging national aspirations.' The risk was more immediate and more real than he recognized. His doctrine did indeed encourage national aspirations, which exploded into rebellion in Easter 1916. In the words of a distinguished Irish historian:

Undoubtedly the Gaelic League was the greatest single force in propagating the separatist ideal among the Irish people during the twenty years before the rising. In February 1914 Pearse wrote as follows:
'The Gaelic League will be recognised in history as the most

revolutionary influence that has ever come into Ireland. The Irish Revolution really began when the seven proto-Gaelic Leaguers met in O'Connell Street. . . . The germ of all future Irish history was in that back room.'[6]

The ' terrible beauty ' of 1916 and the aura that still surrounds it have obscured the greatness of Douglas Hyde as a maker of modern Ireland. In the same way, the brilliance of his literary contemporaries has thrown into the shade his solid contribution to Irish letters. In both spheres, research can but enhance his reputation. In the words of a modern writer:

> Our people do not yet appreciate what a key-figure in our history Dr Douglas Hyde was. At a time of deep depression, it was he alone who saw that Ireland's most urgent need was not material but psychical. Hyde's psychiatry for the nation was to get Ireland to return to her own mind, to know herself as she had been, and to be herself again.[7]

The purpose of this study has been to trace through his diaries the circumstances, the forces and the personal relationships that combined to form the mind and spirit of this remarkable man.

I

Early Days: Discovering the Unwritten Tradition

On 31 December 1878, three weeks before his nineteenth birthday, Douglas Hyde wrote the following review of his life up to then:

> This year is now passed, and glory and praise to God we are still alive and well. Glory to the Lord of the heavens for all his goodness. Many a new and strange thing happened to me in this year that has gone by and I am still safe under the roof of my earthly father. May I be yet and forever under the roof and in the embrace of my father high in heaven. Amen.[1]

> I now think that it is useful and right for me to give a brief résumé of my whole life since I was born, so that I may never be forgetful of the events of most significance as long as this book is in my possession.

> I may begin by saying that I was born in the year 1860, in the first month, the seventeenth day, in Castlerea, but I spent all my life in Kilmactrine in Co. Sligo until I was seven years of age, when my father changed his place of residence and came to this place, Frenchpark in the County Roscommon, two miles from County Mayo and the same distance from County Sligo. We came here in 1866. The old Lord de Freyne was alive at the time, and because he was related to the Master he gave him shooting rights over his lands and, in particular, possession of the Ratra bogs, and after his death his wife did not take these from us. Fowling over these lands was always our favourite pastime.[2]

> My brother Arthur went to college in the year 1871, and my other brother Oldfield likewise in 1875. I stayed at home practically all the time but in 1873 I hurt my left thigh, and it was a great hindrance to my studying, etc., etc. I then went for a short period to a wretched school in Dublin. I wasn't there more than three weeks in all, and I learned

nothing. I had reasonable Latin at that time, but I was without a word of Greek. However, shortly after I came home I began to learn Greek under the direction of my father. After doing Arnold's book and a little of Lucian I began doing Homer in January 1875, and I have continued the study of Greek since then, but I got little or no help in it from my father or from anyone else, or in Latin either, after a start had been put to my learning.

When I was very young I got a little teaching in French from Cecily Hyde at Drumkilla,[3] and I continued on my own at it, but when I started on Greek and Latin I forgot almost all of it. Indeed I never had a great knowledge of it, for all I did in it was the Ollandorf[4] lessons. But in the last month of the year 1876 I began to read the first book I ever read in French, the History of Charles XII by Voltaire, and I finished it on January 18 of last year. To show my ignorance, I found in that book five hundred and fifty words and more which I had to look up in the dictionary. So much for my French. I had not a word at all of German, or knowledge even of the alphabet, before the month of March last year when I was at Drumkilla, and Cecily Hyde began to teach me. With her I did about twenty lessons of Ollendorf, and she gave me a loan of the book to bring back to Frenchpark with me. I continued at it, doing a lesson every day until I finished the book, and just when I had done all but three or four lessons the Hydes of Drumkilla invited me to Germany and France with them to the 'Exposition', and to Switzerland. When I came back on August 8 last year I started reading a German book with notes by Bedecker, and I did a couple of hundred pages of it. Thus my German.

As for my Irish, I began to learn a little of it viva voce from James Hart, the keeper of the bogs, and before he died I had a good deal of it, except alone that I could not understand much when I heard it spoken, although I myself could say every single word, almost, that I wanted to say. But when poor James died, the finest and most gentle countryman I ever saw, and a man for whom I had more respect and affection than I have had for any countryman up to now, or ever will have, when he died in the year 1875, in the month of December, I thought my Irish would go from my memory, but then I began speaking to Mrs William

Connolly when she came to milk the cows in the evening. I wasn't long speaking to her when I found a great improvement in my Irish, because she gave me more opportunity for practice than James—James being too contrary and proud, so that I was afraid to trouble him too much. At times, in the same way, I got words and information from John Lavin and his wife, and from people I met out fowling, etc. It was not long until I was able to understand and to speak the language. As to how I learned to read it, that will be seen at the end of this volume, in the list of books I got, because they are listed in the order in which I acquired them. I got most of my reading knowledge at first from an old New Testament in English characters which I found in the house where Mr Frenan, the previous minister, left it after him. But it is clear that I had not much knowledge of the language up to about a year and a half ago. This can be seen from the book in which I wrote from day to day, for many is the ugly fault in every line of the Irish in which it is written.

When I started learning Irish I had no hope at all that there would ever be any interest in it, or that it would be of any use to me, only that I thought it was a fine worthy language; but when the society for preserving the Irish language started last year I knew then that I had done well in learning it.

Seven or eight months ago I applied for admission to the college as an Irish-speaking Sizar, but my application was turned down on the grounds that my father was too well off. Now I do not know what will become of me.

Now I feel I should put down the amount of knowledge I have of foreign languages. My knowledge of Irish will be seen from this manuscript, and from the list at the back of the book, for I have read most of the books on that list.

In Latin I read four or five books of Livy, the War with Jugurtha, seven books of Virgil, and his Georgics; five or six or seven orationes of Cicero; all of Horace.

In Greek I read sixteen books of Homer; three books of Xenophon; the 'De Corona' and another small piece by the same author; 'Prometheus Bound' and 'Hecuba'.

In French I read 'Charles XII'; a couple of hundred pages of the 'Life of Louis XVII'; 'Paul and Virginia'; 'The Princess of Babylon' etc.; 'Le Diable Boiteux' by de Sage. More than three hundred pages of the 'Confessions' of Rousseau; 'Le Médecin Malgré Lui'; a good part of a story by 'Chartria' entitled 'The Blocus'; and other small pieces which I do not remember now.

In German I did more than two hundred pages of a reading book by Bedecker; a little story of the 'nains', twenty pages; half of 'Undine'. A long story from Fischel's book and a translation of it as well. Three hundred pages of a book of fairy stories, etc., without notes but with a vocabulary at the end of it.

Hyde had had a happy childhood. By the age of fourteen, when he began to keep a diary, he had his own gun and was able to pick off jackdaws and rabbits with a sure aim and even to join his father and his elder brothers on their fowling expeditions. The difference in ages, however, tended to separate the two older brothers from the younger; apart from their passion for fowling the three boys had little in common. On the other hand, a close bond of affection and camaraderie existed between Douglas and Annette, which continued into adult life.

As he mentioned, fowling was his favourite pastime, but he also enjoyed pottering about their small farm. He had a keen eye for everything that happened about him, especially for signs of the changing seasons:

17 April 1876   Saw first swallow.

25 April 1876   Saw first butterfly of the season.

28 August 1876 Finished making the hay on the lawn; began reaping the oats.

21 December 1876 A fine day with a little snow, the first snow this year. I was up on the loft and there are plenty of apples there still. It was the best year for apples I have ever seen.

Winter evenings could be very pleasant indoors, as the following word-picture (with pen and ink illustration) shows. It was written when Hyde was about fifteen, and his imperfect knowledge of the Irish language at the time adds a childish simplicity to the description:

> There is a barrel of porter in the cellar. There are a couple of gallons of whiskey upstairs. Seamus Hart and the Master, Oldfield, Arthur and myself in the kitchen with a good fire in the grate. We sit down and drink a few glasses of punch or grog. Seamus tells us stories and we drink plenty, and go to bed drunk, or nearly drunk, or at least merry.

Greek and Latin appear on a few occasions. For example,

> 19 April   Sunday, went to Church. Ma not able to go. ******[*sic*]. Edidaskon tous paidas [Greek lettering] 'mae hêne'. [mé fhéin = myself]

And

> 10 April   Nova ancilla venit.

It is a curious fact that references to the domestic staff, which are generally confined to their comings and goings, are almost invariably in Latin. This, as well as reflecting the classical education which the boys received from their father, suggests that Latin was the medium of communication within the family when anything was being discussed which was not for the servants' ears. In a tattered little notebook in which Arthur kept a diary for some months the following domestic drama is unfolded:

> 20 August 1872   Out shooting with Pa, O. and Douglas. We got 16 grouse, 4 hares, 2 teal, 2 snipe, 1 curlew. Hodie ego primum flagitium ingens ancillae comperii. Illa enim jamdudum aliquot menses militi cuidam quotidie constituerat.

> 22 August   Pa and Douglas out shooting with the dog. Pater summo imperio saevit in Connelum quia de ancilla non ante divulgaverat. Miles nomine est Reilaios [Greek lettering]. Pa and D. shot six grouse, 1 snipe.

> 23 August   Ancilla expulsa est. O. and I out shooting, got 10 grouse, 1 hare and one snipe.

The first attempt at expressing a thought in Irish occurs on

28 March 1874 Wet day. Thoine Moisther war shane a l'oure ulk Arthure oge.

The first two words are clear enough: Thoine moisther (Tá an máistir) = The master is; 'war' may possibly stand for 'i bhfeirg' = angry; 'a l'oure ulk de Arthure óg' (a labhair olc de Arthur óg) means 'who spoke badly of young Arthur'.

The word 'moisther' is particularly interesting. When Hyde writes in English his father is 'Pa' or, later, 'the Governor', and his mother is 'Ma'. In Irish, on the other hand, they are always 'An Moisther' and 'An Moistrass', 'The Master' and 'The Mistress'. This, of course, is a result of his having picked up his Irish from listening to the servants and the local people who had dealings with the Rectory. In the same way, Hyde always refers to his older brother as 'Arthur óg', 'young Arthur', which is the native Irish speaker's way of distinguishing between father and son of the same name.

Sentences and phrases in this curious 'English' spelling occur with increasing frequency in the following months. Were there no evidence to the contrary, it would be reasonable to assume that Hyde had seen and been influenced by the manuscripts and even printed books in 'English' Irish that were common especially in the west of Ireland at this time. But there is evidence to the contrary. Hyde declares that he learned Irish 'viva voce' from Seamus Hart, Mrs Connolly and the Lavins, and that he taught himself reading with the aid of an Irish New Testament. (The fact that this latter was in English characters is beside the point; it was in formal spelling in Roman type.)

But the clearest proof that Hyde had no experience of books or manuscripts in this irregular spelling at the time is afforded by a remark in the list of books which he gives at the end of the third volume of the diaries (1878-1880). Here, at number fifty-two (the books are in the order in which he acquired them) we find 'Catechism in Connacht Irish written phonetically', and the comment—the only such expression of opinion in a list of one hundred and nine books—'most barbarous'. (By this time Hyde himself was writing in standard spelling.)

The only reasonable conclusion one comes to is that from that first sentence in March 1874 until through his reading he mastered the intricacies of Gaelic spelling Hyde used a system which he invented for himself to put on paper the sounds he learned by ear.

Like all learners of a new language, particularly learners without a teacher, he had great difficulty with the verbs. Tenses and moods are beyond him:

11 May 1874 Ro la brau. rocka mae a Ratra geera cunnein. neil vais-mae obultha worra cunnien—

at this point he gives up the struggle and turns to French—

car Morris avait tiré plusieurs coups. Hart était ici. J'étais estropié de sorte que je ne pouvais pas revenir à la maison.[5]

French and Irish go much together at this period. For example:

8 May 1874 Fine day, no rain. J'aidais Connolly d'élever le foin dans le grenier pendant une heure et demie. Je commencai le Livie ' agus morcreucthmae a goppul, lau beau niel shae fluch guf oil '. Je tuai quatre papillons. Il y avait beaucoup de astres dans le soir.[6]

In 1873, at the age of thirteen, he complains of soreness of the eyes in French verse:

J'ai grand mal aux mes yeux,
Dit le brave D.H.
J'ai grand mal aux mes yeux,
Dit le brave D.H.
J'ai grand mal aux mes yeux,
Aux mes yeux si beaux et bleus,
Mais enfin je suis au bout,
Dit le brave D.H.

The poem continues for another two stanzas but is left unfinished.

Over the following twelve months the proportion of Irish increases and the vocabulary becomes more extensive. At the end of December 1875, in the longest piece he had ever attempted in Irish, he records the death of his good friend Seamus Hart:

29 December 1875 Cold stormy day. Foor sé Sémuis bás naé. Fear oc a ganool sin oc a firineach sin oc a munturach sin ní chonairc mé riamh. Bhi sé tin himpul a teachtgin agus neii sin foor se éag. Sémuis bucht rina mé foghlamin gaodoilig uet. Fear le Gaelic oc a maith sin ni bhi sé 'a teis so. Ni higlum daoine a be dhecall feasda atá beidh dool agum oc a maith lé hu. Shocth seravid leat agus go mae do ainim banni ar neamh anis.

30 December 1875 Dark day. wet & damp. Drimmim mudya iga na suchree na Sémuis bucth. Bhi Shaun an seo.

This little panegyric on Seamus shows a marked improvement in his Irish. His knowledge is still very elementary, but he is getting the feel of the language. It reads easily and naturally:

Seamus died yesterday. A man so kindly, so truthful, so neighbourly, I never saw. He was ill about a week, and then he died. Poor Seamus, I learned my Irish from you. There will never be another with such a knowledge of Irish. I can see no one from now on with whom I can enjoy friendship such as I enjoyed with you. May God seven-fold bless you, and may your blessed soul be in heaven now.

However, he found an able and willing successor to Seamus in Mrs William Connolly.

Later, his Irish improved so much that there is a lyrical quality about his description of a winter evening:

7 December 1876 Fine calm day with a little frost. A & I went out shooting to the lake. A shot a waterhen & 5 snipe & I 3 snipe. O rugadh mé ni chonnairc me leithid a snuaidh air a loch no uisge comh ciún no adharc cho deas. Bhi an t'uisce gus an aéir mar aón rud, 'gus connairc me gach uile oileán sa t'uisce co plánalta gur ni rabh fhios agam cé bhi an oileán, ce bhi an t'uisce. Deirigh ceo ro mhór nuair bhi sinn tioct abhaile ach stiur mid abhaile le realt amháin a bhi ann. ach bhi dansér mor ann.[7]

8

At the same time there is a simple clarity and freshness about his English:

19 December Very rough cold day. I went out shooting to Rathciarri & towards Liosergul. Shot 6 snipe in the rushy fields near Liosachurce & at the rath mor and 9 green plovers nearly all in single shots, flying. Shot three of them very late when I was coming home in about five minutes as they wheeled over my head in the dark.

22 December Snowy day, & snow on the ground. I went out shooting to the Currachs, Ballinphuil, & the river. Shot a wild goose & a hare and six grey plovers & a brace & a half of snipe & a partridge & three lapwings & a waterhen.
I killed the wild goose at Lung river, after a great stalk, behind a low ditch, at about 60 yards, with a green cartridge of No. 1 & shot him pretty dead. It was one of the Scotch Greys & weighed about 7 pounds. I might have fired at him when much closer, but waited for him to turn his side. [Note in Irish:] It is the first one I ever killed. I am very pleased about it.

A few days later he was up early on Christmas morning to examine his Christmas presents. They included the Bible in Irish and, also in Irish, Richard King's history of the Church of Ireland. His interest in Irish was being taken seriously.

He had begun reading the Gaelic New Testament by this time; the result was a quite dramatic improvement in his writing of Irish.

On 18 January 1877 he wrote:

My birthday. Alas! I am seventeen today, and I am afraid I am not as I ought to be (I am writing this under the influence of whiskey.)

In spite of his misgivings, however, a very definite advance towards maturity is noticeable at this point. The neat well-formed writing is in striking contrast to the cramped, untidy, boyish scribble of the earlier volume. The beginning of 1877 sees the emergence of Hyde the serious and dedicated student. His target was the Trinity College entrance examination in which, he had discovered, his Irish might be made to serve a useful purpose:

27 January 1877   I finished Virgil's Georgics today and I did not know what I should do next. In the end I decided to read the New Testament in Greek and in Irish, because there is a lot of talk about my going in for a Sizarship in Irish at the College. I made a start on the Greek version today and it was not too difficult, but I am afraid I have too much to do.

He was working very hard. He aimed at doing a minimum of five hours study each day; every evening he checked on how the time had been spent between the various subjects, and reproved himself sternly whenever he fell short of his target. Here is a fairly typical work programme:

19 January 1877   Before dinner I spent at least two hours at Latin, and between that and supper I did a little Irish. After supper I did Greek for an hour, then an hour at Latin, and before I went to bed I spent a good hour at French. In all, five good hours.

By 18 April he had finished Horace's Odes, Epodes and the Carmen Saeculare, and on the following day he began the first book of Livy

because it is a long time since I did it and it was quite gone from my memory. I found it difficult enough now, and I wasn't able to do more than two hundred and forty lines, but I wrote some Latin verses too, and a Latin prose as I do almost every night. In all, about six hours.

Early in 1877 he sent a specimen of his Latin verse to Arthur in Trinity College for his comments:

Frenchpark.
Wednesday

My dear A

I do not write to you as Ma has done so & the Governor too, but I enclose half note & a copy of original verse. Annette has the keys. Pa's gout is nearly gone & he is almost as well able to walk as ever. There is no news here & nothing to say. You were right as to your letter being kept by Pa & his forgetting to give it to me however he remembered it in a couple of days. Love to O, when will he come back. You know ' The stars looked down on the Battle Plain ' so I dont send the English.

> Sanguineum campum noctis surgentia signa
>   Coelo despiciunt aura levisque crepat,
> Dum recubat juvenis moriens cum cuspide fracta
>   Et bellator equus non procul inde jacet.
> Quod signum supra quondam tremefecerit aura
>   Hoc ad cor gelido [a] nunc tenet ille manu
> Et *prius in* vacuas abiit *jam** spiritus auras
>   Ad cor pro palla signa decora premit.
> Purpureo clypeoque cubat quo labitur Allia
>   Et rapidus torrens volvitur ante pedem
> Et fluit interea fluvius cum sanguine tinctus,
>   Heros purpureo dum cubat ille toro.
> Et multi lachrymis oculi rorantur obortis
>   Sanguinea et vincit [*curat*] vulnera multa manus.
> Sed caput e terra tollit quo corpora multa
>   Nobilium campo fusa cruore jacent,
> ' Non revocando anima est mihi nunc abeatis *amici*
>   ⌀*Desine,* nil lachrumae, nil pia facta valent
> Utque cadunt folia autumno sic gloria magna
>   Nostrum nunc cecidit, Hesperiaeque simul'

Why not put ' quam ' for ' jam '; prius—quam.*
⌀*desine singular would hardly do after amici plural.*

The letter and verses are in pencil. Arthur corrected the verses in ink (indicated here by italics) and returned the letter.

At the same time, he was never in danger of developing into a bookworm. He rarely missed a day's fowling in season; he fished in the nearby lake, and swam in summer. He was a frequent visitor in neighbours' houses, as the following amusing incident suggests:

18 July 1877   After dinner Connolly[8] and I went down to the lake and had a swim. I was fishing but I caught nothing. The water was very cold. I worked a great cure with snuff. When I was at the lake a week ago Mrs Dockrey was in a bad way with a sore nose. There was a little spot on it, and it was so painful she could not sleep at night. I gave her half my box of strong black snuff, and she told me today that it had cured her completely, it caused such a flow of water from her eyes and nose. She had been suffering for years, and she was very grateful to me.

He continued to practise his Irish with Mrs Connolly. An indication of how Irish was ceasing to be the language of the people is the fact that Mrs Connolly herself was out of practice when Hyde began speaking to her. On 23 May 1876 he notes:

Mrs Connolly's Irish is improving; she is better able to get her tongue around it and it is coming back to her memory.

At the same time he worked hard at the grammar on his own. An interesting point here is that up to this time Sunday was very strictly a day of rest: no study, no shooting. Sunday entries have a monotonous regularity:

Sunday. Fine day. Went to Church.
Sunday. Wet day. Went to Church.

At the beginning of 1877, however, he seems to have come to terms with his conscience about Irish: it was not a profane subject like Latin, Greek or French; the study of Irish was not incompatible with the seemly observance of the Lord's Day. The Sunday entry begins to contain a new note:

Sunday 21 January 1877   Very wet day. We went to Church. Took a walk in the evening when it cleared up. I sat up late studying Irish.

Sunday 28 January   There was no service today as the Master's foot was bad with gout. Studied a good deal of Irish, chiefly Neilson.[9]

Towards the end of 1878 his programme of study had to be

abandoned when he began to suffer from soreness of the eyes which grew worse as the months passed. The first mention of this is on 13 November 1878:

> Was not able to read much because of sore eyes, so I went out shooting about 12 o'clock.

Five days later the position was more serious:

> 18 November   A beautiful day, but now my eyes are so painful that I can do scarcely anything; I can hardly read at all. I am doing my best not to let my German slip, but it is only with difficulty that I can manage to read a couple of half-pages each day. As for my French, I have almost entirely forgotten it.

> 19 November   Another beautiful day. I continued in the same way, except that my eyes were a little better. Glory be to God, it is a terrible thing for a person to be without sight!

It was only when reading that his eyes bothered him. He was still able to enjoy his fowling; indeed, it provided a relief and distraction from the enforced idleness to which he was so unaccustomed. But even here the fates were against him, in the person of Lord de Freyne. In September 1878 his lordship forbade the shooting of hares because he wanted to net them and let them loose in the great park of his estate.

Early in the new year it was decided that something must be done about his eyes:

> 7 January 1879   Oldfield and I came to Dublin; O. to his rooms in college and I to Blackrock[10] because I must see an eye specialist. We travelled up with the Catholic bishop of Sligo, a very pleasant man, full of courtesy. . .

> 8 January   . . . I went to Fitzgerald the eye specialist. He told me my eyes were not very strong, and that I must get spectacles and wear them in future when I read. I got the spectacles at Spensers for twelve and sixpence. . . .

He had other worries too about this time:

13

15 August 1878 There was a great argument tonight between Arthur and the Master about the Master's excessive drinking. Arthur said that all the Master's good works and preaching were of no avail as long as he continued like this. . . .

Unfortunately the Master did continue to drink heavily, and Douglas became increasingly critical of the fact. Another cause of friction between himself and his parents was the family practice of playing cards on winter evenings. Douglas seemed to enjoy the cards for a time, but gradually he began to look on them as a waste of time:

17 October 1878 Tonight I kicked up a row about having to play cards every evening, wasting my time when I should be studying. The end of it was that I made the Master and the Mistress angry and that they thought I was an ungrateful son in that I refused to play when they asked me. But, upon my word, it is hard on me too. Because of the cards, bad luck to them, I did hardly anything today. I hate them.

But the greatest cause of contention between Douglas and his father was the Sunday school. His father occasionally asked him to take the children on a Sunday morning, which Douglas did, but as the occasions became more frequent his response became less willing. On Sunday, 27 October 1878, for instance:

I went to Church and to my great annoyance I had to take the Sunday school because the Master got up late. . . .

The following Sunday:

When breakfast was finished the governor told me I had to go and take the Sunday school. I flared up and told him he ought to go himself and not be destroying the school. ' Why wouldn't you go?' he asked. ' Because I hate and detest it ', I replied. ' Don't say that ', he answered. ' Don't say any more; I'll go myself '. I must admit he had reason for asking, because he drank a few bottles of beer last night—small bottles—and he thought his face was too red, although in fact it wasn't. I'm afraid I fell greatly in his estimation over this, because he thought that if I wasn't capable of teaching a

14

small school I could never hope to be a minister. He said too that I was too taken up with languages; that I should learn other things, etc. etc. I was very upset myself because I do not like to refuse him, but I know that it is better that I should stand up to him in the beginning, and maybe he will go himself in future. . . .

In this scene we get a hint of another and a deeper clash between Douglas and his father. The Reverend Hyde naturally hoped that one of his sons would follow him in the ministry. As neither of the two older ones had shown any leanings in that direction, all his hopes were now fixed on his younger son. Douglas wrote, as a postscript, on his seventeenth birthday:

17 January 1877   Throughout this month they have been on to me that I should be a minister and go to foreign lands, but I do not know . . . I do not know at all what I will do.

He had evidently discussed this problem with Cecily Oldfield. In any case, at the end of October 1878 he received a letter from a Mr Welland, a professor of Divinity in England, about his becoming a missioner ' to the black men in foreign lands.' Mr Welland suggested that he should first go to Trinity College, Dublin, or to some college in England.

1 November 1878 . . . When I told the governor this he said, ' T.C.D. be damned! Look at how it made an undisciplined scoundrel of Oldfield, and an agnostic of Arthur. I won't let you through any college! You can be a preacher to your own Irish-speaking countrymen.'

When I offered to show him the letter he said, ' Not at this hour of the night ', and I heard no more of the matter. However, I wrote a long letter to Cecily Oldfield thanking her for her kindness. All I got out of the whole affair was two half-crowns when my father cursed T.C.D.

Mr Hyde had evidently agreed to pay a fine for any curse he was heard to utter!
    All in all, the Rectory was an unhappy household at this period. Mrs Hyde suffered severe attacks of asthma:

24 October 1878   Alas, my mother had a dreadful night last night, with terrible smothering. She was very worn out after it. The trouble continued into the following day. It was painful to watch her; I have not seen her suffer such an attack for four or five years. It started with a cold, and persistent coughing brought on the asthma. . . . The doctor came today. . . .

25 October   The Mistress continues in the same condition. She is not much improved; indeed she spent a worse night than the previous one. She doesn't get a wink of sleep because the smothering wakes her up, and she is exhausted. When she goes into a weakness we have to wake her up or she would die for lack of breath. The doctor was here again with ether which he promised yesterday.

The crowning sorrow of this dark period for the Hyde family was the long illness and eventual death of Arthur. He had been ailing throughout the summer of 1878, and early in October he went to his cousins, the Hunts, at Drumkilla, apparently in the hope that the change would do him good. Douglas also came to stay at Drumkilla on his way home from seeing the eye specialist in Dublin. He was shocked at the change he saw in his brother:

15 January 1879   I got a great fright when I saw Arthur looking so poorly; very weak, very thin; quite worn away.

In his account of the weeks that followed Douglas reveals more of his inner self than he is wont to do. His attitude towards Arthur is curiously ambivalent. On the one hand there is genuine sympathy for his brother's suffering; on the other, there are indications of sharp jealousy at the care and attention which Arthur's illness was gaining for him. It is interesting too to note his frank admission of a desire to be liked and to be thought well of.

18 January 1879   Dr Bradshaw came yesterday to see Arthur and said that his lungs were nothing worse than they were the last time he examined them. He ordered a bottle for him, to be taken for the diphth[11] which was bothering him and weakening him for some time. He continues very weak; to walk down stairs is as much as he can manage. Certainly,

Mr Hunt and his wife are as kind as they can be. His every wish is granted.

19 January   I went to church and stayed at Anna Kane's for dinner. I went a second time to church. A wet day. I met William Jones and he invited me to go to Drumard to kill rabbits. [Anna Kane was one of the local gentry.]

20 January   A little snow fell, and the day was cold and wet. I studied a good deal of German with Cecily.

21 January   Another ugly day. Arthur is still the same way.

22 January   After lunch I went for a walk with Cecily along boreens and bogs to Maehill and home again. A frosty day.

23 January   Anna Kane invited us all to the castle at 7.30. I went, although I didn't have proper dress for the occasion, only my black coat. There were many people there: Jones, Mr Stewart, the Wrights from Cloone, Mr Adams, Captain Crofton, and Mr Smith. I was not very interested in the company, but I drank a lot, three glasses of champagne, three or four of sherry and about six of claret. It was midnight before we were home. A good dinner.

24 January   A hard frost today and yesterday. There is as much as four inches of ice on the small lake, for because of the shade of the trees it never thawed since the heavy frost at the end of last year, almost two months ago.

25 January   Cecily went to Mount Campbell. Hard frost still. While I was skating on the lake the ice broke and I fell in up to the second button of my waistcoat and every stitch on me was soaked. I got a halfglass of whiskey from Frances [Mrs Hunt] and no harm came to me.

26 January   Sunday. All went to church except Emily and me. I stayed back to look after Arthur because he wasn't too well at all and he stayed in bed, complaining that this was his worst day so far. A bright frosty day. Anna Kane invited me to dinner and I went, and to the second service in the church.

27 January   Arthur stayed in bed today as well as yesterday, but I think he was a little better today. I had a long talk with Frances about him; she was very upset. She said to me, with a big tear running down her cheek, ' Oh, if he were my own

son I could not be more fond of him.' She is very kind and very attentive to him, and when he is bad she is very unhappy. She wrote to the Master asking him to come and see Arthur. I heard from home. My mother is better, but she had a severe pain in her back.

28 January   Arthur stayed in bed again today, but I think laziness was the main reason for that, because he is much better today. Frances' kindness to him is indescribable. When dinner was ready today she didn't come downstairs for five or six minutes after it had been served, only trying to get Arthur to swallow a cup of arrowroot, and she stays talking to him for hours at a time. I cannot understand why they have such interest in him, for he makes so little return of kindness or consideration to them that one would think it was all the same to him whether he pleased or bothered them. If I were in his position—little devil that I am—everyone would be against me. A telegram was sent for medicine for him yesterday, and the bottle came today.

The entries become more and more melancholy as the days go by. First Emily and then Cecily retired to bed with colds. Mr Hunt got news of the death of an aunt in Dublin and went off to the funeral. Frances was left with three invalids on her hands.

16 February 1879   Sunday.   Cecily and Emily still in bed and Arthur doesn't get up at all. I went to church and taught school there because the usual teachers were absent. Mr Smith invited me to go to his house with Mr Adams. I went and drank a few glasses of whiskey and water. I didn't stay long there but came back to Emily's school at the gate and taught there too, although I felt somewhat the worse for the amount of drink I had taken.
I gave a lot of help to Frances throughout the day, and I think she likes me. . . .

19 February   When they were all gone to bed I had a long talk with Frances about Arthur and the poor chance he had of surviving, because he is not improving at all but going downhill. She has a fairly good opinion of me, I believe, as regards conduct and piety. I like her a thousand times better than I did before. I give her a good deal of help around the house while the others are sick and most of the work falls on her shoulders. . . .

4 March   Today Dr Bradshaw came again to see Arthur. He said there was a great cavity in his lung, that he had consumption, and that he couldn't live longer than next summer, but that he thought he would not survive even that long, because there was every likelihood, he said, that the diarrhoia [sic] would sweep him before this month of March was out. This news did not come unexpectedly to me, or to anyone else in the house, I believe, not even to Arthur himself, although he was a bit downcast on account of it. 'It is hard', he said, 'to put all hope aside, and to knock down all one's castles in the air in one moment of time.' I felt, and I said to him, that I almost wished I were in his place. 'Ah, 'tis little you know', he said.

After the first shock of the news everything went calmly as before. I wrote home, but without telling the whole truth. I wrote fully to Oldfield.

5 March   A calm quiet day. Arthur in the same condition. I was all right except for my eyes. Went for a short walk.

6 March   . . . A telegram from Mother enquiring how Arthur was, and asking if she might come to Drumkilla. Frances wrote a reply. I hope she will not come. Such a visit would do no good, I believe, only harm, to herself and to him.

7 March   Arthur could not come down but he went for a while into Frances' room. He is in the same way. I wrote a long letter home to my mother, about A. and everything.

8 March   I killed a wild pigeon for Arthur. . . .

Hyde still had a lot of trouble from his eyes, and on 13 May he went to London to see another specialist :

16 May 1879   I went to Critchett the oculist, and after an hour's wait I saw him. He told me I had a fine pair of eyes but that I did not use them to the full.[12] He said it didn't matter even if I hurt my eyes with too much reading— that they were my slaves. He gave me a prescription, something to rub in behind my ears, and something else to apply to the eyes with a brush, under the eyelids. And—oh dear! —he told me to read as intensely as I could for ten days, even when my eyes were as bad as they could be; then to come back to him and he would know, he said, what was wrong with them.

I also went to the dentist and he told me to leave the three eyes,[13] which were very bad, as they were, that I would have no trouble from them. He took no money from me; why I do not know, but I was pleased. He wrote me a prescription for something to kill the pain.

From there I went into the centre of the city and bought some German books, which I shall list in my account of money spent.

17 May Around mid-day I went to visit Anna White. She wasn't in, but after I had waited for a while she returned. She was very kind and insisted that I should stay for dinner and supper, which I did. And, alas, she told me she had had a letter yesterday from Emily Hyde with the news that my brother Arthur had died at last, at about five o'clock on Wednesday, after the Master had been with him for two or three hours.

19[14] Sunday.

> Nil againn anois mo brón
> A n-áit an tsaoi acht caoi a's deór
> Sileadh deór a's gul a's caoi
> Feasta dúinn as briseadh croidhe.[15]

I went to St Mary Abbot's Church, where I met Anna White. I called to her house again in the afternoon, went to church a second time with her, stayed with her for tea and went home about 10.30. I had great fun talking to a young Irishwoman who is staying at Miss Gowring's,[16] and who has spent ten or fifteen years in England, about religion etc. She is very low-church. She said the Prayer Book was full of Popery and Romanism, and that the Archbishop of Dublin had done a great deal of harm imposing Ritualism on us, and so on. I trotted out for her the arguments I heard so often from the Master, but I made no impression on her; she said she was not able to argue. Her thesis was that a person once converted could never be damned. I showed her the chapter in Ezechiel, and the strong verses in Hebrews, but to no avail. Be that as it may, she is nevertheless pleasant company.

19 I met Anna White by appointment at the station and spent a couple of hours going around the shops with her. She went home then and I began reading to hurt my eyes

as Critchett had ordered. I read a good deal of German. I bought an old book on the state of Ireland, written in Latin, for two shillings, a German book for sixpence, Sintram and his companions for 1/8 and a collection of the best Italian writers for two shillings.

20 I stayed at home and read for most of the day, but for all that my eyes were not very painful. I think the stuff I put at the back of my ears and the drops I put in my eyes are doing good. In the afternoon I went out and bought two books: one on ghosts and the invisible world and the other on English battles; a shilling each.

21 I read a lot today. Ten pages of Quintus Curtius, five of the Thirty Years War, twenty of ' Aslang and Ritter ' and more than twenty-five of that excellent book, ' Hauff '. This evening I went to see Anna White and stayed until 11.30. I found her depressed about many things, but she was very kind to me as she always is. I had a letter from Frenchpark telling me that Arthur was buried on Saturday, and that the Master didn't come home until Monday. My mother's health is good, but she is very brokenhearted. They told me that the Master and Oldfield are united again through Arthur's pleading; the poor boy spent his last breath for Oldfield. They say he had a fine funeral. The Oldfields say that he was greatly loved by all who knew him.
It is not so with me. He and the Governor were as if created to be the two most opposed and obnoxious to my way of thinking that could ever exist on the face of the earth.

That strange remark is his final word on his brother Arthur. He remained on in London for a week or so. On his second visit to Critchett he had the reassuring diagnosis that there was nothing seriously wrong with his eyes, and that they would be all right in time. In fact, however, it was several years before he could read for long periods without pain.

It was around his seventeenth birthday too that he took up the writing of verse in Irish and English. The most interesting feature of these verses is the strongly nationalist and bitterly anti-English feeling with which they are charged. This, of course, is not really surprising. His friend John Lavin was a Fenian, and Fenianism was in the air about him. On Sunday, 25 February

1877, there was a Fenian meeting in Frenchpark ' which ', Hyde records, ' was a success.' Another topic he heard discussed was the iniquity and greed of landlords:

7 June 1877   Dockrey was in the kitchen for a long time. He is a terrible man. He can talk of nothing but the land and the landlords.

These two themes—physical force and the plight of the peasants —inspire most of Hyde's verses throughout 1877. The first poem, in English, was composed in March:

Do scriobh mé an abhrán seo misi fhein[17]

' Graun 'a Peeca Géur '[18]

Those damnable English and traitors and all
　　　　Says Graun a peeca géur,
I'll close with them soon and I'll give them a fall
　　　　Says Graun a peeca géur.
　　　　And I'll bid them beware
　　　　And I tell them take care
　　　　For I'll come like a snare
　　　　On the face of them all
　　　　And I'll give them a fall
　　　　Says the peeca géur.

Chorus:　　　Graun a peeca géur,
　　　　　　Graun a peeca géur,
　　　　　　Le eerin foor be E'rin seer[19]
　　　　　　Says Graun a peeca géur.

Take care of yourself when the bullets are flying
　　　　Says some to the peeca geur
But the danger of falling, the danger of dying
　　　　Is nothing to peeca géur.
　　　　For air Dhia we swear it[20]
　　　　No longer we'll bear it
Of wrongs and destruction we've had our share.
　　　　No longer we'll bear it,
　　　　We boldly declare it,
　　　　Says Graun a peeca géur.

Chorus

And what will you get by such shedding of gore
                    Mo graun a peeca géur[21]
I'll get what I can and I'll ask no more
                    Says graun a peeca géur.
                    But I'll clear the land
                    Of their ravenous band
                    And I will not spare
                    A in troth I wont back them
                    When next I attack them
                    To stand the peeca geur.

Chorus: Graun a peeca géur,
             Graun a peeca géur,
             Le eerin fuar be Eirin seer
             Doort Graun a peeca géur[22]

And when the Red Army is drawn 'cross Ocean
                    Says Graun a peeca géur,
It's then we'll rise up and there'll be a comotion [*sic*]
                    Says Graun a peeca géur.
                    We wont let the occasion
                    Pass without raging
                    With fury amazing
                    And from their lair
                    We'll drive them and hack them
                    And smash them and rack them
                    And crush them
                    Says peeca géur.

His next poem, dated 2 April 1878, is headed:

Irish Alcaic Verses

Och Eire bochd ta náire le fad agad,
Cailte mo léan faoi slabhra na Sasanach
Mar sin budh choir gach Eirinach fhior
Bronach is tuirseach a beith ariamh.

Achd éirigh nois 'gus duisigh a' tire seo
Connachd le Mumhan Laighean agus sean Uladh
Na bidhi sclábhuidh feasda, duisighe,
S' cailte do thir agus briste faraor.

Och sbochd a nidh é, s' minic a ccuala mé
Caint ar do chliu, s' umradh le na seinsearibh,
Achd brisde nois faoi chuing na Galda
D imtigh do chroidhe is do meisneach, uaitse.

(Literal translation)

Ah, poor Ireland, you are a long time in shame,
Wretched, alas, neath the chains of the English,
      And so every true Irishman
      Should be sad and weary.

But rise up now and wake up this country,
Connaught with Munster, Leinster with ancient Ulster,
      No longer be slaves, wake up!
Your country is ruined and broken, alas.

Ah, it is a sad thing! It is often I heard
Talk of your fame and tales of the elders;
But broken now under the yoke of the foreigner
Your heart and your courage fail you.

In August he wrote a poem in Irish expressing the sentiments of a young man forced to emigrate from County Mayo. The last verse is:

Oileán Sacsan, Oilleán Sacsan [*sic*]
Dearg le fuil, ann sin, an seo,
Mo mhallachd aidhbheil, éifeachtach, boagalach
Sios ort feasta, go deo, deo, deo.

(Literal translation)

Island of the Saxons, Island of the Saxons,
Red with blood, there and here,
My terrible, effective, dangerous curse on you
      Now and forever more.

A poem of sixteen verses written at the beginning of 1878 bewails the plight of the Irish peasantry:

> faoi bhochdanus scriosta
> S' a sinsireachd, bfhéidir, bhi righthe gus prionnaidh [*sic*]
> ruined under poverty
> And their ancestors, perhaps, were kings and princes.

He laments the fact that the people have lost their spirit; that they are bending their necks to the yoke without hope or thought of resistance:

(Translation)

> And in their power to free their country
> By rising and drawing their blades like men,
> To show the Saxon that each man is ready
> To break the yoke with which he is bound;
>
> To frighten that most hateful country—
> Believe, oh believe that she will not withstand force,
> But she will grant easily, meekly, to arms
> What she will never grant to truth or to right.

The poem ends in a fierce declaration of hatred:

> I hate your law, I hate your rule,
> I hate your people and your weak Queen;
> I hate your merchants who have riches and property
> Great is their arrogance, little their worth.
>
> I hate your parliament, half of them are boors
> Wrangling together without manners or respect—
> The men who rule the kingdom are liars and scoundrels
> Skilled only in trickery and humbug.
>
> Smoke rises over no city more accursed
> Than London, for all its grandeur, its pomp and fame;
> It deserves from God the most severe chastisement
> Like ancient Rome or great Babylon.

It is extraordinary how early and how instinctively Hyde became a collector of folklore. He had only the most rudimentary knowledge of Irish, and yet he had a sense of the value of these stray shreds and fragments of tradition. In September 1877 he took down from a neighbour, Mrs O'Rourke, the first recorded version of ' Mo bhrón ar an bhfarraige ' (' My grief on the sea '):

> Mo bhron air an bhfairge
>   As e 'tá mór
> As e ta eadar me
> S' mo mhile stóir.

> Cuige na Laighean agus
>   An condae Chláir
> Ta eadar misi 'gus
>   Mo mhuirnin bháin.

Ta tuileadh an creidim ach ni bhfuair misi e.[23]

His surmise was soon proved correct. In December of the same year he writes:

Fuair me o seanbean siar ag Baile n locha e seo[24]

> Mo bhron air an bhfairrge
>   Is é 'tá mór
> Is e 'tá eadar me
>   S mo mhile stór.

> D fágadh sa mbaile mé
>   Deunamh bróin
> Gan aon shúil tar sáile liom
>   Couidhe na go deó

> Mo léun nach bhfuil misi
>   Gus mo mhuirnín bhán
> A gcuige Laighean
> Na a gcondae Chláir.

26

Mo bhrón nach bhfuil misi
  Gus mo mhile grádh
    Air bord luinge
Tríall go hAimeriaca.

Leabuidh luachra
  Bhidh fú'm a réir
S chaith me amach é
  Le teas an lae.

Tháinic mo grádh sa
  Le mo thaobh
Guailin ar ghualain
  Sis' beil air béil.

Hyde's translation of this song has found its way into many anthologies.[25]

A year or two earlier, probably in 1875, he wrote down the titles of stories that James Hart told around the fire. The writing is very small and the spelling is erratic, but one can make out enough to see that they are mainly concerned with 'tyevshy' (taibhsí = ghosts), 'deenee moich' (daoine maithe = good people, fairies), and strange supernatural happenings:

(Translation)

> The man in the cornfield and his coat, and the good people gathering round him.
>
> Shamus (James) and the good people and the noise of the dog.
>
> Charlie and how he went (or, it could be, 'played'— 'drimis se'—) with the good people.
>
> Shamus and the ghost and the potatoes.
>
> Shamus and his brother and the thing making noise around them.
>
> The ghost we saw five or six times.[26]
>
> Strong Thomas Costello and the lady and the ash tree.

Thomas Costello and the bully and his horse, and the man that fought with him.

It is interesting that 'Strong Thomas Costello' should have featured in these stories. Nearly twenty years later Hyde was to recall these same stories in his introduction to the love-song 'Úna Bhán' (Fair Una) (*Love Songs of Connacht,* pp. 47 ff.):

> But I do not think there is any love song more widely spread throughout the country and more common in the mouth of the people than the poem which Tumaus Loidher (strong Thomas) Cosdello, or Coisdealbhach (foot-shaped?), as the name is often written, composed over the unfortunate and handsome girl Una MacDermott, to whom he had given love. There was no man in Ireland in his time of greater strength and activity than this Tumaus, and that was why he got his nickname of Tumaus Loidhir. The Shanachies [traditional storytellers] used never be tired of telling wonderful stories about him. . . . I heard these stories about Tumaus Loidhir from Shamus O'Hart, from Walter Scurlogue (or Sherlock), both of them dead now, and from Martin O'Brennan, or Brannan, in the County Roscommon. . . .

Another example of the young folklorist at work is this barely recognizable version of a poem by Raftery:

> Nis a tiachd a Naruch, Be a la shimu
> Nis a tiachd na Fail Briduch
> 　　Erro me mo glorh.
> Ohil me ann mo cean e
> Ni a sdupa me riamh
> Go shas a me hiar
> 　　Lar annda Mio.

About two years later he took down a more intelligible version:

> Nois a teacht an earraigh
> 　　Beidh an la sínte
> Nois ar teacht na feile Bhride
> 　　Eireocha me mo ghlór

O thug me ann mo cheann é
  Ni stopfa me choidhche
Go seasfa mé shiar
  Lar chondae Mhuighe Eo.

Years later Hyde was to bring out the first edition of the poems of blind Raferty. He tells of how he found the words of this song:

I had risen out of a fine frosty day in winter, my little dog at heel and gun on shoulder, and it was not long I had gone until I heard the old man at the door of his cottage and he singing sweetly to himself,

Anois ar dteacht an earraigh beidh an la sineadh
  Nois ar dteacht na Feil Brighde 'seadh thogfad mo cheol,
O chuir me in mo cheann e ni stopfaidh me choidhche
Go seasfaidh me shiar i lar Chonndae Mhuigh-Eo.

The words pleased me greatly. I moved over to the old man, and ' Would you learn me that song?' says I. He taught it to me, and I went home, and with me a great part of 'The County Mayo' by heart. That was my first meeting with the wave that Raftery left behind him. I did not hear his name at that time, and I did not know for many years afterwards that it was he who had composed the piece which had pleased me so well.

Songs Ascribed to Raftery, pp. 3, 5,

Thus, even before he fully understood the language in which it was preserved, Hyde had an ear for the unwritten tradition which lived only in the memory of people such as that old man who sang to himself by his cabin door.

D

II

The Written Tradition

'As to how I learned to read Irish, that will be seen at the end of this volume, in the list of books that I got, for they are listed in the order in which I acquired them. . . . I have read most of the books on that list.'[1]

The list to which Hyde refers is found at the end of volume 3 of his diaries (1878-1880). There are in fact three lists. The first contains one hundred and nine books written in Irish, the second is a list of twenty-four books, mainly in English, but on Irish subjects, and the third consists of eighteen items of manuscript. This collection of Irish and Anglo-Irish books is an impressive one by any standards; it is an extraordinary library for a young man of twenty who never had a formal lesson in Irish language or literature. In a remarkable way it draws together all the threads of Irish literary endeavour of the preceding decades; every learned Irish society of the nineteenth century is represented here.

1. The Gaelic Society, founded in 1807. Theophilus O'Flanagan was the outstanding scholar in this pioneering group. The volume of Transactions (number 34 on the main list) was the only publication of the Society, but O'Flanagan also published a translation of *Cambrensis Eversus* in 1895 (number 9 on the second list).

2. The Iberno-Celtic Society, founded in 1818. This society also published only one volume (number 3 on Hyde's second list).

3. The Irish Archaeological Society, founded in 1840, and

4. The Celtic Society, founded in 1845.
   These two groups came together in 1853 to form

5. The Irish Archaeological and Celtic Society.
   This was a much more high-powered organization than any of its predecessors. It had for patron His Royal Highness the Prince Albert; for president, His Grace the Duke

of Leinster. Vice-Presidents were the Marquess of Kildare, the Earl of Dunraven, Lord Talbot de Malahide and the President of the Catholic Seminary, Maynooth. Its council included the greatest Irish scholars of the day: Eugene O'Curry, John O'Donovan, George Petrie, James Henthorn Todd of Trinity College, Dublin[2] and Thomas Larcom.[3]

At the time of their union, the two societies separately had published a total of twenty-one volumes. The aims of the new joint society were set out as follows:

> The immediate object of this Society is to print, with accurate English translations and annotations, the un-published documents illustrative of Irish history, especi-ally those in the ancient and obsolete Irish language, many of which can be accurately translated and eluci-dated only by scholars who had been long engaged in investigating the Celtic remains of Ireland; and should the publication of these manuscripts be long delayed, many most important literary monuments may become unavailable to the students of history and comparative philology. The Society will also endeavour to protect the existing monumental and architectural remains of Ireland, by directing public attention to their preserva-tion from the destruction with which they frequently are threatened.[4]

Five important publications of this Society, or of the societies from which it was formed, are in Hyde's list (numbers 33, 36, 58, 67, 68).

6. The Ossianic Society.

' On the 17th of March, 1853, a few individuals interested in the preservation and publication of Irish Manuscripts met at No. 9, Anglesea-Street, for the purpose of forming a Society whose object should be the publication of Fenian poems, tales, and romances, illustrative of the Fenian period of Irish history, in the Irish language and character, with literal translations and notes explanatory of the text, when practic-able; and at a subsequent meeting, held on the 9th May following, the Society was formed, and named the Ossianic Society. . . .'[5]

There was, in fact, no overlapping or danger of collision

between the Ossianic and the Archaeological and Celtic Societies. The latter was concerned with rather abstruse and academic aspects of archaeology and philology, while the Ossianic Society, as its name implies, confined itself to one area of Irish antiquity, the Fenian Cycle,[6] and its object was to provide texts and translations for non-specialist readers.

John O' Donovan of the *Annals* was also on the council of this society, as was Standish Hayes O'Grady, a fine classical and Oriental scholar as well as being an eminent authority on ancient Irish literature; he compiled the first catalogue of Irish manuscripts in the British Museum. John O'Daly, the prolific publisher of popular Irish texts, was Honorary Secretary and publisher to the society. Another notable member was the Reverend Euseby Digby Cleaver, a man of extraordinary generosity towards the cause of the Irish language. He spent thousands of pounds in providing financial rewards for teachers, prizes for pupils and free text-books for schools. It was at his suggestion that Douglas Hyde wrote his first book, *Leabhar Sgéulaigheachta*, and Cleaver paid for its publication. In dedicating the book to him Hyde wrote: ' Of you that saying of the Roman is true— except to change one word: " nihil Hibernicum alienum a me puto." '

Six volumes from the Ossianic Society feature in Hyde's list, including the collection of Fenian poems (number 24) in which first appeared the legend of Ossian's journey to the Land of Youth which was to inspire Yeats's 'Wanderings of Oisin'.

7. The Society for the Preservation of the Irish Language.
This society differed essentially from all that went before it in that its object was the revival, or at least the saving from extinction, of Irish as a spoken language. It grew out of the enthusiasm of two men in particular: David Comyn, a Clareman who was a clerk in the National Bank in Dublin, and Fr John Nolan, a Carmelite priest. Other men who were prominent in the early days were Thomas O'Neill Russell, who spent many years as a commercial traveller in the USA, and Canon Ulick Bourke, author, editor and president of St Jarlath's College, Tuam.

Many years later Hyde was to describe the Society for the

Preservation of the Irish Language as 'the first attempt that was made to involve ordinary people in the cause of the Irish language'.[7] There is no doubt that it was a powerful influence on his thinking in the years that followed, and that in spirit and organization it was a model for the Gaelic League of some fifteen years later.[8] In this context it is interesting to read Hyde's account of his first contact with the society.

In June 1877 his mother was ill, and it was decided that she should see a specialist in Dublin. She did not feel well enough to travel alone, so Douglas accompanied her. They stayed for a week with the Oldfield cousins, and while her sister Cecily attended to Mrs Hyde's needs Douglas was free to browse around the bookshops and do some personal shopping:

18 June 1877   I went into Dublin and bought two Irish books, snuff, etc. . . .

19 June   I went to Dublin again and bought two more Irish Books, and an oak stick. Then I went into the place where this new society established for the upkeep of the language was gathered together. I was listening to them for a good while, and when I was leaving one of them came outside the door with me and asked me if I could go down to Kingstown tomorrow and see him and have tea with him. I thanked him and said I would come, and I came home.

20 June   A fine day. After an early dinner Cecily and I went to Kingstown and I visited the Mansfields.[9] I left them after a short time and went to Mr Russell's house (that is the man's name) and had tea with him and his wife, a nice woman, French. We talked for a good while, and there was a great welcome for me. Afterwards I went back to Mansfields and walked with them and Cecily on the pier until well on in the night. It was fairly late when we got home—eleven or so. 'If you are at the end of Leinster Street at eleven o'clock tomorrow', Russell said to me, 'I will meet you and show you the Academy.'[10] I thanked him and said I would be there if I could.

21 June   I went to Dublin and met Mr Russell and he showed me the Academy and was very kind to me.[11] I saw a lot there: ancient books, eight hundred years old, spearheads, harps, swords, the Tara brooch, the Cross of Cong, bog

butter, and many other things I cannot remember. I met Mr Mangan also and he was very courteous to me. He told me that if I came to him he would give me every help he could to learn Irish, and he took a pinch of snuff from me. Mr McSweeney too told me I could come in any time I wanted in future, that I had only to ask for him. We spent three hours there, after which I left Mr Russell, had my dinner, bought some things I needed and came home.[12]

One of the immediate objects of the society was the provision of 'cheap elementary works, from which the language can be easily learned. . . .' In the autumn of 1877 the *First Irish Book* appeared, a very elementary little grammar with a simple vocabulary; the second and third were published in the following two years. They are numbers 15, 21 and 79 in Hyde's collection.

Particularly important for Hyde's later work as editor and translator of the traditional songs of Connaught is the impressive collection of *editiones principes* of Irish poetry. The first of these, in importance as well as in time, was Charlotte Brooke's *Reliques of Irish Poetry* (1789). Miss Brooke declared that she undertook this work 'in the hope of awakening a just and useful curiosity on the subject of our poetical compositions'.[13] In this she succeeded admirably. She was the first to draw attention to Irish mythology as the source of a literature in English; she 'opened the way that Ferguson, Mangan, and Yeats would follow. Certain names had been uttered that would not remain forgotten . . . Conor, Cu Chulainn, Emain Machae, Deirdre, Tara, Finn.'[14]

Miss Brooke's translations are stiff and prosaic, but her enthusiasm for the native language was simple and sincere:

It is really astonishing of what various and comprehensive powers this neglected language is possessed. In the pathetic, it breathes the most beautiful and affecting simplicity; and in the bolder species of composition, it is distinguished by a force of expression, a sublime dignity, and a rapid energy, which it is scarcely possible for any translation fully to convey; as it sometimes fills the mind with ideas altogether new, and which perhaps, no modern language is entirely prepared to express. One compound epithet must often be translated by two lines of English verse, and, on such occasions, much

34

of the beauty is necessarily lost; the force and effect of the
thought being weakened by too slow an introduction on the
mind; just as the light which dazzles, when flashing swiftly
on the eye, will be gazed at with indifference if let in by
degrees.[15]

The most important collection of Irish verse was James Hardi-
man's *Irish Minstrelsy* (1831). In the preface to his own *Love
Songs of Connacht* Hyde refers to the 'gems of lyric song' in
Hardiman's two volumes, and adds:

It is to them the student should first look for the very highest
expression of the lyric genius of our race.[16]

Miss Brooke was an Ulsterwoman, and Hardiman was a
Connaughtman. It was now the turn of Munster. *Reliques of
Irish Jacobite Poetry* first appeared in 1844; *Poets and Poetry of
Munster* in 1849; a 'Second Series', an entirely new collection, in
1860. Edward Walsh[17] translated the Jacobite relics, James
Clarence Mangan[18] the first series of the poetry of Munster, and
Dr George Sigerson[19] the second.

The name of John O'Daly is closely associated with these
three collections, either as editor or publisher. It will also be
noted that a surprisingly large number of the books on Hyde's
list were published by O'Daly. Hyde says of him that there was
no one in his time who did more, in his own way, to popularize
and cultivate Irish than he.[20]

O'Daly was born in County Waterford about 1800, and
educated at a hedge-school. He spent some years teaching Irish
at a Wesleyan school in Kilkenny before moving to Dublin
where he set up as a bookseller and later as a publisher. It was
at his house in Anglesea Street that the meeting was held in
1853 out of which developed the Ossianic Society, to which
he was both honorary secretary and publisher.

He was a keen collector of manuscripts, especially of the
popular poetry of the eighteenth century; it was in this way that
he provided the material for the three volumes.

In *Mise agus an Connradh,* Hyde stated that he used to visit
O'Daly, then a little old man, in his bookshop in Anglesea Street,
and that O'Daly recalled to him how Mangan, who knew no

Irish, used to come into the shop, stretch his droll figure across the counter and put into verse O'Daly's literal prose translations of the Gaelic poems.[21]

John O'Daly died in 1878, and in due course Hyde received notice of the auction of his books and manuscripts. His account of the auction is interesting. It explains how he acquired some of the most valuable books in his collection, as well as all the manuscripts; it also shows what a shrewd and discriminating buyer this lad from the country was, in competition with Trinity dons and Dublin booksellers.

14 August 1878 . . . I got a list of books and manuscripts which are to be sold at O'Daly's auction. I said it would be a pity if I weren't present when they were being sold, and when the Master heard that he kindly said that he would give me six pounds to go to Dublin and buy what I could. I accepted his offer gladly, and I am, D.V. to go to Dublin on Saturday.

17 August I got up very early, about five o'clock, and drove with Connolly to Boyle, where I took the eight o'clock train to Dublin. I travelled third class for the first time, and found it comfortable enough. I left my 'impedimenta' in the cloakroom at Westland Row and I went to D'Olier Street to look at the books which are to be sold at Monday's auction. There is a great variety of books there, but I will not bother with any but the Irish books. I stayed examining them until near six o'clock, and then I went to Westland Row and from there to Blackrock to the Oldfields. I found them hale and hearty, especially my grandmother; I never saw her looking so well.

19 August In the morning I went to the auction. It was about 1 o'clock when it began, and I did not leave it until six o'clock except for a couple of minutes to squeeze my knees. I bought 'Keating's History of Ireland', translated by O'Mahony the Fenian, in America, for five shillings and ninepence. I also bought a fine new copy of 'Hardiman' (two volumes) for twenty-three shillings; Keating's 'Foras Feasa ar Eirinn', in Irish and English, a very good copy, for thirteen shillings; 'Leabhar na gCeart' for four shillings and a New Testament in Munster Irish by O'Catháin for a shilling. 'Oidche (sic) Cloinne Uisneach' &c published by the Gaelic Society in 1808, for six shillings and threepence;

36

'The Celtic Miscellany' for 1849 for one and six, and O'Reilly's Dictionary with O'Donovan's supplement, published in 1864. There was a lot of money going on Irish books, and I was lucky to get these as cheaply as I did. There was many a book on which my heart was set but which I had to let go because I couldn't offer as much as the others did. There was one man in particular, a bookseller by the name of Traynor, who was very interested in Irish books. But for him I would have got the books I bought more cheaply, only he raised the price on them. I raised the price on him in turn. I was on the point of taking the Annals of the Four Masters for 30/- and he beat me, but he would have got them for a pound if I had not been there.

Dinner was finished again when I got home. I had a heavy load of books to carry.

20 August I went in to the auction again. I met a good many people I knew in Dublin today. . . . I bought O'Reilly's Irish Writers; poems in Old Irish by the Dean of Lismore; the first for six shillings and the second for six shillings and sixpence. O'Sullivan Beare's Historia Hiberniae for fifteen pence, very cheap; the Catechism in Irish by Ua Eodhasa (Romae 1707) very cheaply entirely at ninepence. I also bought Hardiman's book again, although I had bought a copy of it yesterday, but I got it five shillings cheaper today for eighteen shillings. I also bought a lot of ten books, and among them was a book in Scots Gaelic called 'Leabhar na Cnoc', and another Scots book 'Duain Gaelic le Livingstone', and The Book of Common Prayer in Irish; Bunyan's 'Pilgrim's Progress' in Irish, and three other books in English: 'Ireland Sixty Years Ago', 'Callanan's Poems' and 'Stories of the Geraldines'. I offered three books out of the lot to Traynor if he would stay out of the bidding for them. He agreed, and I got the lot for two and sixpence, and I gave him the three worst books among them. . . .

21 August I went into the auction again and bought O'Brien's Irish Grammar for 1/6. Then the manuscripts started and I bought the first lot, a miscellaneous bundle of pages in Irish and English.[22] There were several manuscripts in the lot, but these are the most noteworthy: A collection of songs, one eleven, one twelve, one fifteen, one eight verses long; well

copied out. The titles were 'Naomh Smuainte' [Holy Thoughts], 'A Naomh Mhuire Matar (*sic*) Dé' [Holy Mary Mother of God], &c, &c. A fine copy of Cormac MacArt's Instruction to his son, written in 1838, copied from the Leabhar Breac.[23] Excellent copies of Carolan's songs, twenty-seven[24] of them. A collection of songs, most of them written about the noble families of Co. Leitrim, with 'Uilleacán Dubh O', ' Ceann Dubh Dílis ' &c, some of them written and all copied by P. O'Flainn.[25] An English translation of Echtra [*sic*] an Bhais[26] by O'Daly. A fine copy of Eocair Sgiatha an Aifrinn.[27] Two good copies of Cuirt an Meadhon-Oidche.[28] An old story copied for John O'Donovan in the year 1837. 'Cuirt an Meadhon Oidche' translated into English verse by Wolfe.[29] A manuscript of English verses, 40 pages, on the people of County Clare. Religious poems written by Michael O'Longain in 1796, 8 pages. A poem or satire on the Arch-bishop of Cashel, by Eoghan McCraith, a hundred verses. Manuscript of the Battle of Cnoca[30] 33 pages. The battle of Magh Mocruime,[31] a very old manuscript, bound. Eachtra Triar Cloinne, 24 pages, etc., etc. Also I bought a nice bound book in O'Donovan's handwriting, for five shillings, in which there were many religious poems. A very fine book indeed.

I sat up late reading my manuscripts and putting them in order.

In teaching himself to read Irish without a master Hyde adopted a very sensible approach. He chose either texts with the substance of which he already had some familiarity (the Scriptures and the Iliad) or books in which an English version was printed side by side with the Irish. This latter is the case in most of the texts (as distinct from grammars and dictionaries) in the first half of his list.

His Sunday reading for most of 1878 was Dr O'Gallagher's sermons, with Irish and English on facing pages and a vocabulary at the back. On Sunday, 27 October he writes:

> . . . I finished the last sermon of O'Gallagher's today, and I cannot sufficiently praise them, or the manner in which they are edited by Fr Bourke . . .[32]

It is interesting to note Hyde's commendation of the editing of the sermons. No doubt he read with particular satisfaction the Canon's ideas on 'The Language of the Gael' in a long appendix to the main text. 'In reply to letters from young men in several counties' as to the time and manner best suited to learning the Irish language, the Canon writes:

> The period of youth is the best time to learn Irish. When one is young the organs employed in articulating are flexible; the ear retentive of sound; the memory fresh . . .
>
> If people are in earnest, and if this desire for learning the language of our nation, and of teaching it, be not a passing fit of laudable fervor or of patriotism, they will, whenever they can, endeavour to form classes for learning Irish Gaelic, amongst the young children attending those schools taught by religious ladies of conventual institutions, by the Christian brothers, or, if possible, by the teachers of National Schools. The two languages—Irish and English—can be taught. English is necessary; Irish, however, ought not to be passed over in silence. The use of two imparts a fuller utterance . . .

Future Gaelic League policy is particularly clearly foreshadowed in the following paragraphs:

> It is only right, then, that those who, as you say, speak Irish, and who wish to see a knowledge of it spread, should form clubs and frame a rule that no language but Irish Gaelic be spoken during 'club' hours. This practice could be extended to the home circle. . . .
>
> It is certain, therefore, that in order to learn Irish, one must, whether he is still young or advanced to the years of maturity, make, at any cost, an attempt to speak it, otherwise the accent and the Gaelic idioms, which are all quite opposed to everything of the kind in English, can never be learned.

The idea of festivals or *feiseanna* which were to become such a feature of Gaelic League policy was also put forward by the Canon:

> Annual meetings like the Eisteddfodan should be held, and prizes awarded in public.

He ends with an exhortation:

The dying language cannot be restored to anything like a vigorous state in a year, nay,—nor in ten years. Let each act as if its restoration depended upon himself alone.

This was the gospel which Hyde professed and practised, and which he preached throughout the country for over twenty years.

On 30 July 1878, on his way home from a holiday in France and Switzerland, Hyde spent a few hours browsing around secondhand bookshops in Dublin. Among his purchases was Donleavy's Catechism, first published in Paris in 1742; there were two subsequent editions in Dublin, in 1822 and 1848. (As the auction catalogue includes the Paris edition, it seems reasonable to presume that this was the one Hyde bought in 1878). It is a large volume, as catechisms go: lvi + 518 pages octavo. Indeed the author, the Reverend Andrew Donleavy, begins his Advertisement with a defence and justification of the size of his book:

> The Bulk of this *Cathechism* will probably, at first View, afright such as are used only to little *Abridgments, meerly* calculated for *Beginners,* and *Chiefly for Children at their Horn-book,* or thereabout. But in opening it, they will find, it is in *two Languages,* and that, consequently, they have but *Half the Work* on their Hands. . . . They will likewise see, that the Print is large, and much Waste occasioned, through the Necessity of placing the Questions and Answers of both Languages, directly opposite to each other. . . . Lastly they will, towards the End, meet with an Abridgment of the *Christian Doctrine* in *Irish* Rhyme, composed upwards of an Age ago by the zealous and learned F. *Bonaventure O Heoghusa* of the Order of S. *Francis;* and also with the Elements of the *Irish* Language, in Favour of such as would fain learn to read it; and thereby be useful to their Neighbour. . . .

This latter part of the book must have been of particular interest and encouragement to Hyde. The author bewails the fact that Irish is now ' on the Brink of utter Decay ',

> to the great Dishonour and Shame of the *Natives,* who shall always pass every where for *Irish-Men*: Although *Irish-Men*

without *Irish* is an Incongruity, and a great Bull. Besides, the *Irish-Language* is undeniably a very Ancient *Mother-Language,* and one of the smoothest in *Europe,* no Way abounding with Monosyllables, nor clogged with rugged Consonants, which make a harsh Sound, that grates upon the Ear. And there is still extant a great Number of old valuable *Irish Manuscripts* both in publick and private Hands, which would, if translated and published, give great Light into the Antiquities of the Country, and furnish some able Pen with Materials enough, to write a compleat History of the *Kingdom* : What a Discredit then must it be to the whole *Nation,* to let such a *Language* go to Wrack, and to give no Encouragement, not *even* the Necessaries of Life, to some of the *Few,* who still remain, and are capable to rescue those venerable *Monuments of Antiquity* from the profound Obscurity, they are buried in?

Another book which must be presumed to have quickened Hyde's resolve to work for the restoration of the native language and literature was Hugh MacCurtain's *The Elements of the Irish Language,* printed at Louvain in 1728. In his ' Preface to the Ingenious and Generous Reader ' the author explains his purpose:

. . . to use all my Endeavours and Industry, to publish a more full and correct Grammar of the said language, now in its decay and almost in Darkness, even to the Natives themselves. . . .

It is certain, most of our Nobility and Gentry have abandoned it, and disdained to learn or Speake the same these 200 years past. And I could heartily wish, such persons would look back and reflect on this matter; that they might see through the Glass of their own reason, how strange it seems to the world, that any people should scorn the Language, wherein the whole treasure of their own Antiquity and profound sciences lie in obscurity . . .

I know there are some ridiculing wits, that condemn as vain and useless, the labours of those who would Endeavour to preserve this Language; but no wise or knowing person ought to take Notice of such Criticks. And there are many that take great liberty in talking after such a manner, yet some of the Nobility, Bishops & Doctors of our European Colledges, most Extensive Capacities in all kinds of litterature, are the most Zealous in promoting the language and preserving its monuments.

Another interesting feature of Hyde's library is the number of books in Scots Gaelic: almost a third of the total. His interest in this branch of Gaelic literature started from the chance discovery of some books from the Scottish Highlands in O'Daly's stock. He bought three, and some weeks later he records in his diary that he read three or four pages of Scots Gaelic with much difficulty. But his interest was awakened, and soon afterwards we find him writing to Edinburgh and Glasgow for particular books.

Most of these books were collections of popular poetry, and there is no doubt but that they influenced Hyde's decision to publish the songs of Connaught.[33] Also from his reading at this early stage he gained a good deal of the knowledge of Scottish Gaelic literature which he displays in Chapter XXXIX of his *Literary History of Ireland*.

His reading of passages such as I have quoted confirmed something that was becoming evident to Hyde in his daily life: that when an Irishman lost his native language he lost much more than a medium of communication; he cut himself off from his cultural roots and suffered a deterioration of his national character. This was to be the quintessence of Hyde's philosophy. It is the theme of his historic speech on ' The Necessity for De-Anglicising Ireland ':

> I believe it is our Gaelic past which, though the Irish race does not recognise it just at present, is really at the bottom of the Irish heart. . . ; do what they may the race of to-day cannot wholly divest itself from the mantle of its own past.

It was in the seclusion of his study in Frenchpark that Hyde discovered for himself the past in which lay the hope of Ireland's future. While he worked away in lonely isolation he kept in touch, by correspondence and occasional visits, with O'Neill Russell and Comyn of the Society for the Preservation of the Irish Language. For instance, on the morning on which he got notice of the O'Daly auction, by the same post he received an Irish-American newspaper from Russell:

13 August 1878   Russell sent me a paper from America yesterday
   with Irish print and a lot of news about how the Irish
   language is coming on in that country. It raised my heart
   greatly. When I came back from France I heard that Russell
   and his group had won a great victory: that the Irish
   language is to be taught in the schools in future with awards
   for successful teachers. This was a great achievement, and
   Fr O'Nolan told me that many people believed the Irish
   language was saved by that fact.

The great victory to which Hyde refers was the decision of the
Commissioners of National Schools 'to grant Result Fees for
proficiency in the Irish language on the same basis as applicable
to Greek, Latin and French.' This first official recognition of the
Irish language by a department of government was the result of a
Memorial forwarded to the commission by the Society for the
Preservation of the Irish Language in June 1878.[34]
   On the evening of the final day of the auction he dined with
David Comyn, co-founder of the society. Hyde's account of the
occasion, apart from its historic interest, reveals a new facet of
his character: his fastidiousness. It is amusing to note how his
patrician sensibilities were offended by the plebeian manners of
his host:

28 August 1878   . . . I left my books in the care of a man at the
   auction room and went at about six o'clock in the evening to
   113 Gardiner Street to have dinner with Comyn, the influential man in the Irish Society. I wasn't keen on visiting
   him at first, but he would take no excuse from me, so I went,
   and Oh! when I knocked at the door a slovenly girl opened
   it and when I asked if Mr Comyn was in she said he was not,
   but that he would be home very soon if I would wait. 'Go
   upstairs', she said 'and you will find the drawing room.' I
   went up and found a drab untidy room in which there was a
   man with no shoes on his feet. He went out and shortly
   afterwards Comyn came in and shook hands with me. A few
   minutes later he said 'Let's go to dinner', without even saying
   'Would you like to wash your hands?' or anything. Down
   we went and found a long table with a very dirty cloth on it,
   a woman at the head, an unshaven man at the opposite end
   and two or three people at each side. We began, I eating like
   a christian while Comyn showed more interest in his knife

than in his fork, putting it in his mouth like a shovel. Dinner finished, we left the others still at table and went to his own room. He showed me his books, made me a present of one of them and promised to send me 'Cúirt an Meadhon Oidhche'. He was kind. It was close to ten o'clock when I finally got home.

Something of the same fastidiousness is reflected in the final sentence of the account of his homecoming a fortnight later:

9 October 1878   I found the people at home well. The master was pleased enough with the arrows I brought—seven of them. What a change from the elegance and tidiness of Blackrock [his cousins' place in the suburbs of Dublin] to the slovenly disorder of this place.

Over the next two years he made time from his studies for regular outings with the gun and for convivial sessions with his friend Lavin:

16 November 1878   [English] Went up in the evening to Seaghan Ua Laimhin's [John Lavin's] to see why he was not coming down. I searched the rushy fields and shot a brace of snipe, and then coming home in the evening a golden plover in the turlough field [Irish] When Sean came down tonight we played cards and drank whiskey. I showed him several of my Irish books and read out for him some of the songs from Hardiman's collection. He said there were many of them he had heard before. It was eleven o'clock when he left and I went with him to the top of Cunningham's boreen. We had a pleasant evening.

He welcomed every opportunity of speaking Irish, and every trace of the old native culture which was disappearing so fast:

4 December 1878   . . . I met a blind piper from Co Galway and had a long talk with him about his travels. He had been in twenty-seven Irish counties. His favourites were Mayo, Kerry, Tipperary and Dublin; those he liked least were Longford and Limerick. He spoke Irish well.

The following month he went to Dublin to see the eye specialist, and as usual he availed himself of the opportunity to visit the Irish bookshops:

9 January 1879   I went into Dublin and bought Oh! a book that
     brought joy to my heart: The Munster poems by O'Daly,
     translated into English by Clarence Mangan. I paid seven
     and six for it and thought it cheap at the price.

At Traynor's bookshop he met Fr O'Nolan, secretary of the
Society for the Preservation of the Irish Language, and gave him
ten shillings, his subscription as a member of the society.[35] In
June 1879, on his way home from London, he visited Traynor
again and bought six volumes of the transactions of the Ossianic
Society for fifty shillings.

     While I was buying them an old man dressed in black came
     in and began speaking to me about Irish books in general
     and about O'Callaghan's 'Green Book' in particular.[36] I told
     him I did not think the latter was a decent or proper book
     because of certain things in it which I mentioned. Imagine
     my surprise when he roared at me in a voice like thunder,
     'Damn it, Sir, I wrote those pages myself! It was I wrote
     every line of them!' I was greatly taken aback to find that
     it was O'Callaghan himself who was there. He spent an
     hour talking to me, fiercely anti-English, etc. An extra-
     ordinary man!

In August 1879 he suffered a bout of pleurisy. At the end of the
month he sums up:

Sunday 31 August   This month is now past, and I am grateful
     to be as well as I am. There is no doubt about it, I was in a
     bad way, and only that the Master sent for Dr O'Farrell
     when he did there was every likelihood that I would be
     swept off. Because I was in that condition I did not do much
     reading: I wasn't able to. I read some German, but very
     little Greek or Latin. It was a bad month out and out.
     I'm afraid the people will be ruined, without a sod of turf
     or anything.
     The spirit of poetry rose strong in me during my illness.
     Most of the poems were in Irish, with a few in English, but
     it doesn't come half as easily to me as the other language.

It was at this point that Hyde adopted the pseudonym that was to
become so famous in later years:

E

18 January 1880 A fine frosty day. I had a slight cold so I didn't
go out. I have nothing to do—my eyes are too sore for reading. I had a letter from Comyn yesterday : he has printed
my third poem, ' eisd liom a oigfir '. [sic] He told me Russell
had written to him from America asking who was the
'Craoibhin Aoibhinn'. To-day I received from Russell himself
an American paper in which he had written that I would be
the great Irish poet of the future.[37]

7 February My poem, ' O tiocfaimid is troidfimid ' was printed
in The Irishman and I had a long kind letter from Comyn.
He was asking me to write prose.

Next month, on 6 March, he had his fifth poem printed in
the *Irishman*—' Mo bheannact leat a thír mo grádh '. Three days
later :

9 March Russell sent me from America a paper in which there
was a letter from himself about my Irish poems in *The
Irishman*. He said they were very good, especially ' Eisd liom
a Oigir ' [sic], and that the Craoibhin Aoibhinn was the
best Irish writer they had today; that he knew me, and was
proud of the fact, but that he wouldn't reveal my name, and
much praise besides. . . .

In the *Irishman* of 10 April 1880 Hyde published a toast in verse
to O'Donovan Rossa the Fenian :

Ólaim deagh-shláinte Ua Dhonabháin Rossa,
Ca bhfuighfead a shamhuil anall no abhos o,
Do thiománfadh na daoine gan armaibh gan éudach
A g-ceart-lár na saighdiúr na g-claideamh 's na m-baynets.
Do cheannuigh 's do chonnmhaigh an púdar 's na gunna
Nach d-tig leis a chur cum ma n-daoine bocht'loma.
Do bhrostuigh d'aimhdeóin sin ár bpobal bocht lom
Saighdiúra na Sacsan do sgapadh tar tonn.

(Translation)

I drink to the health of O'Donovan Rossa,
Where will I find his like at home or abroad,
Who would drive the people without arms or uniforms

Into the midst of the soldiers, the swords and the bayonets.
Who bought and kept the powder and the guns
Which he could not send to the poor defenceless people,
Who nevertheless urged our poor unarmed peasantry
To drive the Saxon soldiers away across the sea.

Such were his sentiments in his twenty-first year, when he enrolled as an undergraduate at Trinity College, Dublin.

III

At Trinity College, Dublin

In June 1880 Douglas Hyde took the entrance examination for
Trinity College. Out of a hundred candidates he came seventh,
and that in spite of a wretched performance in mathematics.

22 June 1880 I was examined in four texts I had chosen:
Horace's Odes, four books of Virgil, three of Homer and
three Xenophon. I got eights in them all except for Horace,
in which I got seven. Then I had Euclid, viva voce, eight
again, and Euclid written, seven. . . .
(He chose ' Oliver Cromwell ' for his English essay, ' and
gave him hell for an hour ').

23 June 1880 I went in again today and had three papers on
classics and History, and then a paper on which there were
sixteen questions in Mathematics. The moment I saw these I
knew I would do no good on them so I left the hall. The
others had two and a half hours to do them.

Being an undergraduate made little change in his way of life;
he continued to study at home. College regulations at the time
allowed the option of attending lectures or sitting an examination
at the end of each term in lieu thereof. Hyde chose the latter
course, which was popularly known as ' the steam-packet degree
course ' from the number of British students who crossed the
Irish Sea for the termly examinations. The result was that for
most of his undergraduate years he had little social contact with
his fellow-students, no community life and no real sense of
belonging to the college.

For the first three years of his course references to Trinity are
confined to records of examinations passed and prizes won. In
his first term he gained first class honours and second place in
German with a prize of four or five pounds (he wasn't sure at
the time of writing); a year later he gained first class honours
in French and German, with a prize of four pounds for each.
In April 1884 he came first in Italian with 75%, and at the end

48

of the same year he graduated B.A. with a Large Gold Medal, ' a great honour, for only three were awarded this year.'

He had his first experience of college life in the Trinity term of 1882:

6 May   I came to Dublin to put in lectures because I was afraid of the examination. Cam O'Kane[1] gave me the use of his rooms as neither he nor O'Farrell is staying there. I wasn't half an hour in the city when I met Oldfield who had come up today also. I went to bed early. The reason I came to Dublin was that I thought it would be much easier on my eyes to attend lectures than to have to pass an examination.

After the years of isolation and solitary study, college life was a new and stimulating experience for him, and he revelled in it:

June 6   Last evening after I had come back from the train and eaten my dinner I met Johnson and went and drank a glass of punch with him. Then we went to Richards' rooms where we found quite a gathering. They all called on me to sing. I refused at first, but when we all had drunk a good share I sang ' Beannacht leat, beannacht leat, a chondae Mhuighe Eo ', and according to them I sang well, although it was without a tune of any kind.[2] Coffey and Richards sang too, and afterwards I gave them ' Trinquons et toc '.[3] I stayed until the end. I attacked Lawson for something he said to me earlier, that he would drink me under the table if I bought the claret, at 7/6 a bottle. I shamed him properly.
I went to bed at about 1.30 and when I woke up in the morning I had nothing on except my boots.

In his summing up at the end of 1882 he wrote:

31 December   Thanks be to God, the old year is past and the New Year finds us more or less as we were. Oldfield left Carndonagh this month and is now in Dunlavin, while the rest of us are in the same old way.[4]
I did not do very much this year. I took a general examination at the College in January and made up another term by lectures which began on May 9 and ended on June 8. I stayed in Cam O'Kane's rooms where I had a gay time and an opportunity of widening my circle of acquaintance.

49

It was in these lectures that I first met young McDonnell, and through him I got to know his family. Around the same time I had the very satisfactory experience of getting to know Frances Crofton and her cousin Miss Westropp.[5]

In all, I think the term in College was the happiest time in my life.

The Reverend Hyde still hoped that his youngest son would follow him in the ministry. Douglas never really accepted the prospect of a career in the church, but to avoid an open clash with his father he took lectures in Divinity at the beginning of his third year.

2 November 1882   I went in at 11 o'clock for my first lecture in Divinity School. There were fifty or sixty people there, and the lecturer was a man named Lee. Oh, how my heart sank at hearing the same boring old phrases I had heard with loathing so often before. It was, in fact, a very fine lecture, but I hadn't the slightest interest in it, alas. When the lecture was finished we had to sit an examination in Greek, with a lot of grammar. I did not do well. . . .

6 November   I went in for my second lecture in Divinity. I hated it, and hated the people who were with me. They are not refined or well-bred. . . .

During the following summer vacation he had several blunt confrontations with his father:

21 July 1883   The day was wet and showery. I drove to Boyle and left the small carriage with Black to be painted and fitted out. Mr Burke invited me to lunch with him, which I did, and I rode home in an hour and 40 minutes.

When I arrived home I was not too tired, but my father began talking about the life and work of a minister. I said I would never be a minister, and I told him why. With great difficulty I succeeded in convincing him, but when I said that I wanted to be a doctor he swore most positively and solemnly that I would never get another farthing from him. We had it out thoroughly between us. I said that in that case I would have to emigrate to find a livelihood. 'Tell me when you are going', he said, and we left it at that, except that he promised me seventy pounds from this out if I went into the church, a thing I refused to do. I did not tell him that it was unfair of him to cast me out into the world without a profession when he had spent five hundred pounds on my brother and not as much as a hundred and fifty on me.

Although he busied himself with saving the hay and other summer activities on the farm, and with his reading and writing, he could not shake off the concern he felt about his future:

28 July 1883 Bringing home the turf today and yesterday. [In German] A beautiful heavenly day. Drank with Seaghan na Pighne. Did not read much. Wrote down 'Monachar and Manachar' from the lips of Brennan.[6] Read fifty pages of Craik[7] and wrote until late in the night an essay on 'Why I do not want to be a Minister in the Irish Protestant Church'.

9 August We began cutting the hay. My father and I had a terrible row tonight about belief in the Bible and about angels. He lost his temper completely and threatened me, and I did the same, so that we almost had an irreconcilable break. However, when he came to himself he shook hands with me and we made it up. I spent a couple of hours trying to make him understand my arguments against Christianity, which he answered very feebly. It was late in the night—12.30 or so—when I went to bed, and if I was no worse in health as a result of the squabble I certainly was no better. . . .

Towards the end of this summer vacation he finaly wrung reluctant approval from his father for his plan to become a doctor:

2 October 1883 I had an éclaircissement with the Master about my becoming a doctor, and when I threatened to go to London and become a Bohemian he yielded at last, but only grudgingly.

However, he still had the more difficult task of convincing himself:

7 October Sunday. Church. I walked with the dogs to Lung Bridge and back. [German] I spent a terrible day, in the

most dreadful doubt about my future, as I endeavoured to decide either to become a Minister of the Church or to train for a profession, but to no avail. For no sooner had I thought to have chosen the one than the other seemed more attractive, so that I just could not decide. For a week now I find myself in this state of self-torment so that life became sheer hell. Never before did I experience the like and today especially it was simply terrible, cruel beyond measure. If I were sure that my health would not collapse under the strain of the Medical School I would not hesitate a moment to become a doctor. But I am practically sure (although not quite—hence my wavering) that it would bring about my death, and even if I did save my health I know that my eyes are so weak that I could hardly gain for myself a reputation. On the other hand, I always feel a secret aversion against the clerical life, inspired in my childhood by my father's inexcusable conduct. I still cannot free myself of this feeling. Hence my state of mind which is so awful that I would not wish it on a dog.

In the end he continued at the Divinity School, and despite his unease and his distaste for the subject he got a first in his finals in 1885 and went on to win a special divinity prize the following year.

As it happened, Hyde's choice of Divinity, however reluctant and misguided, was to play a major part in his development as a student of Irish. The reason was, as he scathingly remarks in the preface to his *Literary History of Ireland* (1899), that Trinity College, Dublin,

by far the richest college in the British Isles, one of the wealthiest universities in the world, allows its so-called ' Irish professorship' to be an adjunct of its Divinity School, founded *and paid* by a Society for—the conversion of Irish Roman Catholics through the medium of their own language![8]

In November 1883 Hyde got his own rooms at Trinity: number 24 on the ground floor. These rooms soon became a centre for typical undergraduate symposia: debates and discussions into the early hours, sustained by glasses of punch and pipes of tobacco. Such a programme was not conducive to the regular keeping of a diary, and it is not surprising that at this time, after ten years of remarkable fidelity to the day-today record, the first substantial gaps occur. The whole of November and December 1883 are summarized in one long entry and, whereas January is fully written up,[9] another lapse occurs from 3 February to 10 April 1884. The summary of this latter period indicates how much more involved he had become in college activities:

> I stayed in Dublin, at the College, until the end of term, from February 1st to March 26th, and I was in my own rooms throughout this time. The rooms were comfortable enough eventually. I bought a very nice carpet for £2; a couple of cabinets for my books, one for £2 and the other for 28 shillings; three or four nice pictures. They re-papered the walls for me and gave me a new grate.

> Sheehan[10] was the best friend I had in the college. I used to be in his rooms while my own were being done up. I went to Mass with him a couple of Sundays, and another day we went for a walk to Castleknock. I took a great liking to him.

> Another man I know well is young Moffat. He is often in my rooms, and he came with me to the Discussion Club in York Street, i.e. Young Ireland, to my great amusement. He is a Conservative.[11]

> Two old friends of mine are Wilson and Wright, but I did not see much of them.

> I went to a very enjoyable dance at Wrights house. I went to an ' Afternoon ' at Connors, to two at Oldfields, and to a couple of dinners at Croftons. I took dancing lessons twice a week, and learned the Cotulis [Cotillion?], or almost.

> I am a member of the Historical Society and I know most of the people in it. I am also in the Theological Society and in the Chess Club. . . .

The first mention of the Historical Society occurs on 9 May 1883:

> I went to a meeting of the Historical Society and gave my

vote to O'Connell who stirred up a great row among them with his fooling. Rowe got first prize and O'Connell second.

A fortnight later he records a special occasion at the 'Hist.':

23 May . . . I went to a meeting of the College Historical Society. The speeches were very good. Lecky, the distinguished historian, spoke from the chair. I myself spoke, as did O'Connell, Sheehan and Dillon. I came home on the last tram at 11.45 with Dillon.

At the inaugural meeting in November 1883 he was a steward in evening clothes but he makes no further reference to the society until June of the following year:

11 June 1884 . . . I was at a meeting of the Historical Society. Lyster was elected auditor, with twenty two votes more than Dillon. I got twenty-three votes; I was surprised to get so many. I was the highest of those who failed to get a place.

He records a number of meetings in 1885:

3 March . . . I spoke on 'Celts and Teutons' at the Historical Society and did wonderfully well. Everyone said I was the best speaker.

13 May . . . I opened the debate at the Historical Society arguing that England was going downhill.

3 June I gave a very good talk in the Historical Society on 'Irish Rule in Ireland'.

17 June I spoke at the Historical on Classics and it went quite well.

At the same time he was a regular speaker at the Theological Society:

1 March 1885 I read my paper on 'The Attitude of the Reformed Church in Ireland' at the Theological and the reading lasted an hour and a quarter. Stockley and Hackett took my side, while many more spoke against me. Salmon in particular said he would not have come had he known what I was going to read. I got a place on the committee.

His paper on this occasion won favourable notice in the *Dublin University Review* of April 1885:

> At the next meeting held on March 2nd, an essay was read by Mr Douglas Hyde (Sen. Mod.), B.A., on ' The Attitude of the Reformed Church in Ireland'. The title was, as the essayist himself allowed, a little misleading. The first part of the paper was a historical account of the rise and development of the three largest Christian bodies in this country —the Roman Catholic, the Presbyterian, and the Church of Ireland. The latter part of the Paper gave the essayist's own opinions as to the position the Irish Church clergy ought to take up with regard to the present Nationalist movement. This position, according to Mr Hyde, should be one of approval, implicit if not avowed. Such opinions are not very common in the Theological Society, and their expression evoked against the essayist many hostile criticisms. . . . On one feature of Mr Hyde's essay we have not touched, namely, its style. It is not often that an essay is read in College where clearly-defined views are expressed in language so beautiful and simple.

Hyde himself was soon closely involved with the *Dublin University Review*: it was in its pages that he first propounded his philosophy of nationalism. The *Review* was founded by Charles Hubert Oldham[12] in February 1885 as ' a monthly magazine of literature, art and university intelligence'. The editorial of the opening issue states the aim of the new journal:

> . . . It is believed, therefore, that without sinking into mere provincialism, without discussing too exclusively purely Irish topics, without giving undue importance to the writings or achievements of Irishmen, the *Review* can assume and maintain a distinctly national tone; and in its pages Irish writers can express to Irish readers their views on the social problems of the day, and on the phases and aspects of contemporary art and literature. It cannot be too emphatically declared that with the vexed questions of current politics the *Review* has nothing whatever to do.
> Such an organ, we hold, can with propriety be issued from the institution from which we have derived our title. We assume that Dublin University is, or in the nature of things

ought to be, the true centre of culture and educated opinion in Dublin. Many there are who regret that it does not exert a more direct and permeating influence. An influence it undoubtedly has, but it is of a fragmentary character, the effect rather of individual members than of the institution itself. We see no good reason why it ought to continue to be so.[13]

After the first few months T. W. Rolleston[14] took over the editorship, while Oldham continued as Managing Director. It was probably through Rolleston that Hyde was introduced to Oldham and became involved in the *Review*. In 1885 Rolleston was living in Delgany, a village in County Wicklow some twenty miles south of Dublin. Hyde records his first visit to the house:

13 March Sunday After chapel in College I went with the Stockleys and a man named Wynne to Palmerston Park. We had lunch there and took the train at Miltown and went on to Bray. We then walked with the two dogs until we came to Delgany to the de Burgh's house. We went in and had tea with them and then the elder Stockley and I went to Rolleston's house which was not far from the other. We found himself and his wife at home, and Standish O'Grady. I spoke German with Rolleston and he gave me a book, an essay he himself had written. We were more than two hours walking back to Bray where we arrived at 8 o'clock, really tired.

Some weeks later Rolleston introduced Hyde to John O'Leary, recently returned from five years' penal servitude followed by fifteen years' enforced exile in Paris for his part in the Fenian conspiracy:

8 May Lecture from Salmon and another from Wallis on Hebrew. I had an invitation to dine with Rolleston and John O'Leary at Bern's Hotel and I went. Rolleston gave us a very fine dinner and a bottle of wine, and I talked with him and with O'Leary for a couple of hours, but then I had to go to Crees for a reading of the Picolimini and the Verre d'Eau. Stockley was with me at Crees and I walked part of the way back with him. O'Leary was a grey-haired

old man with a long beard. He spoke bitterly against the League and I defended it. His politics are O'Brien's.

The first mention of Oldham and the *Review* occurs on

2 June   Lectures and grinding. I was devilishly tired. I spent the night in Oldham's rooms with Cherry, Yeats, a man named Gregg, the elder Stockley, Coffey and someone called Stokes, discussing how to introduce an Irish national spirit into the Revue. I went to bed at 12.30, worn out.

There were several such meetings over the following weeks:

6 June   I stayed at home. Rolleston and Coffey came to me and we discussed things in my rooms. I was at a meeting of the Gaelic Union in the Mansion House.

12 June   A meeting in Oldham's rooms. Coffey, Stockley, Rolleston, Fitzgerald the eye-specialist, a man named Pearceall, Falkiner and one or two others. I stayed until midnight. Fitzgerald invited us all to have dinner with him.

15 June   Working hard. Long talk with Oldham.

18 June   I went to a big dinner which Fitzgerald the eye-specialist gave. The guests were Oldham, Stockley, Coffey, Falkiner, Prof. Armstrong, A. Webb, Mr Pearceall, Rolleston, myself and another man. We had champagne and everything, and much discussion of the Revue. I went home at 11 or 12.

23 June   . . . In the evening there was a meeting in Oldham's rooms; eight or nine people and myself. Great talk about the Revue. The meeting went on till midnight.

24 June   A little tennis with young McDermott in the morning. To F.C. at noon, but it was a wet day so we could not go for a walk but we came back to Dublin together. I went to dinner with the Stockleys at 6.30. Oldham, Osborne and Miss Dowden were there. Then at 8.30 we all went to Dowden's house and spent three hours smoking and talking with him. Dr Storey, Coffey, Lyster, and young Gwynne[15] were there also. We had a good supper. I came home at about 1.30.

These meetings, especially that of 2 June at which they discussed 'how to introduce an Irish national spirit into the Revue' are significant. In the July issue of the magazine the editor introduced not only a new format but, more important, a radical change of policy:

> We also intend to open our columns to a temperate discussion of certain public questions by representatives of the different parties or social movements in Ireland. The first article of this description will appear in our August issue, and will be contributed by Mr Standish O'Grady. It will deal with Conservatism in Ireland—its Policy and Future.

O'Grady's article duly appeared. In it he castigated the landlords, not for rackrents and oppression of their tenants, but for failing to provide aristocratic leadership:

> The grand opportunity was theirs of harnessing, bitting and bridling this wild, tameless democracy—tameless but tameable, and in its heart desiring to be tamed—of controlling it, and by methods democratic inevitably as belonging to these centuries, but aristocratic too, leading forward this people to higher and ever higher stages.[16]

Needless to say, such patrician condescension infuriated the Land League. O'Grady's arguments were contemptuously dismissed as outworn and anachronistic by Michael Davitt in an article under the same heading in the following issue.

Of more relevance in the present context, however, is an article in the August issue on 'The Irish Language and Literature'. The author, Justin Huntly McCarthy, appeals to all young Irishmen to learn something at least of the language which might have been their native language, and to become familiar with 'the splendid stories of legendary Irish history.' Having stated that there are Irishmen who are familiar with Greek and Roman literature but who would be hopelessly puzzled to explain the identity of the heroes of Irish myth and legend, he goes on:

> I should not, for my part, wish Ireland to be behindhand with any other country in what is called classical culture. . . .

One of the finest translations of the *Iliad,* or rather of portion of the *Iliad,* into any foreign language is the late Archbishop M'Hale's Irish rendering of some of the early books of the great epic. But what I should like all Irishmen, and especially all young Irishmen, to remember is, that Ireland would not lack poetical literature of the finest and of the noblest, even if the hexameters of the singer of Smyrna—

' The old man who, clearest-souled of men,
Saw the wide prospect and the Asian fen,
And Tmolus Hill, and Smyrna Bay, though blind '—

had never been rendered in the language of Oisin.

To my mind there are no more fascinating legends in any literature that I know of—and I have studied the literatures of many countries—than the legends which deal with Finn, the son of Coul, and the Feni, his companions. The Feni, as I have written elsewhere, are strange and shadowy figures, Ossianic ghosts, moving in dusky vales, or along hillsides clothed with echoing woods, and seamed with the many-coloured tides of rearing streams. . . .

Cucullain is as fine a hero as Theseus; Queen Maev is no less marvellous than Helen; the fate of the children of Tureen is as grim as the fortunes of the Heraclidae. Nor must I forget that wonderful story of the adventures of Oisin in the Land of Youth, a legend which, for phantasy, for the magic of poetic imagination, and for sweet sadness, has not to my mind, its superior among all the legends of the earth—all that I, at least, am acquainted with.

The publication of this article is an important event in the history of the Irish literary movement. W. B. Yeats had been a contributor to the *Review* from the beginning, but his themes were exotic, such as ' The Island of Statues: an Arcadian Faery Tale '. Here, for the first time, he caught a glimpse of the ' fountain of Gaelic legends ' from which he was to draw so freely in the coming years. It is surely more than a coincidence that it was just at this time that he began the long poem which was to become ' The Wanderings of Oisin ', and the turning-point in his career:

Many of the poems in *Crossways*, certainly those upon shepherds and fauns, must have been written before I was twenty, for from the moment when I began *The Wanderings of Oisin,* which I did at that age, I believe my subject-matter became Irish.[17]

Yeats was twenty on 13 June 1885.

McCarthy's article, which appeared in August, certainly inspired Douglas Hyde to take up his pen. In the October 1885 issue of the *Review* there was an article from him which might be described as an outline draft of *Love Songs of Connacht*:

The sympathetic letter [*sic*] of Mr Justin Huntly McCarthy on the subject of the Irish language and literature, in the August number of this *Review* gives encouragement to draw attention to another and humbler field of our literature which few have thought worthy of being laboured in, but which nevertheless is generally interesting, and always instructive enough to repay any trouble spent upon it. This field consists of the songs and folklore of our peasantry as preserved in the Gaedheilg tongue, which form a kind of literature in themselves, none the less real for never having been committed to writing, and which owing to the inexorable connection between thought and language, will last exactly as long as the tongue of Oisin lasts, and will die when it dies. After gleaning for several summers in central Connacht, round the haunts of Turlough O Carolan, the last of the Irish bards, and collecting such scraps of old songs, ballads, proverbs, and stories as chance threw his way, the writer thought that to contemplate the result from a literary point of view might possibly be of interest to some of those (he thinks, an increasing class) who take an interest in this oldest surviving branch of Aryan languages, which a hundred years ago was spoken throughout the length and breadth of our country, even up to the walls of Dublin.

Hyde contrasts the simple charm of these Connaught verses with the over-elaborate style of the Gaelic poets of Munster with which he was familiar, as we have seen, from the volumes in his own library:

As to the verses themselves, they are generally full of simplicity and naivete, and as such they form the most extreme contrast to the poems of the regular bards, which are refined and polished away to a ruinous extreme, making, in too many instances, the sense subservient to the sound; for the regular versifiers have too often preferred a luscious sweetness and a delicious softness in numbers and rhythm to sound sense and striking thoughts.[18] The poems by the Munster bards printed by O'Daly, in two volumes, and the two large volumes of Hardiman (unfortunately long out of print), afford the student a very good idea of what Irish poetry is really like; but most pieces contained in these publications are drawn from manuscripts, and few from the mouths of the peasantry.

He gives a general description of the types of song that he has collected, remarking on the total absence of the true ballad or narrative poem, and then goes on to treat in detail of the love songs:

But of all the verses in which the peasantry delight, the love songs are by far the best. Many of them are genuinely pathetic, and speak the very excess of passion in nearly all its phases—generally its most despairing ones. A few verses are jotted down here, nearly at random, from these unknown and unpublished songs, and the wish to preserve what a score or so of years will find disappeared off the face of the earth must serve as an excuse for reproducing the *ipsissima verba*,[19] for slowly but surely those who know them are disappearing; those who sung them are passing away; and soon, very soon, the place that knew them shall know them no more. Here is a song in which a lover, having opened all his mind to his mistress for the first time, and apparently meeting with a favourable answer, becomes suddenly enraptured with the beauty of everything around him, and exclaims twice—

> Oh, the kine they are lowing,
> And the calves are at play,
> And you, white pulse of my bosom,
> You have had my secret today.

In another poem the lover seems to have been less sucessful, for he cries in agony—

F

Oh, my heart is breaking slowly, breaking in the
midst of me.
As the roots on some wild mountain give beneath
the lonely tree.

. . . Another song sings the beauty of some ' Girl of the nine
Gold Tresses', of whom her admirer cries with more than
Celtic hyperbole that there existed not

In the valley of starlight
Such splendour of beauty
There shines light for a hundred from each gold hair.[20]

Here is another verse from a lovely song, the 'Drinawn
Donn', in which a peasant girl regrets having set her affec-
tions on an object too high for her. In the original it is very
affecting—

He is foolish, he who attempts the first high wall
he sees,
When a low wall stands beside him he could vault
across at ease;
The rowan-tree clusters be bitter, though stately the
tree and tall,
Oh, the low-bush berries beside it are sweeter
after all.

Tears actually stood in the eyes of the old woman from
whom this was taken down as she sang the words. . . .

Every separate locality has its own favourite traditions, songs,
and stories, often descending to us from the dim twilight of
antiquity; and whoever will take the pains to examine them
will find them remarkable for a generosity of sentiment and
an absence of vulgarity, which have done much to leave their
impress upon the character of our nation. But, alas, all these
traditions are so inextricably bound up with the tongue in
which they are preserved, that as our language wanes and
dies, the golden legends of the far-off centuries fade and
pass away. No one sees their influence upon culture; no one
sees their educational power; no one puts out a hand to
arrest them ere they depart for ever.

AN CHRAOIBHIN AOIBHINN

A remark in the editorial columns of the *Review* some months later prompted Hyde to take up his pen in defence of the national language. In 'Notes of the Month', June 1886, reference was made to the Centenary Dinner of the Royal Irish Academy which had taken place on 12 May. While congratulating the Academy on its achievements over the past century, the editor regretted that its activities had been so one-sided.[21]

> Except in name the section for Polite Literature hardly exists. A nation without a literature of its own, an imaginative literature stamped with the characteristics of its own genius, illustrating and ennobling its own history, topography, etc., is a nation without a soul.

He goes on, however, to query the aims of the language revivalists:

> But we should like to see more definiteness or more common-sense in the aims of *An Chraoibin Aoibinn* [*sic*] and his friends. Do they wish to make Irish the language of our conversation and our newspapers? Impossible, and wholly undesirable. Do they wish to make us a bilingual people in the sense that everybody should know two languages? But peasantry and artisans cannot be expected to know two languages except at the expense of both. Would they separate Ireland into an English-speaking country and an Irish-speaking country? But how seriously this would affect the free circulation of thought: —
> 'Shooting in pulses of fire, ceaseless, to vivify all'.
> What is there left except to treat Irish as a classic, and leave it to the Universities?
> Sufficient endowments will secure their attention to its interests.

In July the editor announced a reaction to these remarks:

> Certain questions which in our Notes of last month were put to enthusiasts for the revival or preservation of Celtic as a living language, have, we are glad to say, called forth an answer from one of the Celtic scholars best fitted, in every respect, to deal with them. . . .

The 'Celtic scholar' was, of course, Douglas Hyde, and his answer entitled 'A Plea for the Irish Language', filled ten pages of the August issue. It is an article of major significance in the study of Hyde's political and cultural development. Here for the first time he had occasion to formulate his ideas about the language and its contribution to the Irish ethos. Most of the ideas expressed here were to become fundamental principles of his Gaelic League propaganda in the years to come, while one important detail, which will be noted in due course, was to be substantially modified. As a policy statement of the future president of the Gaelic League the article deserves to be quoted at considerable length.

I cannot avoid saying a few words in deprecation of the editorial censure, and explaining why it is I do not share the wish to see my language dead and decently buried—to 'leave it to the universities', as they call it. We know what that means. We have seen our very numerous, very ancient and very interesting MSS. handed over to the safe keeping of the colleges already. There they lie in their companies:

'No one wakes them, they are keeping
Royal state and semblance still ',

and mildew on their pages, the dust upon their covers, in the utmost repose and dignity, where we are requested to leave them, 'to the universities',—where their placid rest may be disturbed only once or twice in a generation.[22]

Now if we allow our living language to die out, it is almost a certainty that we condemn our literary records to remain in obscurity. All our great scholars, nearly all those who have done anything for the elucidation of our MSS., O'Connor of Ballingar, O'Donovan, O'Curry, Petrie, Hennessy, all these spoke the language naturally from their cradle, and had it not been so they would never have been able to accomplish the work they did, a work which first made it possible for a Jubainville or a Windisch to prosecute their Celtic studies with any success.[23]

There is no use in arguing the advantage of making Irish the language of our newspapers and clubs, because that is and ever shall be an impossibility; but for several reasons we wish to arrest the language in its downward path, and if we cannot spread it (as I do not believe we very much can), we will at least prevent it from dying out and make sure that those who speak it now, will also transmit it unmodified to their descendants.

This last paragraph is especially noteworthy. It shows that at this time Hyde's aim was to preserve the language where it survived rather than to revive it where it had died. Had he persevered in this policy, the Gaelic League would have taken an altogether different course from that which it in fact pursued; it would have had as its aim the social and economic development of the Gaeltacht (Irish-speaking) areas rather than the restoration of the language throughout the country as a whole. The former course would seem to have had more promise of success, but the economic measures it called for were beyond the means of a voluntary organization such as the Gaelic League.

In the following paragraphs Hyde aligns himself steadfastly on the side of Gaelic Ireland, and traces the outline of his momentous manifesto of six years later, 'The Necessity for De-Anglicising Ireland':

To be told that the language which I spoke from my cradle, the language my father and grandfather and all my ancestors in an unbroken line leading up into the remote twilight of antiquity have spoken, the language which has entwined itself with every fibre of my being, helped to mould my habits of conduct and forms of thought, to be calmly told by an Irish Journal that the sooner I give up this language the better, that the sooner I 'leave it to the universities' the better, that we will improve our English speaking by giving up our Irish, to be told this by a representative Irish Journal is naturally and justly painful.

Englishmen have very noble and excellent qualities which I should like to see imitated here, but I should not like to imitate them in everything. I like our own habits and character better, they are more consonant to my nature; I like our own turn of thought, our own characteristics, and above all I like our own language and do not wish to see the effacing hand of cosmopolitanism prevail against it. . . .

He goes on to argue that the decay of the native language inevitably leads to a decline in moral qualities among the country people:

> . . . When they lose the language they lose also the traditional unwritten literature which, inculcating and eulogising what is courteous, high-minded, and noble, supplied continuously an incentive to the practice of those qualities.

With regard to the editor's misgivings about restricting ' the free circulation of thought' Hyde makes a surprising admission:

> . . . If by ceasing to speak Irish our peasantry could learn to appreciate Shakespeare and Milton, to study Wordsworth or Tennyson, then I would certainly say adieu to it. But this is not the case. They lay aside a language which for all ordinary purposes of every day life is much more forcible than any with which I am acquainted, and they replace it by another which they learn badly and speak with an atrocious accent, interlarding it with barbarisms and vulgarity.

He then proceeds to emphasize the essential relationship that must exist between language and culture:

> The language of the western Gael is the language best suited to his surroundings. It corresponds best to his topography, his nomenclature and his organs of speech, and the use of it guarantees the remembrance of his own weird and beautiful traditions. Around the blazing bog fire of a winter's night Dermod O'Duibhne of the love spot, Finn with his coat of hairy skin, Conan the Thersites of the Fenians, the old blinded giant Esheen (Ossian), the speckled bull with the moveable horn, the enchanted cat of Rathcroghan, and all the other wild and poetic offspring of the bardic imagination pass in review before us. Every hill, every *lios*, [' fairy fort'] every crag and gnarled tree and lonely valley has its own strange and graceful legend attached to it, the product of the Hibernian Celt in its truest and purest type, not to be improved upon by change, and of infinite worth in moulding the race type, of immeasurable value in forming its character.

But where the language dies, these folk memories scarcely survive one generation, as in the east of County Leitrim and in
County Longford:

> . . . There Dermod of the love spot is unknown, Finn
> MacCool is barely remembered as ' a giant ', Ossian is never
> heard of, the ancient memories have ceased to cling to the
> various objects of nature; the halo of romance, the exquisite
> and dreamy film which hangs over the Mayo mountains has
> been blown away by the brutal blast of the most realistic
> materialism, and people when they gather into one another's
> houses in the evening for a *cailee* [céilidhe—a night visit]
> can talk of nothing but the latest scandal or the price Tim
> Rooney got for his calf, or the calving of Paddy Sweeney's
> cow.

Having dealt with the various other arguments and comments
of the editor, Hyde makes an impassioned plea that, after centuries of suppression, the language be given a fair chance:

> I do not believe in resuscitating a great national language
> by twopenny-halfpenny bounties. If the Irish people are
> resolved to let the national language die, by all means let
> them; I believe the instinct of a nation is always juster than
> that of an individual. But this at least no one can deny, that
> hitherto the Irish nation has had no choice in the matter.
> What between the Anglo-Irish gentry who came upon us
> in a flood after the confiscations of 1648, and again after
> 1691, whose great object it was to stamp out both the
> language and institutions of the nation, with their bards and
> shanachies and ollamhs and professors; what with the brutal-
> ized sensual unsympathetic gentry of the last century, the
> racing, blasting drunkard squireens who usurped the places of
> the O'Connors, the O'Briens, the O'Donnells, the O'Cahans,
> and the MacCarthys, our old and truly cultured national
> nobility who cherished hereditary poets and historians; what
> with the purblind cringing pedagogues of the present cen-
> tury whose habit it was to beat and threaten their pupils for
> talking Irish; what with the high-handed action of the
> authorities who with a cool contempt of existing circum-
> stances surely unequalled in an European country, [*sic*]
> continued to appoint English-speaking magistrates, petty

session clerks and local officials among a people to whom they cannot make themselves intelligible; what with the hostility of the Board of Education who do not recognize the language of those baronies where no English is spoken even to the extent of publishing school books in it; what with all this and our long slavery as a nation, we assert that the Irish language has had no chance of showing its capabilities, or those who speak it of taking their own part and making their voice heard.

The next paragraph reminds us that in 1886 Home Rule was confidently expected:

Our emancipation as a nation is at hand, a few short years will surely see the dreams of centuries fulfilled, and then it will be the duty—can anyone deny it?—of our rulers to see that our language is treated as the language of any other country of Europe would be treated in like circumstances; to see that those who learn no other language shall be taught to read the one they do know, and that as much encouragement be given to it by the Government as is given to English.

He ends with a renewed appeal for the preservation of the surviving Irish-speaking communities, even if practical considerations demanded that they should become bi-lingual:

In conclusion we may say this, that while our social and commercial relations make it a necessity for every man woman and child in this kingdom to learn English sooner or later, reverence for our past history, regard for the memory of our ancestors, our national honour, and the fear of becoming materialized and losing our best and highest characteristics call upon us imperatively to assist the Irish speaking population at the present crisis and to establish for all time a bilingual population in those parts of Ireland where Irish is now spoken, from whom all those who in the distant future may wish to investigate the history or the antiquities of our nation, may draw as from a fountain that vernacular knowledge which for such purpose is indispensably necessary.

AN CHRAOIBHIN AOIBHINN

Three years later when Hyde published his first book, a collection of folk-tales entitled *Leabhar Sgeulaigheachta* (Dublin, 1889), he appended to it a note ' On the reasons for keeping alive the Irish Language ' which is, in fact, an abbreviated but otherwise almost word for word reproduction of this *Review* article, which is, in effect, the manifesto of the future president of the Gaelic League.[24]

Across the road from the main gates of Trinity College, over what is now the office of American Express, Charles Oldham had his rooms. Here, on 21 November 1885, Oldham established what came to be known as the Contemporary Club:

> At 8.30 I went with Joynt to the new club in Oldham's rooms. People gathered slowly and only thirteen came. Talk at first de omnibus rebus et quibusdam aliis. . . . Dr Fitz- gerald, Walker, Taylor, the two Stockleys, Lipmann, Eyre, Cherry and two or three others present. There was a long argument about the name of the club, Bailey in the chair. In the end it was adjourned until next Saturday. When the others left and the meeting broke up, Cherry, Taylor, Lip- mann, another man and I stayed on and we had a very heated argument about the present state of Ireland. It was two o'clock in the morning before we went home.

Forthright and full-blooded wrangling was to be a feature of the Contemporary Club, as W. B. Yeats recalls:

> In Ireland harsh argument which had gone out of fashion in England was still the manner of our conversation, and at this club Unionist and Nationalist could interrupt one another and insult one another without the formal and traditional restraint of public speech. Sometimes they would change the subject and discuss Socialism, or a philosophical question, merely to discover their old passions under a new shape. *Autobiographies,* p. 93

Even the spirited Maud Gonne was surprised at the vehemence of the debate. She relates that when she first made up her mind to work for Ireland's freedom a friend brought her to consult Mr Oldham. He in turn decided that she should meet John

O'Leary, and invited her to a meeting of his then exclusively male club.

> In his original way, Oldham introduced me to the Club in this fashion:
> 'Maud Gonne wants to meet John O'Leary; I thought you would all like to meet Maud Gonne.'

The debate that evening, as on most evenings, was on current Irish politics. Miss Gonne's first surprise was to hear the great O'Leary bitterly denounce the Land League and pour scorn on the Irish Parliamentary leaders.

> There were men of all shades of political opinion at the Club, even one or two Unionists, and the debate became very vehement. My kind friend and introducer, Mr. Oldham, was ferociously attacked when he took the side of the Parliamentary Party and defended John Dillon and William O'Brien. I felt sorry for him, but soon realised I need not; attacks, even personal ones, rolled off him like water from a duck's back as he smilingly put on the kettle and refilled our tea-cups. *A Servant of the Queen,* pp. 84-88

Some time later the rules were modified to admit ladies once a month. Professor Mary Macken, who attended many meetings, was left with a similar memory of fiery polemics, but found that Oldham, far from needing sympathy, was able to give at least as good as he got:

> Oldham constantly gave offence in debate when he least intended it. At heart the kindest of men, he was himself invulnerable to wordy attack and must have assumed that others had bathed in the dragon's blood also. *Studies,* March 1939, p. 138

Hyde's interest in the Contemporary Club is proved not only by his regular attendance at meetings ('I went to the club every Saturday but one'—diary, 19 March 1886), but also by the painstakingly detailed notes he made of the matters discussed. Here he had an opportunity of hearing contemporary political issues argued not only between nationalists and unionists but, among nationalists themselves, between advocates of constitutional methods such as Oldham and champions of physical force like O'Leary. (Incidentally, it is interesting to note that Hyde did not share in Yeats's hero-worship of O'Leary. Indeed, he has some trenchant remarks on the old Fenian's political views.)

Apart from its function as a school of contemporary politics, the club provided Hyde with an opportunity of doing something he thoroughly enjoyed at this time, that is, of making new acquaintances. After his years of almost monastic seclusion up to 1883 when he took rooms in college, he was now avid for company. Moreover, he was enjoying the discovery that he was a social success. His life at this time was a busy round of meetings, 'At Homes', dinners, poetry and play readings, not to mention his assiduous courting of Frances Crofton.

For the new light they throw on this lively forum at which opinions were expressed and friendships forged which influenced the course of the literary revival, it seems worth while quoting at some length from Hyde's record of these Saturday evenings in Oldham's rooms overlooking College Green.

5 December 1885 [Irish] I went to the club at 9.30. Bryce, the man who wrote The Holy Roman Empire, was there and O'Leary, Murrough O'Brien, Dr Fitzgerald, Falkiner, Russell, Walker, Cherry, Bailey, Stockley (senior), Rolleston, Crooke, Lipmann and about 20 altogether. Bryce said Parnell had made a mistake in not supporting and strengthening one party or the other, as he had nothing to hope for now from either side; neither party could join with him without losing the votes of the country. [English] O Laoghaire said the priests were all powerful on educational questions [Irish] but that they had no influence at all on the question of nationality. [English] He admitted that if the land question & the educational one were settled the priests would become as cold to the national cause as the tenant farmers. All admitted that. The Educational schemes were discussed & most agreed that TCD must go to the Catholics. [German] But, as Cherry said, as soon as they would get TCD the first question would be (as is now the case in the Roman Catholic university) 'to what faith does he belong?', and Bryce was of opinion that a university which would reject men like Darwin and Huxley because they did

not share the same beliefs in religious matters would lose its status among the universities of the world.[25] Most agreed too that the country would reject whichever party made terms with Parnell, & that an agreement might be made to discard the Irish vote, since the country would back up the ministry in rejecting it & carrying on office in the teeth of a majority composed of the Irish vote and the Opposition. Alfred Webb gave a high character to the present Irish representatives & said they were much more earnest straightforward unselfish men than the Callans & Pat O'Briens of the past. [Irish] When the meeting broke up O'Leary, Cherry & a couple of others stayed to drink a glass of punch. O'L. said there were 8 Fenians in the last parliament, & 18 or 25 in this one, [English] but that they must be acting immorally [Irish] in giving their oath to a country they aimed to destroy. I walked home part of the way with Cherry.

On 12 December 1885 he records another meeting:

All the lions were there: Davitt,[26] O'Leary, Russell,[27] a man named Williams who stood against Bradlaw in Finsbury,[28] Alfred Webb,[29] Coffey, Dr Sigerson, Hazlitt, &c, &c. . . .

The discussion, as usual, was on politics:

Davitt was very moderate, so much as to astonish the Englishman. ' 3 pledges will be required of us I understand', said he, ' and I do not see any objection to giving them. 1. That we will not confiscate private property 2 nor interfere with personal or religious freedom.'[30]

20 December 1885 [Irish] Sunday. I was at the club last night. Williams the Englishman there. O'Leary, Russell, the Stockleys, Cherry, Coffey, Gaussen, etc., etc. Much talk on [English] representative Government, single and double chambers etc. I never came across so complete a Tory as O Laoghaire [O'Leary], he did not think that the masses have a right to the franchise, it was not expedient he said, forgetting that he constituted himself the judge of the expediency.

There was also much discussion on the advisability of 2nd chambers, and as to whether we ought to have one here.

O Laoghaire true to his ultra Tory principles contended strongly for them, as did Gaussen & Patton. Stocley [*sic*] Walker and myself against. We were of opinion that biennial or triennial Parliaments would prevent legislation in haste upon subjects about which the country had not pronounced, that a second chamber must be a class chamber, that the difficulty of getting one exactly so constituted as to act as a drag on hasty legislation without coming into collision with the lower house or injuring the unity of the nation was very great, that they would be when once constituted irresponsible and would represent no one except themselves, and to me the danger of bribery with such a class seemed very great, ' they would sell us again said Stocli and we would have another Union.'

On New Year's Day 1886, in his review of the year just ended, Hyde summed up:

The most significant things I did were to join the Mosaic and the new club that Oldham founded.

The Mosaic was a literary circle which met fortnightly at the homes of members.

One of his social calls around this time is particularly interesting:

23 March 1886 I called on the Wilsons, had a long talk with them and drank three glasses of wine with Mackey. Went for a walk with Cree and Coffey. I met Coffey's wife and walked back with her, and she invited me to visit them this evening. I went, and enjoyed myself very much. M. Close was there, and Standish O'Grady and his sister, and Lipmann, and voilà tout. I spoke a good deal and well with S. O'Grady and found him very interesting. I drank tea with seven others in Lunn's rooms. A great night.

' M. Close ' is, of course, the Reverend Maxwell H. Close, M.A., M.R.I.A., (1822-1903), a Church of Ireland clergyman who, like his contemporary and confrère the Reverend Euseby D. Cleaver, was an exceptionally generous benefactor to the cause of the Irish Language. ' Our Maecenas ' Hyde calls him in *Mise agus an Connradh* (p. 21). He was a founder-member of the Society for the Preservation of the Irish Language, and among his donations to the society was a gift of twenty pounds for the publication of *The Third Irish Book* (1879). He also to a great extent financed the publication of *Irisleabhar na Gaedhilge* (*The Gaelic Journal*) from its establishment in 1882 until it was taken over by the Gaelic League in 1893. Over forty years later Hyde wrote of him:

> Without the help, the financial backing and the good-will of Maxwell Close we could not have carried on. He was always ready to assist every good cause. . . . Without him perhaps the Gaelic League would never have come into being. *Mise agus an Connradh,* pp. 26 *passim.*

Standish James O'Grady (1846-1928), historian, storyteller, political journalist, was born in Castletown, Berehaven, in the western corner of County Cork. Like Hyde, he was the son of a Protestant clergyman. His *History of Ireland: Heroic Period* was published in two volumes in 1878 and 1880. The following year he published *History of Ireland: Critical and Philosophical.* One of his most popular works was *The Bog of Stars* (1893), a series of short stories from Elizabethan Irish history. His views on the politics of his day are found in *Toryism and the Tory Democracy* (1886). W. B. Yeats says of him that he was a man to whom ' every imaginative Irish writer owed a portion of his soul ' (*Autobiographies*, p. 220), while Vivian Mercier describes his ' Heroic History ' as ' the fuse which exploded the long-awaited Literary Revival.'[31]

An interesting insight into O'Grady's approach to history is found in a book review which he wrote for the *Dublin University Review:*

> History is, we believe, the same word as story, and certainly the most universally interesting historical works are those of the story-telling sort. . . . Indeed, the more professional and didactic the historian, and the greater his dignity, the more he seems to miss his true aim. All of us without exception are curious to *see* our ancestors, *see* the men of old times, and it is not the rhetorician or philosopher who enables us to do this, but the story-teller.

Hyde took a keen interest in the socialist gospel preached by

William Morris during his visit to Dublin in 1886, and made detailed notes of Morris's basic principles. One of these entries, though exceptionally long, seems to be worth quoting in full as showing not only Hyde's ability to grasp and memorize an argument but also his own reactions to the socialist doctrine. (He also gives an interesting account of the reactions of Dublin workingmen to Morris's ideas!)

10 April 1886 The substance of Morris' (W) lecture last night was that art would not exist at all if it did not give pleasure. 2 obj[ect]s to it: 1. Ascetic, 2. Utilitarian.

Man has his energetic mood and his idle mood. The curse of his idle mood is vacancy. Art if it interests him ought to attract him in his idle mood and by interesting him supply pleasure instead of vacancy. In his active mood it it [*sic*] excites him and gives whereupon to expend his activity with interest and profit. Machinery has destroyed art, the work man of the middle ages is now the 'factory hand', and works without care or interest or enjoyment. He thinks the over-employment of machinery will bring about a revulsion & that the world will go back to hand industries again (in which I cannot agree with him). England was a much more beautiful and pleasant place 40 years ago. It will be still worse in forty years more, getting more vulgar & ugly every day.

Now every man can produce much more than is wanted for his own support & could give the rest of his liesure [*sic*] to art & pleasure. Why does he not? It is because he does not reap the fruits of his own work, other people who do nothing get the benefit of it. All the work (rather energy and activity) of this second class is absolutely wasted. They do not support themselves, they are supported by others. They ought to be *made* to support themselves. Then man would be on a par with man and the burden of the now overworked lessened & he could give himself to amusement and art. At present our work is excessive and unpleasant and our rest is unfruitful.

Of course it seems to me that there can be very little art & still less interest in turning things out by machinery, while in the middle ages the workman spending weeks & months in the hand-manufacture of an article which we would now produce in minutes and days, grew interested over his work

75

and produced with pleasure to himself an artistic production. But, (and here I think Morris burked the hinge and turning-point of the whole question) is it more advantageous to humanity at large or is it not, that we should turn out a large number of articles, unartistic it is true & hideous, but undeniably cheap & useful, and allow these to permeate among the masses, and be within reach of every one, is this more useful than the production of the scanty number of artistic and highly wrought goods of the middle ages. In other words is our whole so-called civilisation a step backwards or forwards? (I think from what I have heard him since say that he would call it in many respects retrogressive).

Next evening he went to hear Morris speak at a working men's club:

Morris was there but his speech was finished before we arrived. In the end he got up to speak again, to answer points raised and great heavens!—it was then the uproar and pandemonium started. They would not listen to him on any account. A man by the name of Twomey got up and he was shocking.

[English] The row lasted about twenty minutes before he got a hearing. The 700 or 800 proletarians declaring and exclaiming against Atheism which some of the previous speakers said was inherent in Socialism, and the vast majority being unwilling to hear any thing [sic] about Socialistic doctrines either. I am sure that in no workmans club in any city of Europe would the same things have happened or such a religiously ignorant pro-Catholic anti-doctrinarian feeling have been displayed. Walker prisided [sic]. [Irish] When he finally finished speaking they came out and brought myself and Gwynne into the Gresham hotel for a drink. We went by car to the Contemporary Club. There was a great crush there; the room was more crowded than I have ever seen it. For two hours or so they continued to put questions to Morris about his plan and his work, but there was not much sense to the questions. [English] They all even men like Patton manifested an utter inability to think themselves into the socialist programme. They could not for instance even imagine a state in which gold & precious stones would have no peculiar worth. . . . As far as I could gather from Morris [*sic*] answers to the questions put him he looked forward to a time when there would be no rich and poor but all men equal, no accumulation of capital in the hands of any one. No laws and consequently no criminal classes, for just as a sense of honour now prevents an officer for instance from running away from his post so a sense of honour and morality & the general high tone prevalent among all men would keep them from crime. There would be no contracts enforced by law, and no marriage contracts, but bean le fear [a woman with a man] according as inclination or any other cause mutually welded the pair. The children would not belong exclusively to the parents. Dirty work would be done by machinery or by volunteers. Great works of art would be public property. Doctors would do their work but would be in no way superior to or richer than, say, the men that blackened their shoes, & they would do their work not for profit or aggrandisement but because they were fitted for it. The whole thing sounded most extraordinarily fantastic & strange. Morris does not believe in State Socialism & would not like to see the advocates of his principles in Parliament, but he believes that the rationality of mankind will teach them gradually that in working out these principles they will be really consulting their own happiness and they will even from a selfish point of view be benefiting themselves more than they are at present, riding in their carriages and lording it over their inferiors. If however all legislation were placed in his hands he would begin by fixing a minimum below which wages should not fall, and a maximum above which the price of commodities should not rise. For example Guinness would have to give his dray-men, say, 30 shillings a week, never less & sell his porter at say 1d a pint, never more, which would speedily reduce Guinness to the condition of one of his own workmen, and make him live on say, 30s a week himself. [Irish] It was 2.30 a.m. when we broke up and I went with Crooke to Herdman's rooms where we talked till 4 a.m. and I was exhausted.

Early in July 1886 he went for a holiday in Scotland with his friend 'Mackey' Wilson. They arrived back in Dublin on 31 July, and after various visits to friends Hyde went home to Frenchpark on 6 August. A few days later he wrote the following:

77

GAELIC IN SCOTLAND

I found Gaelic in much healthier and more vigorous state than Irish is Ireland [sic]. Where the people seemed to speak it at all both old and young seemed to speak it and were rather proud of it than the reverse. They did not hang their heads as if ashamed and answer in English, as is generally the case at home. In Sky & especially in Rossshire Gaelic seemed universally spoken and I met several people who did not understand any English. In Perthshire and Stirling it was less spoken especially about Loch Earn Loch Katrine & Loch Lomond, but even here the genuine crofters spoke it still. Dumbarton Stirling and Callander are all entrances to the Highlands and in their neighbourhood English was in the ascendancy completely. Round Dunoon very little Gaelic was spoken but even then they had Gaelic Services. At Glencoe all the quarrymen in the slate quarries seemed to speak Gaelic, and round Oban it was (except in the town) universal. At first I found it difficult to understand but soon got used to the peculiar pronounciation [sic]. The most curious particularity of it was the sound of ao in such words as saoghal daor saor &c., which is exactly like the sound of eu in French feu or feuille or the ö umlaut in German. Besides this & the *mi* for mé & é for sé, there were special words which it was positively necessary to know before one could carry on a conversation, as *giulàn* for iomchar, *Rathad* for Bothar which was unknown, cu for madadh though the latter was used in some places. *faotan* for fághail, *cha nil me i n-urraim* for ni fheudaim, *báta* for bád, *feumaidh é* for caithfidh se = he must. The word *fós* they thought ridiculous & scriptural, and drásta was what they seemed to use for it. They never said na bi ag cathadh tabaic but na bí a smóc! The sound of á in such words as báta latha &c was just like the sound of a in father.

There are several influences at work in keeping up Gaelic which do not operate in Ireland, and of these the principal is the Presbyterian religion which being of so popular a character encourages everyone to take a part in the singing of Gaelic hymns and the elders to take a part in extempore prayer in their own language which is a most powerful

instrument both in cultivating the language and in familiaris-
ing the people with it in its purest form.

The whole Presbyterian service consists of Psalms sung in
Gaelic, the precentor repeating the first line & the congregation taking it up & repeating it with a peculiar wailing
intonation much more resembling an Irish funeral cry than
a the [sic] singing of a church psalm, then extempore prayers
by the minister in Gaelic, then a chapter from the Gaelic
bible and more psalms & an hour-long sermon in Gaelic.
I was present at the service in Gairloch. Most of the people
had Gaelic bibles & hymnbooks & the way they sang the
psalms was most impressive. Each line was first sung by the
whole congregation even where the first line by itself had no
meaning and made no sense. The English service which
followed was attended by relatively very few.

The Churches seem to attend well to their spiritual wants
wherever Gaelic is spoken, & to provide them with pastors
who use it. On the other hand the priests in Ireland discredit
the language all they can as a general rule & preach in
English even where English is not spoken.[32] Then too most
of the landlords are of the old race and are not ashamed of it,
or ashamed of keeping up the old language and customs,
while in Ireland it is just the contrary. In the third place
Gaelic has a strong position in the curriculum of the national
schools which it has not in Ireland, and lastly there is not
that perpetual migration of the people to reap the harvest in
England which occurring perpetually in Ireland makes the
people learn English and drop their own language. Gaelic
will probably die out in the course of years but it will last
for generations after the last word of Irish has been spoken.[33]
Even the Scottish maps respect Gaelic orthography and Beinn
fada or Loch Dearg or Sliabh-nam-ban, instead of those
utterly meaningless barbourous [sic] disgraceful caricatures
of Irish names which deface our own maps.

The remainder of these ' Impressions de Voyage ' are concerned
with general topics:

I heard scarcely any distinctively Scotch pronounciations
[sic], only one man speaking of Irishmen in Parliament &

redress of grievances said, 'Ye cry oot for it, but we maun thole it.' *Ut & doon* for out and down were generally said, but in the Highlands they either spoke Gaelic or else very fair English. 'Vera gude' however was of everlasting occurrence, and a 'gude few', the gude being sounded like the u in French je *fus* or *excuse*. [Irish] Dinner a crown; double room & servants 8/6; breakfast three shillings.

The hotels were considerably more expensive than the English hotels. Almost as much so as first rate London hotels.

The established Presbyterian Church has I believe the most members, and next to that the Free Church, which differs from the other in that its members have more direct control over their ministers & are out of the reach of the civil law in case they get rid of them. The United Presbyterian church seems the least powerful. The Episcopalians I was informed are only 2 per cent.

The leading papers seem to be the Scotsman & Glascow [*sic*] Herald two rabid anti-Irish pro-Union papers, & the North British Mail a Gladstonian anti-Union one. They struck me as being rather fuller & better edited than our Irish papers.

Sky has the fame of being exceptionally clever, and shaming the mainland in talents of all kinds. A Skyman they said never made a fool, but always carried a head on his shoulders. With Mull it seemed the oposite [*sic*] : Sacsanach a mhuintir Mhuile was an old reproach.

The Highland costume seemed confined to the pipers who always wore it, and in Rossshire I saw two or three of the peasantry dressed in it.

An itinerant conjuror I met at Loch Earnhead informed me that after having gone the rounds of great Britain over and over again, there was no place that payed [*sic*] him better than the Highlands but for the bad roads. The North of England he said was fonder of amusement than any other spot, except perhaps Cornwall, where they were too poor.

The condition of the Crofters seems to have been steadily improving of late years, and their landlords *dare* not take the liberties with them which they took 30 years ago, when they turned whole families and villages adrift to make their deer-forests. The Irish land agitation has given them the cue. And there is growing feeling that to get justice they must take the law into their own hands. It would in most places be very hard to carry out an eviction, and the crofters in Ross will not pay more than 9d a head for the grazing on the mountains of their little black head sheep. The people seemed to think that if molested much more they would act like the Irish shoot the factors and baliffs [*sic*]. They regularly burn the heather on the mountains when it gets too long for the sheep to eat. Even for grouse feeding however it would require to be burnt every 13 or 14 years.

On 25 August he was about to leave for the Horse Show in Dublin when his mother was taken seriously ill and lapsed into unconsciousness.

27 August 1886 At 8 o'clock this morning my mother died. She had been forty-eight hours unconscious, straining hard under the spasms, struggling and wrestling with death. I sat by her bedside all night but she never recognised me. Her death was painful and distressing as she fought to the last minute.

I cannot say that I am sorry she is dead. Even if she had lived a little longer, she would have been in a bad way. It is better for herself that she suffers no longer, and it is better for us. To Annette especially it is a relief not to be any longer as she was, trying to look after her every hour of the day.

My mother was in her fifty-second year; as selfless, disinterested a woman as ever walked this earth.

I had a difficult and exhausting day, writing to all those who had to be informed, ordering the coffin, the mourning coach, meat, wine, etc., and keeping the people away from the place. I wrote ten letters and sent five telegrams.

For the next six weeks Douglas was alone with his father. The atmosphere in the house was bleak; the relationship between father and son very strained:

30 September 1886   The month just ended was a miserable month for me. Still, I am not as lonely after my mother as I thought I would be. I have the whole place to look after. I leave out the daily measures of tea and sugar and flour, and nothing goes to waste without my noticing it. I cut the mutton and the bacon, order the dinner, look after the servants, supervise everything. It is good practice for me.

I seldom talk to my father. I cannot bring myself to speak to him or to keep up a conversation with him. That way at least I have no rows with him. Besides, I still have a certain fear of him, and some of the old hatred, and I have little enough sympathy for his pains and his grief.

I read a lot. Not, alas, theology, but Mill and Mansell, some French, and so on. Only for the Frenches of Ratra I would surely die of ennui. My father reads a little to me almost every evening, since he cannot get me to talk; some Copperfield and some Lecky.

At twenty-six he was still without a career. He could no longer pretend any interest in Divinity; at the start of the new term he returned to Trinity College and took up the study of law.

IV

Among the Literary Nationalists

The main interest of the diaries for his latter years at Trinity College is the light they throw on Hyde's relationship with the group of literary nationalists who formed the nucleus of what came to be known as the Irish literary revival. Names which occur frequently at this period are those of John O'Leary and his sister Ellen, Dr George Sigerson, Katherine Tynan, Rose Kavanagh and, though somewhat less frequently, that of W. B. Yeats.

Yeats's own account of this period (mainly in *Reveries over Childhood and Youth*) is dominated by the Olympian presence of John O'Leary, but for Hyde the outstanding figure in the group was Dr Sigerson. The reason is obvious. Hyde's passionate interest was not the anti-imperial struggle personified by O'Leary, nor the mainly political, propagandist Anglo-Irish literature to which O'Leary introduced Yeats and his other disciples, but the native language which he saw dying throughout the country and the traditional lore that must die with it, unless the language could be saved at the eleventh hour or, at least, the songs and stories enshrined in it could be collected before they disappeared forever.

In Hyde's eyes no living Irishman had done more to preserve the oral tradition than Dr Sigerson. It was he who, as a young medical student, had succeeded James Clarence Mangan as translator and versifier of the Irish poems which John O'Daly published in *Poets and Poetry of Munster. Second Series* (1860). (This is No. 13 in the list of Irish books which Hyde had read by the age of twenty). Sigerson went on to complete his medical studies in Paris and published several tracts and treatises in his professional field. His most important publication, however, in the present context, is *Bards of the Gael and Gall* (London, 1897), which Hyde described as ' a contribution to the so-called Celtic revival the importance of which it would be difficult to overestimate ', adding generously, in view of his own *Love Songs of Connacht* published four years earlier, ' his translations may be

83

better relied on by the English reader for their accuracy than those of any other who has ever attempted to turn Irish into English verses."[1]

It was during these years from 1886 onwards that Hyde's initial reverence and respect for Sigerson, who was twenty-two years his senior, developed into a warm personal friendship. Hyde dedicated his *Love Songs of Connacht* to Sigerson:

> Allow me to offer you this slight attempt on my part to do for Connacht what you yourself and the late John O'Daly, following in the footsteps of Edward Walsh, to some extent accomplished for Munster, more than thirty years ago . . . not for its intrinsic worth, if it has any, but as a slight token of gratitude from one who has derived the greatest pleasure from your own early and patriotic labours in the same direction. . . .

Sigerson, in turn, dedicated his *Bards of the Gael and Gall*[2]

> To Sir Charles Gavan Duffy, President of the Irish Literary Society of London, a representative of the Gael, and to Dr Douglas Hyde, President of the Gaelic League of Dublin, a descendant of the Gall.

Katherine Tynan, now largely forgotten except perhaps as a friend and correspondent of W. B. Yeats, once enjoyed a considerable measure of fame in her own right. In 1885 she published her first volume of poetry entitled *Louise de la Valliere and other poems* of which a critic wrote in the *Dublin University Review*:

> . . . Miss Tynan has faults: her expression is often wanting in power; her epithets are often borrowed from Rossetti; but she is a poetess: she has
> ' The vision and the faculty divine '.
> What she has already given to the world is worth having. What she will give will, we believe, be much more worth having.

She produced several more volumes of her own verses as well as anthologies of Irish verse, five volumes of memoirs and several novels. Her home, a fine farmhouse at Clondalkin a few miles south of Dublin, was a favourite meeting place for literary nationalists on Sunday evenings. In 1893 she married Henry A. Hinkson, a graduate of Trinity College, Dublin.

It was after the publication of her first book of poems that Katherine Tynan became acquainted with Douglas Hyde, and W. B. Yeats has the following interesting observation on the influence of Hyde's Gaelic verses in translation on her later work:

> No living Irish poet has learned so much from the translators as Mrs Hinkson, and the great change this knowledge has made on her verse is an example of the necessity for Irish writers to study the native tradition of expression. Her first two books, ' Louise de Valliere ' and ' Shamrocks ', contained here and there a moving lyric, but were on the whole merely excellent in promise. . . . The work of the Irish folklorists, and the translations of Dr Hyde and of an earlier poet, the village schoolmaster, Edward Walsh, began to affect her, however, soon after the publication of ' Shamrocks '; and the best of ' Ballads and Lyrics ' and cuckoo songs have the freedom from rhetoric, the simplicity and the tenderness, though not the passion, of the Gaelic poets.
> *The Bookman,* September 1894. [*Cuckoo Songs* was the title of Miss Tynan's fourth book of verse.]

Rose Kavanagh (1860-1891) was regarded by her contemporaries as a young poet whose early promise was cut off by an untimely death. Under the pseudonym of ' Ruby ' she contributed stories, articles and poems to a variety of Irish newspapers and magazines and for some years before her death she conducted a children's section in the *Weekly Freeman* where she signed herself ' Uncle Remus '. Yeats wrote a warm tribute to her under the heading ' Rose Kavanagh: Death of a Promising Poet ' in the *Boston Pilot,* 11 April 1891.

These are the people whose names occur most frequently in the diaries from 1886 to 1890. Other names will be noted as they occur in the text. Needless to say, not all the entries for this period are of equal interest. I have chosen those which throw light on Hyde's relationship with the pioneers of the ' revival ' and on the beginnings of his own career as a writer. I have also included, as far as possible, references to other social and cultural circles to which Hyde belonged at this time, his journey to Paris, and personal experiences such as his first meeting with Maud Gonne, his unsuccessful efforts to teach her Irish, and his intense grief at the death of his closest friend of college days, 'Mackey' Wilson.

3 November 1886 To Lipman in the evening at the Russell Hotel.[3] Talking to Katherine Tynan. A good number of people there: Coffey and his wife,[4] Johnston Ballykilbeg[5] etc.

20 November I went to 'Young Ireland'. A lecture from Taylor, the best I ever heard, on Eoghan Ruadh.[6] I was the first speaker from the floor, and Sheehan was second.[7] I walked home with Rose Kavanagh.

24 November This evening I went to 40 Leinster Street [sic] to John O'Leary's house. There were many there whom I knew: Sigerson, Rose Kavanagh, young Yeats, Coffey and his wife, etc. I stayed until 12.30 and walked home with Sigerson and Rose. She is a very nice girl, and it was she who edited *United Ireland* while O'Brien was in prison.[8] I liked her very much and had a long talk with her and Katherine Tynan.

25 November I went to the University College, Stephen's Green. I had a platform ticket. O'Maolmhuaidh, Sexton, John Dillon, T. D. Sullivan and Delany spoke. Dowden was there and I had a few words with him.[9]

27 November Sheehan gave a paper on Grattan to 'Young Ireland' and I spoke on it—very well, as I thought myself. I went home with him and Herdmann and we spent the night at Henrietta Street [Sheehan's home] until 2 a.m. We walked home.

4 December A visit to Baker; he filled a tooth for me. Yeats came to me this afternoon and we spent three hours together reciting our poems to each other. Then we went to the Club. There was an interesting debate on Archbishop Walsh's manifesto.[10] Walker said [English] that the dual ownership existed only as long as the rent was paid; that the moment it ceased to be paid the tenants [sic] half of the ownership lapsed. On the other hand the fall of prices is looked upon as a kataclasm [sic] which interfered with & rendered nugatory the judicial courts, etc.

At the Gaelic Union.

7 December   I went to Lipmann's conversazione at the Russell Hotel. The two Johnsons [*sic*] and their sister; O'Leary and his sister, Yeats and I. There until midnight. It wasn't good.

11 December   . . . Great discussion with Yeats at the Club on historic dramas, Yeats insisting that one might violate historic truth ad lib. so that the sentiments were good, we denying the same. There was little or no political discussion & a small meeting. . . . Got home about 1.30 a.m. and spent an hour with Herdmann over a glass of punch.

15 December   I spoke on the closing of public houses and the prevention of sale of drink, and when that was over I went to John O'Leary's house in Leinster Street at 10 o'clock. Katherine Tynan, Rose Kavanagh, Mrs Sigerson, J. F. Taylor, etc. there. I brought with me three or four of my own English poems and I had to read one of them, ' O'Mahony's Lament '.[11] I do not know if they liked it, but I think they did. I walked back with Taylor at 12.30 and then spent another couple of hours in Herdmann's rooms. It was 3 a.m. before I went to bed.

During the Christmas holidays he did a lot of reading, writing and shooting. He wrote a thousand-line poem in English on Deirdre for the Vice-Chancellor's Prize, and an essay of thirty-five pages on ' Dangers and Safeguards of Modern Democratic Government '. In his summing up on the last night of the year he reflected: ' Glory be to God, we are here again and another year over us, and I am still going on in the same old way, doing nothing for myself. . . .'

He returned to Dublin on 14 January 1887.

23 January   Sunday   Church . . . Yeats the poet[12] called in to me and we walked the four miles to Katherine Tynan's house at Clondalkin; her four sisters, a brother and her father, an old man, were there. They were at dinner when we arrived and we sat in with them. Katherine showed me her own room, her pictures, books, etc., and I had a long conversation with all of them. They all have a frightful brogue. Her father is a farmer with three hundred acres . . .
I had a good drink and they drove us as far as Roundtown.

I walked home from there and upon my word I was tired enough.

25 January   I met Katherine Tynan and her sister by arrangement at 2.15. I brought them around the college and showed them everything, and all the time I was terribly embarrassed lest anyone should see me talking to them.[13] Katherine was all right but her sister was a sight. I gave them tea, cakes and sweets, etc., and Yeates [*sic*] came in at the same time.

Hyde's meetings with Yeats at this period are particularly interesting. The first mention of Yeats occurs on 13 December 1885 when he was one of a group that met for a social evening at the home of Hyde's friend George Coffey.

Some days later:

18 December 1885   Went with Joynt to Young Ireland. Very good paper from Oldham. Gregg, A. Webb and Joynt spoke. I went back to Oldham's rooms where I drank a glass of punch and spent three hours talking to Yeates [*sic*].

Yeats was then twenty. As a boy he had sat by cottage firesides in Sligo and heard tales of ghosts and fairies, but he had been unaware that he was touching the fringe of a distinctive native culture. As he wrote years later:

When I was a child I had only to climb the hill behind the house to see long, blue, ragged hills flowing along the southern horizon. What beauty was lost to me, what depth of emotion is still perhaps lacking in me, because nobody told me, not even the merchant captains who knew everything, that Cruachan of the Enchantments lay behind those long, blue, ragged hills![14]

Now he was a reluctant art-student, whose real enthusiasm was for the writing of poetry 'in imitation of Shelley and Edmund Spenser', while his interest in ghosts and fairies had led him to psychic research and mystical philosophy.

Yeats himself declared that it was through the old Fenian leader John O'Leary that he found his theme. This, I suggest, is a stylized version of the real situation. The patriarchal figure of O'Leary added elegant detail to Yeats's self-portrait:

> His long imprisonment, his longer banishment, his magnificent head, his scholarship, his pride, his integrity, all that aristocratic dream nourished amid little shops and little farms . . .
>
> *Essays and Introductions,* p. 510

Beautiful lofty things . . . dream of the noble and the beggarman . . . it was the perfect back-cloth!

This is not to question the fact that O'Leary's dignified nationalism, and the Young Ireland literature which he lent him, had a profound influence on Yeats and inspired him to become an Irish poet, to be counted one with Davis, Mangan, Ferguson. However, when it came to finding the material on which an Irish poet might work, the folk literature, 'a new fountain of legends, and, as I think, a more abundant fountain than any in Europe'. (*Essays and Introductions,* p. 186). John O'Leary, who saw no purpose or value in the Irish language except as a specialist subject for scholars,[15] was hardly a competent guide. On the other hand, there was no man in Dublin, or indeed in Ireland, better qualified than Douglas Hyde to lead the young poet to his sources. He was equally well versed in the written tradition and in the unwritten.

It is easy to imagine the delight with which Yeats read Hyde's English rendering of the living Gaelic tradition in the *Dublin University Review* of October 1885:

> Oh, the kine they are lowing,
> And the calves are at play,
> And you, white pulse of my bosom,
> You have my secret today.

or

> Oh, my heart is breaking slowly, breaking in
> the midst of me,
> As the roots on some wild mountain give beneath
> the lonely tree

or, in the description of a girl's golden hair, that there was not

In the valley of starlight
Such splendour of beauty:
There shines light for a hundred from each gold hair.

Hyde was also well qualified to introduce Yeats to the hidden
Ireland of the eighteenth-century Gaelic poets of Munster, of
which Yeats was to write so authoritatively a couple of years
later:

> Andrew Magrath, surnamed 'The Merry Pedlar'; O'Sullivan
> the Red, pious and profligate, John MacDonnell of vision-
> seeing memory; John O'Cullen, who lamented in such
> famous words over the Abbey of Timoleague; and O'Heffer-
> nan the blind, who in his old age loved to stand listening
> while the ploughboys in the hedge school droned out some
> Greek poet; and many another.[16]

Needless to say, Yeats was quite incapable of appreciating a line
from any of these poets. In Hyde, however, he had an expert
guide, for Hyde had been enjoying John MacDonnell's vision-
poetry or *aislingí* and John O'Cullen's lament over Timoleague
Abbey and the rest for several years. Indeed, all the knowledge
that Yeats displays here and elsewhere[17] may be traced to two
books which feature in Hyde's first list: *The Poets and Poetry of
Munster* (First Series) and *Reliques of Irish Jacobite Poetry*. Yeats's
remarks on the Gaelic poets constitute little more than a para-
phrase of John O'Daly's notes to these two bilingual collections.

One wishes that Hyde had given details of his discussions with
Yeats as he does of debates at the Club and of Morris's lectures.
It may be that he did not share Yeats's interest in the occult,
and found his mysticism tiresome. Or it may be that he regarded
Yeats the newcomer as a rival for the limelight at these literary
gatherings. Whatever the reason, there is a distinct note of pique
in the entry for 29 January 1887, the last mention of Yeats before
the latter left Dublin to return with his family to London:

> Sunday. Visit to Dowden for a few hours. Yeats was there;
> I was bored to death with his blather.[18]

On 19 May 1887 he returned home after an absence of over four
months. A few days later he erected a headstone of Sicilian
marble over his mother's grave. The inscription reads:

In memoriam Elizabethae J. O. Oldfield
    archidiaconi Elphinensis filiae
quae hanc flebilem vitam Aug 27 1886 reliquit.
    Finita est militia ejus.

He spent most of the summer and autumn of 1887 poring over
lawbooks, and on 9 November he came to Dublin to read for
the LL.B.

9 November . . . I was just in time to get my dinner and a bed
at Morrison's Hotel before the big meeting of the Historical
Society. I went there to receive my two medals: a silver for
oratory and a gold for my English essay—not knowing I
had won the latter until that very morning. There was a
big crowd there. Lynch, Q.C., Walker, Weldon and someone by the name of Bayer [the name is indistinct] spoke.
I spent the night until 2 a.m. in Herdmann's rooms, talking
to himself and Sheehan.

3 December   To the Mosaic. A paper from Berry on the Irish
poets; it was very good. I spoke and said it was a scandal
that half the people present had never heard of Thomas
Davis, after his poems had gone through fifty editions. I
went on to Coffeys where there was a big party. I met
King, John O'Leary and his sister, Katherine Tynan, Rose
Kavanagh, etc . . .

On 6 and 7 December he sat the examination for the LL.B.
On the evening of 7 December as he was about to start for the
Shakespeare Club dressed in his ' frack ',[19] he got a letter telling
him that his friend Mackey Wilson was dying in Bournemouth.
Next day he describes his reaction to the news:

8 December   I was so shattered at the news of poor Mackey that
I cried like a child, and had to turn to the punch to calm
myself. I drank half a pint and more, and smoked until my
mouth was sore and raw. O God, I was miserable. I do not
ever remember crying so much, even when my mother died.
Then I began arguing with myself as to the cause of my
sorrow: was it selfish (the loss of a good friend who was
rich and influential) or was it for Mackey himself, and this
heart-searching left me worse than ever. . . .

9 December Sunday. After Chapel I brought Sheehan with
me and we walked to Katherine Tynan's. We arrived there
about 3.30 and found Yeats and a friend of his, Russell, an
art-student,[20] there before us. There was also two sisters,
Misses Lynch, from Dun Laoghaire, one of whom spoke
intelligently enough. She had lived in the Aegean and in
Greece for a long time, and spoke modern Greek. She had
written a novel.[21] Dinner with Katherine and a very long talk
with her father. . . .

13 December I WAS CONFERRED LL.B. SPENT THE
AFTERNOON WITH LARMINIE IN BRAY, with the
Hewetsons. I do not remember what I did during the day.[22]

19 December I read a paper on old Irish poems at the Mosaic at
Hull's house and got tremendous applause. I spoke in Irish
also. Afterwards I talked with Miss Oldham and—a long talk
—with the two Hulls. Music from Miss Hull and Miss
Oldham that was well worth listening to. Miss Hull read my
poem Deirdre and praised it highly. She is friendly towards
me now.[23]

20 December I went at midday to Rose Kavanagh's office. Miss
O'Leary and another girl came in and we had a long talk,
and Rose and I were invited to spend the evening with them
[the O'Learys]. Rose had offered a prize to the member of
the Club who would send her the best Irish story and I was
to be the judge.

21 December I left Dublin at 9 a.m. and came to Enfield where
I took a car for myself and drove to Culcarrigeen [the Wilson
family home]. When I arrived there I found only the father,
the father's brother and the family; nobody at all from the
district around; it was a very small funeral. My friend
Mackey was buried beside his younger brother, close by the
little church he built himself, and there were only nine
of the gentry in the church and twenty peasants. I was afraid
I would break down, but I wasn't affected as much as I had
feared; I had already suffered too much when I heard the bad
news. O Lord, what a good friend I lost there. He had a very
great love for me, and there was nothing on earth I could
ask of him that he wouldn't do for me. He was rich, but at
the same time he put no store on riches, and he was wont to
think not of himself but of other people. I never heard an

unkind word about him from anyone. I was desolate at losing him. May God grant him a home in heaven, and may He reward him for his life on earth from which he had so little satisfaction. His burial today was a milestone in my life. O Christ, make me as good, upright and christian as he was, and grant me a place beside him in Your kingdom.

From the funeral he went home to Frenchpark.

In his review of the year he wrote:

For myself, this past year was a fairly happy one, but instead of settling down and earning my living I was amusing myself and whiling away the time. . . .

The following term he was back in Dublin studying for the LL.D. He was also preparing his first book for the press:

12 April 1888 Grinding again. A beautiful day. I walked to Gills[24] with Sheehan and the man in charge brought us around and showed us everything: the printers and the binders, the type, the presses in action, etc. I settled with him to print my book for me: 160 pages and a thousand copies at £32. That seemed cheap to me. We spent an hour and a half talking to him, then I walked home with Sheehan, dined with him and drank two or three glasses. We had a long talk de omnibus rebus, after which I walked home at 1.30.

15 April Sunday. Chapel in College. Afterwards I walked with Sheehan to Katherine Tynan's. It was a beautiful day. There were a lot of people there. We had dinner and a good talk. We started for home at 10.30 and I took a good stiff drink. Gregg and Johnson from Ballykilbeg and a man named Piper were with us and we walked home singing and shouting as I had never done in my life before. It was a natural reaction to K.T.'s aestheticism! It was 1.45 before I got home.

On 26 and 27 April 1888 he sat the examination for the LL.D. and on 30 April he got the result:

30 April I discovered that I had come first in the LL.D. exam with 55 marks, more than I needed. I went to visit the Dowdens and had a long talk with the Professor on Matthew

H

Arnold, etc. Then I went down to Gywnns but they were not at home. Afterwards to the Mosaic where we had an enjoyable evening. I spoke on Lord Lytton. . . .

Throughout the summer he worked on folk-tales and wrote a good deal of poetry in Irish. He records what was probably the first earnings from his pen:

17 September   Making a stack of hay. I got £2 from Boyle O'Reilly for my poem Colmcille's Journey from the Old Irish.[25]

In October he came to Dublin for a fortnight to read in the libraries of TCD and the Royal Irish Academy. He visited the Dowdens and noted: 'I never saw the professor looking better.' On 14 October the Frenchs of Ailesbury Road gave a big dinner:

Ingram and his daughter, Falkiner, Dixon, the Crookes and others present. Stockley sang Who fears to speak of 98 in Ingram's presence.[26] Home at 12.30.

15 October   Stockley lunched with me. Talked with Webb and Galbraith who came in while we were at lunch. Dinner, and a good one too, with O'Leary this evening. Stockley and Coffey were there and we had a bottle of wine. O'Leary gave me several books.[27] I walked back with Stockley from O'Leary's house to Ailesbury Road. Home at 12.30.

16 October   Writing at the Academy. . . .

17 October   Visited the Conners, Lysters and Coffeys, and Miss McDowell.... I went from there to O'Mulrenin who brought me along to the Pan-Celtic but there was no one there but Wyer B.L. and a couple of other men.[28] On the way home I called on Larminie at Blackrock and had a very long talk with him and his mother (who is as crotchety a woman as ever I met), I got a couple of books from him. Home at last at 1.30.

On Sunday, 16 December 1888, he records his first meeting with Miss Maud Gonne:

16 December   Sunday. Church; St, Matthew's. A beautiful day. I met the Wilsons and went home with them and had lunch

(the first time since Mackey's death). Afterwards I walked to St Margaret's and back with them. To Sigersons in the evening where I saw the most dazzling woman I have ever seen: Miss Gonne, who drew every male in the room around her. She was wonderfully tall and beautiful. We stayed talking until 1.30 a.m. My head was spinning with her beauty!!![29]

Two days later he met her again:

18 December   Talking to Miss Kavanagh and Sigerson in the office for a couple of hours. Then I went to Miss McDowell and had a long talk with her, after which I walked with her to some club which the boys established between the two Mount Streets. Conversation, dancing, playing, etc., etc. To Sheehan at 8 p.m. and had a drink with him. After that I went to Miss Gonne who was giving a party. I wasn't as dazzled as I was the first time. I had a long talk with Miss O'Leary and Rose Kavanagh. Home at midnight. I recited an Irish poem for them.

19 December   I got a hood and gown for 10/- and got my LL.D. at last. I had to pay £22 for it. Dear enough. The Dillons were there to see me conferred. I was exhausted. Then to the dentist but he did nothing for me. Dinner with the Fellows in the evening; it lasted till 9. Afterwards I went up to Bernard's room and spent a couple of hours with him, smoking and discussing his course of lectures. It was all very pleasant. . . .

Some weeks later Miss Gonne became his pupil:

4 February 1889   I went to Miss Gonne at 11 a.m. to give her her first lesson in Irish. She received me graciously. I stayed for lunch with her and we toasted cheese together by the fire. We talked about all sorts of things: le brave General, the state of Ireland, etc. We did not do much Irish. She is vivacious, talks well and has travelled a lot. I left at 3 p.m. and went to buy a suit of clothes for 30/- and some other things, and I had a word with the printers. This evening I went to the Mosaic. Spoke to Miss Hull and Miss Jameson.[30] Walked home with the latter. A fine evening. Home at midnight.

5 February   I went to a party at Miss Purser's[31] and, this evening, to dinner with Miss Gonne. John and Miss O'Leary were

there, Sigerson and his daughters; Coffey and his wife came later. We stayed till 11.

7 February Giving Miss Gonne her second lesson; with her from 11 to 2.30. We lunched on omelets we had made together at the fire. Had a long talk with her. With Baker [the dentist] again. Spent a couple of hours with Sheehan this evening and did a bit of work at home.

9 February After lunch at the Bodega I went for a walk with Sheehan to Glasnevin. A very heavy frost. Back again at 5 p.m. and to the Gaelic Union at the Mansion House. Then to Doherty on the quays and I spent four hours with him,[32] talking and reading old manuscripts, etc. To Dr Sigerson's with him, and finally to the Club. Home at 1.15.

11 February I went to Miss Gonne; gave her a lesson and stayed for lunch. In the afternoon I went to Lady Naughton but because she was not well I went on to the Dillons and spent a couple of hours talking to them. To the Franco-German Society with the Jeremys. Reading Le Diplomate by Scribe. I read part of it. Home at 11. Heavy snow.

12 February Snow on the ground still. Visited the Wilsons, stayed for dinner with them and went with Mrs Wilson and the young Signorina[33] to a lecture against drink by some General Gunne, and such rubbish I never heard in all my life. Home at 10.30. I *very much* enjoyed my visit to the Wilsons.

13 February This morning I went to Miss Gonne, gave her a lesson and stayed for lunch. I called on Miss Kavanagh and met Carroll there. Had a talk with him. I went with Miss Gonne to a meeting of the Theosophical Society and heard a paper on Sixth Sense from a Mr Dix. I drove home in a cab with Miss Gonne at 10.30.

15 February . . . To the Shakespeare Society this evening; read the part of the clown in Twelfth Night, and read it well I thought. . . .[34]

18 February To Miss Gonne in the morning to give her a lesson. I stayed for a couple of hours but we did not do much Irish. A beautiful day. I wrote a fair amount. I read my essay on George Sand to the Mosaic Club at Hicksons. I walked home

with Miss Orr. A good number of people there, but Miss Hull was ill and didn't come.

21 February   I gave a lecture on early Irish literature to fifty or sixty working men in Coffey's club on the quays. Cusack[35] was there and made a speech in which he praised me highly. I got enormous applause. To Herdmann's rooms afterwards and spent three or four hours with him and Sheehan. Home at 2.15.

24 February   Katherine Tynan invited me to go out to her so I got up early, went to College chapel and then took a tram to Rathmines where I met a young man from the college named Hinkson and his sister (a B.A. from the ' Royal ').[36] We went together on the steam-tram to Tallaght and from there we walked with a man by the name of Dallinger (an Englishman) to the house of the poetess. A good dinner and much talk, etc., etc. Home on the steam-tram at 10, to the college, and I spent the night until 1.30 in Hinkson's rooms, smoking and drinking beer.

13 March   To F.C. in the morning and went for a walk with her. Afterwards I visited Miss Gonne and talked with her for two hours. She was very cordial [' an-charthanach '] and made me a present of her portrait.

The Irish lessons had evidently petered out![37]

21 March 1889   Visited Miss Gonne this morning and had a long talk with her. I did a little reading and visited her again in the afternoon and had another talk with her. Dinner with F.C. and I left her at 9 o'clock and went to the Pan-Celtic where I met Miss Gonne for the third time today. Singing, conversation and so on. I heard my own song, ' We the numerous men' being sung by thirty voices. A Miss Roche put it to music.[38] I conveyed Rose Kavanagh home. Back at 1 o'clock.

29 March   Went to F.C. and had a singing lesson from her. I spent two hours with the printers. I went to Stillorgan and saw the Hayes's there. At 8 o'clock I went with the Hulls to see the pictures [at the Academy?] and at 9.30 to the Pan-Celtic. There I spoke on Walt Whitman and on old stories, and I read a story in English. Home at 12.30 [Note in margin: Visit to Rose Kavanagh.]

30 March   To F.C. this morning but I didn't stay. Read for a couple of hours in the College. Then I visited Dowdens and had an amusing talk with them. Mrs Dowden said I was the only Nationalist she could stand. Then to the Gwynnes and had a talk with them. Young Gwynne and his fiancee were there, and Miss O'Brien. To F.C. then, and to Miss McDowell, and from there to the 'Sunrise' ['Eirighe na Gréine'] Club where I spoke for almost an hour on '98. Fifty or sixty people there. F.C. came with me, and there was a Mrs Maunsell (the wife of the editor of the Express) with Miss McDowell and she was absolutely disgusted.[39] They were satisfied with the lecture. I came home with F.C. A fine night. Home at 11.

2 April 1889   I spent the morning and until 6 o'clock with F.C. I had an invitation to Dowdens but I did not go. I went to Doherty-Contractor [*sic*] afterwards and stayed at his place on the quays until 11 o'clock, talking about the book he is writing, etc. I drove home.[40]

5 April 1889   I spent the day with F.C. again and stayed for dinner. Went to the Pan-Celtic in the evening and read some of my 'Oidhe Cloinne Lir' to them.[41] A long debate, and I spoke to them. We were to have gone to the races at Leopardstown but the day turned out too wet.

13 April 1889   I came home after being in Dublin for two months and a fortnight. I found Annette in a rather bitter mood, and not looking well, the old man drinking too much, and the place untidy (or so it seemed to me, but that is perhaps because I am accustomed to neatness and good order). A fine day. There hasn't been for a long time a year as slow as this year; neither oats nor potatoes are sown yet.

He lost no time in settling down to work, dividing his time between folklore (collecting new material and preparing the English translation for his second book, *Beside The Fire*), farm work and general reading.

15 April   A fine day at last. Writing out properly Blake's stories.[42]

23 April   Writing and translating Irish stories into English. A fine day. A little tennis.

24 April   Reading Anna Karenina and Greek Literature by Jebb, and writing. We walked to Biddy Cosroe's.[43]

5 May   . . . I finished the second volume of Campbell.[44]

10 May   . . . I found old Seaghan Ó Conangáin [sic] from Baile an Phuill here and I got three or four old stories from him but I didn't write down anything.[45]

15 May   I went with Annette to Sean Ó Conganáin's [sic] house. I got two stories from him: The King of Ireland's Son and Oisin. I was three hours with him writing.

16 May   A wet day. Writing out my stories.

20 May   I went to the fair in Frenchpark. I was there at 6 a.m. A beautiful day. I bought a small Kerry cow full of milk for £8-15 and a young calf for £4, and I sold four sheep for £10-10-0 and a yearling calf for £7-2-6. . . .

30 May   A fair in Boyle. I left the house at 4 o'clock in the morning; I had a cow to sell there. I spent nearly four hours at the fair. I was offered only £14 and I would not sell her for that.

In June he went with Annette and Frances Crofton for a fort-night's holiday in Paris. The day after their arrival Hyde called on Maud Gonne, who was then staying at 61 Avenue Wagram. Miss Gonne invited them all to lunch:

27 June 1889   We went to lunch with Miss Gonne at midday. There was a little Serb there who was in Paris for an agrarian congress. He spoke no English, and we all had to speak whatever much or little French we had. Miss Gonne speaks like a Parisienne. I caught only a little of what they said. We had a very good lunch with black coffee and liqueur[46] and cigarettes. F.C. and Annette said that Miss Gonne was the most beautiful woman they had ever laid eyes on. I had a long talk with the Serb who told me about the hunting of wolves and bears in his country. We left at about 2.30. We then took a cab to Shaws where we had tea. Afterwards we went around Notre Dame. I forget what we did in the evening.

They left Paris on 3 July for London, and on 7 July Douglas

crossed to Dublin. Three days later he was home in Frenchpark.

It was a beautiful summer. Tennis at Ratra almost every day. Hyde read *Sapho* by Daudet, *The Four Georges* by Justin McCarthy, *My Religion* by Tolstoi, *Aurora Leigh, Mansfield Park,* and works by Herbert Spencer and Macaulay. He also did a good deal of writing.

19 July 1889   Dinner at Ratra. Writing an essay on the Celts.

26 July   Writing an essay on the Celtic Mind in Literature and Art.

28 July   I wrote an Irish poem, the first for a long time, for a couple of years almost. Reading Aurora Lee [*sic*].

1 August   Tennis at Ratra again. I wrote part of my essay on Gaelic poetry. A fine day.

On 9 August the fine spell broke with a cold, wet, windy day.

10 August   Another wet day. Writing an essay on the Irish poems of the country people.

10 August [The date is repeated]   I killed a crow with a bullet at 85 yards. Writing my essay on the minor Gaelic poems. I finished McCarthy's The History of the Four Georges. A showery day.

15 August   Writing on Irish songs and reading Mansfield Park.

16 August   A stormy day. Reading Mansfield Park and writing a poem in English, a translation of my ' Smaointe bróin '.[47]

17 August   A wet enough day. Drawing in the turf for a week.

18 August   SUNDAY. Church. The Frenches came up and brought me to Ratra. Dinner there. Heavy rain. Home at 12.30. Punch.

5 September   Out fowling. I killed two curlews at the lake. A beautiful day. Translating my book into English.

6 September   Another fine day, but dark. Putting English on my book.

14 September   I went to Seán Ó Cuineagáin a few days ago with Annette and got from him the story of the Tailor and the Three Beasts.[48] We met the Blakes on the road.

On 14 October he came to Dublin, but it was no longer to study
or grind for examinations. Despite his academic qualifications in
Divinity and Law, it was becoming increasingly clear that he
saw his future in neither of these fields. He was devoting
himself more and more to the subject in which he found satisfaction and fulfilment, traditional Gaelic culture. At home he had
busied himself with what he could extract from the living
memories of old singers and storytellers; now his target was the
manuscript material in the library of the Royal Irish Academy.
At the same time, he naturally availed himself of the opportunity
to resume his old social and cultural rounds.

7 October 1889 Reading and writing in the Academy; then
visited Mrs French. J.J. Stockley came. Long talk with him.
To Oldham in the evening. I taught him a little German
and we had a great talk until 3 a.m. I had punch with him.

8 October Lunch with J. J. Stockley. I went with him and
Coffey to the meeting of the National League, and I shook
hands with Tim Harrington.[49] Speeches from John Redmond,
Professor Galbraith and Swift McNeill. Whist in Oldham's
rooms afterwards. Dinner at Gwynnes; Miss Osbourne, J. J.
Stockley, May Gwynne and her fiancé. Much talk, etc. Home
at midnight.

13 October Lunch with King[50] at Blackrock. Katherine Tynan
was there, and a Miss Cantwell who spent five years in Spain.
Fine old whiskey, Chartreuse, Cigarettes—everything very
pleasant. I left them at 5.30 and went to F.C. by cab. Dinner
with her and I brought her and Miss Townsend to the
Ancient [sic] Concert room to hear a lecture by Colonel
Olcott on Theosophism. It wasn't very good at all, and I,
having wined and dined well, kept dozing off all the time.
Home with F.C. To bed early.

14 October . . . Three hours at the Academy. . . .

16 October Stockley left. Reading at the Academy. After dinner
with Frances Crofton I drove with her to the Workingmen's
Club in Wellington Quay where Ashe King gave an
excellent talk on Irish industries. Home with her afterwards.
I never heard a better speech.

18 October Reading at the Academy. Spent the evening with
F.C. I did not go to the Club.

19 October   To Baker at 9 a.m. and spent two hours with him; he hurt me a lot. Reading at the Academy afterwards. Dinner with F.C. and I went with her to a lecture by Colonel Olcott on Irish Fairies at the Ancient Concert Rooms. I spoke, and had a few brief words with the Colonel.

21 October   Reading and writing at the Academy. Long talk with Fr Hogan.[51] Meeting of the Franco-German Society; talk with them afterwards, and with Miss Orr in particular. Dinner with F.C. I was to have brought her to the Theosophical Society but she wouldn't come and my evening was wasted.

28 October   I CAME HOME after being twenty-four days in Dublin. A very wet day. Everybody well.

He spent a month at home, reading and writing, with occasional fowling expeditions and a day at the fair:

7 November   I got up at 4, ate my breakfast and went off in the dark to the fair at Castlerea. I sold an old cow for £14-10 and bought two good heifers, a year and a half old, for £19. Home at 1.30, tired enough. . . .

He was back in Dublin on 4 December, preparing a lecture on Irish folklore.

10 December   Reading and writing without going out. I finished my essay on traditional Irish stories. Good dinner with Sheehan: bottle of port, champagne, glass of brandy. Then we went to look for the place in Rathmines where I was to speak. About eighty people there. I delivered my lecture without reading it; it took an hour and a quarter and went very well.[52] Great praise on all sides. Home at 11.30. Wyer, O'Carroll, Stritch, etc, there.[53]

On 20 December he came home. A few days later he sent Christmas cards to Oldham, Mrs Crofton, Cleaver, J. J. Stockley, Crooke, Hewetson, Katherine Tynan, Yeats, Larminie, W. Stockley, F. C. Sheehan, Miss F. O'Connor, Miss Jeremy, Miss Orr, Fr O'Growney,[54] Fr Keegan,[55] Rose Kavanagh and Cecily Hyde.

The year just ended had been a significant one in his life. It launched him on his career as a writer with the publication of his first book, *Leabhar Sgéulaigheachta*. For one reason or another, he omits his customary review of the past twelve months, but at the end of this volume of the diaries, side by side with his usual meticulous record of income and expenditure, he writes:

Sent copies of my Leabhar Sgeulaigheachta to

1. Hewetson, 2, O Flannery, III Sigerson, IV. Seághan Pléimionn, V. O Maolbhrandán, VI. Maud Gonne, VII. King, VIII. Maxwell Close, IX. J. J. Stockley, X. W. Stockley, XI. John O'Leary, XII. Goodman, XIII. Pádraig O Brian, XIV. T. O'Neill Russell, XV. Atkinson, XVI. Max Nettlan, XVII. Pan-Celtic, XVIII. Gael, XIX. Echo, XX. Freeman, XXI. Irish Times, XXII. Nation, XXIII. United Ireland, XXIV. Irish Monthly, XXV. Limerick Reporter, XXVI. Cork Examiner, XXVII. Catholic Times, XXVIII. Dublin Review, XXIX. Athenaeum, XXX. The Pilot Boston, 31. Morris, 32. Father Hogan, 33. Cusack, 34. Dogherty.

Further evidence that he regarded writing as, at least, an important part of his career from that time on is provided by the list that follows. The first title was already in print; the remainder were projects some of which were realized in the years that followed:

Leabhar Sgéulaigheachta.
Translation of Irish Folklore.
Dánta leis an gCraoibhín Aoibhinn [Poems by the C. A.]
English Poems.
Three Sorrows of Storytelling.
Gaelic Essays.
Leabhar Sgéulaigheachta, vol. 2.
Essay (perhaps) on Raftery the bard. Essay (perhaps) on Fermanagh MS. Essays (perhaps) on Some Irish poems, i.e., Miler McCraith, Elegy on Owen Roe O Neill.
Essay (perhaps) on Irish fairy tales.
Essay on Genius of the Celt in literature and Art.
Unpublished Literature. Irish Folksongs. Irish Language. The southern ? Gaelic folksongs.
Apology for the Pan-Celts.
Leaves from the Irish MSS.
Medieval Irish Romances.

V

Hyde the Writer

Douglas Hyde's first book, *Leabhar Sgéulaigheachta* (1889), a collection of folk-tales, rhymes and riddles, all in Gaelic, was the first of its kind ever published in the native language. This was followed, a year later, by *Beside the Fire,* in which he presented English translations of about half the stories in his first book together with some half dozen other traditional tales in the original Irish with English translations.

Several collections of Irish folktales in English had appeared in the years immediately before 1890, 'but', says Hyde in the preface to *Beside the Fire,*[1] 'these attempts, though interesting from a literary point of view, are not always successes from a scientific one.' He cites, for example, ' Crofton Croker's delightful book " Fairy Legends and Traditions of the South of Ireland " ', but draws attention to a serious flaw in the work:

> The fact is that he learned the ground-work of his tales from conversations with the Southern peasantry, whom he knew well, and then elaborated this over the midnight oil with great skill and delicacy of touch, in order to give a saleable book, thus spiced, to the English public.

He has words of praise too for Patrick Kennedy's ' The Fireside Stories of Ireland ', but points to the same defect:

> Unfortunately, the sources are not given by him any more than by Croker, and we cannot be sure how much belongs to Kennedy the bookseller, and how much to the Wexford peasant.

The next compiler of folklore, Lady Wilde, comes in for even more severe censure. Not only does she fail to give ' the least inkling as to where such-and-such a legend, or cure, or super-stition comes from ', but

> Her entire ignorance of Irish, through the medium of which alone such tales and superstitions can properly, if at all, be collected, is apparent every time she introduces an Irish word.

In spite of these serious shortcomings he gallantly adds:

> Lady Wilde's volumes are, nevertheless, a wonderful and copious record of folk-lore and folk-customs, which must lay Irishmen under one more debt of gratitude to the gifted compiler.

Finally he deals with the collection of Irish folktales compiled by ' an American gentleman, Mr Jeremiah Curtin '. The stories ' are told very well, and with much less cooking and flavouring than his predecessors employed ', but, alas, Mr Curtin's ignorance of the commonest Irish words ' is as startling as Lady Wilde's.' Furthermore, like all his predecessors, he leaves the reader ' in profound ignorance of his authorities.'

> In this he does not do himself justice, for, from my own knowledge of Irish folklore, such as it is, I can easily recognise that Mr Curtin has approached the fountainhead more nearly than any other.

It is highly significant that from his review of existing collections of Irish folklore Hyde goes on directly to declare his unbounded admiration for the compiler of *Popular Tales of the West Highlands*:

> We have as yet no folk-lorist in Ireland who could compare for a moment with such a man as Iain Campbell, of Islay, in investigative powers, thoroughness of treatment, and acquaintance with the people, combined with a powerful national sentiment, and, above all, a knowledge of Gaelic. It is on this last rock that all our workers-up of Irish folklore split.

As a folklorist, Hyde manifestly modelled himself on Campbell of Islay. For instance, in his table of contents Campbell gives, in five columns spread across two pages, the title of the story, the name of the traditional storyteller, the date on which it was written down, the place, and the name of the person who recorded it. Hyde saw the value of this scientific method of presentation, in contrast to the haphazard approach of the Irish writers. It was the example of Campbell that made him declare in his preface to *Beside the Fire* :

In the present book, as well as in my *Leabhar Sgéulaigh-eachta,* I have attempted—if nothing else—to be a little more accurate than my predecessors, and to give the *exact language* of my informants, together with their names and various localities—information which must always be the very first requisite of any work upon which a future scientist may rely when he proceeds to draw honey (is it always honey?) from the flowers which we collectors have culled for him.

In this context, a fact not hitherto sufficiently noted is the extent to which Hyde, as an author, was influenced by the work of Scottish Highland writers. It is a significant fact that of his original collection of Gaelic books, one quarter is made up of Scottish works, and these are mainly collections of folk literature. The similarity between these publications and Hyde's own is striking. For example, in the preface to *Oráin Gae'lach le Uilleam Ros,* the editor, John Mackenzie, writes:

> Previous to the publication of the first edition of Ross's Songs the only record of their existence was their floating through the district on the memories of the people, and the only method of their publication was by the lips of fair maidens and fond admirers.

It can hardly be doubted that the example of men like John Mackenzie inspired Hyde to do for his corner of Ireland what they had done for the Highlands of Scotland. His growing interest in the work of the Scottish folklorists is proved by the fact that whereas the first five or six books in Scottish Gaelic that occur in his list were acquired by chance (at the auction of John O'Daly's library), the remaining twenty or so volumes were ordered expressly from Scotland, and these, acquired between August 1879 and July 1880, when he was about twenty years of age, made up almost the whole of the final quarter of his basic Gaelic library. It is surely more than a coincidence that it was around the same time that he began seriously to devote himself to rescuing from oblivion the songs and stories of the native Irish speakers around his corner of Connaught.

Next to guaranteeing the authenticity of his Gaelic originals, Hyde's main concern was to find the form of language best suited to their presentation in English. Here we come to one of the most important aspects of Hyde's work, the fact that he pioneered a manner of speech that was to become the vernacular, so to speak, of the Anglo-Irish literary movement, the model for Lady Gregory's 'Kiltartanese', Synge's plays and indeed the standard speech of the early Abbey Theatre.

The first thing to be said in this regard is that nothing could have been further from Hyde's conscious mind that the evolution of a distinct idiom for Irish poets and playwrights who worked in English. First and last, Hyde's aim was to convey, as far as any translator could, to those who could not experience it in the original Gaelic, the genuine essence and flavour of the people's songs and stories. He was in no way satisfied with ' the various garbs in which the sophisticated minds of the ladies and gentlemen who trifled in such matters, clothed the dry bones ' of the traditional tales. In his estimation, ' when the skeletons were thus padded round and clad, although built upon folklore, they were no longer folklore themselves.' Hyde's principle was that

> folk-lore can only find a fitting garment in the language that comes from the mouths of those whose minds are so primitive that they retain with pleasure those tales which the more sophisticated invariably forget. For this reason folk-lore is presented in an uncertain and unsuitable medium, whenever the contents of the stories are divorced from their original expression in language.

While once again finding fault with his predecessors in this regard, he acknowledges that the problem is a difficult one:

> It is not very easy to make a good translation from Irish into English, for there are no two Aryan languages more opposed to each other in spirit and idiom.

Hyde even makes so bold as to find fault with the great Campbell of Islay in this field,

> for in order to make his translations picturesque, he has rendered his Gaelic originals something too literally. Thus, he invariably translates *bhain se an ceann deth,* by ' he reaped

the head off him . . .' but *bhain,* though it certainly means 'reap' amongst other things, is the word used for taking off a hat as well as a head.

In this and similiar ways Campbell gave his 'excellent and thoroughly reliable translations' a scarcely legitimate colouring which Hyde sought to avoid in his.

For Hyde, the solution to the problem lay in distinguishing between those Gaelic turns of speech the literal translation of which had been adopted spontaneously into the English of the people and the very many other idioms which had not passed over into the new language of the countryside.

> I do not translate, for instance, the Irish for ' he died ' by ' he got death ' for this, though the literal translation, is not adopted into Hibernian English; but I do translate the Irish *gnidheadh sé sin* by ' he used to do that', which is the ordinary Anglo-Irish attempt at making—what they have not got in English—a consuetudinal tense. I have scarcely used the pluperfect at all. No such tense exists in Irish, and the people who speak English do not seem to feel the want of it, and make no hesitation in saying, ' I'd speak sooner if I knew that', where they mean, ' if I had known that I would have spoken sooner.' I do not translate (as Campbell would), ' it rose with me to do it ', but ' I succeeded in doing it '; for the first, though the literal translation of the Irish idiom, has not been adopted into English;[2] but I do translate ' he did it and he drunk ', instead of, ' he did it while he was drunk '; for the first phrase (the literal translation of the Irish) is universally used throughout English-speaking Ireland. Where, as sometimes happens, the English language contains no exact equivalent for an Irish expression, I have rendered the original as well as I could, as one generally does render for linguistic purposes, from one language into another.

Hyde, of course, was particularly well placed to note these subtle turns of phrase in the speech of the people which one born and reared among them would take for granted. He was fourteen years old when he became interested in the different language of the small farmers and labourers around his home. By then, with his natural flair for language, his ear was well attuned to the more or less cultured English spoken within the family circle. The result was that when he began to go among the people it was not only the totally new and strange Irish language that caught his attention, but also the curious, colourful phrases that he found in their use of English. In a sort of commonplace book that he kept in 1887, when he was seventeen, he wrote down some of these:

Phrases used by the peasantry in speaking English which are translations of Irish idioms.

Don't let on that it's true = A translation of the Irish
    na leig ort gur is fireanach é.

Are you ready with it, i.e. are you done with it.
    Réidh is the Irish for ' done ' & also for ' ready '. So that they translate it ' ready ' in the sense of ' done '.

He put a shout out of him = He shouted.
    Tr' of *chuir se éighm as.*

He's getting it tight, i.e., He's hard put to.
    Tr' of *tá se dhá fhagháil druite é.*

The hound tightened the hare
    Translation of *Do thean an cú an gearrfhiadh.*

He did it & he drunk—i.e., He did it when drunk.
    Tr' of *rinne se é 'gus é ar meisge.*

It's he that has the wisdom i.e. in perfection.
    Tr' of ' *is aige ata an chrionacht* '.

Strike him ' out of face ' = *Buail as eadan é*

Be on your keeping = Mind yourself.
    Tr' of *Bi air do choimhead* [*sic*].

Listen to it yet = Bear with it for a while.
    Tr' of *eisd leis go foil.*

He's lost for it, i.e., eager for it.
    Ta se cailte le faghail e.

He looked from him = He looked about him.
    dhearc se uadh [*sic*].

I

I'm between two thoughts = irresolute.
Ta me eadar dha comhairle.

Dont break the stick on me = i.e. break it to my loss
Na bris an bata orm.

Hes [*sic*] proud out of it = He's proud of it.
                    straic
    Translation of, *ta stro aige as.* [*sic*]

He did good business = came on well.
    Tr' of *rinne sa gnach* [*sic*] *maith.*

What's on you = What's the matter with you
    Tr' of *'ca ta 'rt'.* [*sic*]

I've no touching on him = I cant hold a candle to him
    Tr' of, *nil aon bhaint agam do.*

Isn't well your not afraid [*sic*] = I wonder you're not.
    Nach breagh nac bhfhuil eagla ort [*sic.*]

There's anger, shame etc on him = He's angry, etc.
    Ta fearg, náire &c air.

Its very cold *itself.* It killed i am itself [*sic*] etc
This common use of the word itself is a translation of the
Irish word *fein.*

Its not trusting to that much = He has more, He's not on
this side of that much.
    Nil se taobhuil le noirid sin.

Going over the gap of me = While I was going etc.
    Dul thairis an bhearna dham.

There will be old trouble, old work etc. i.e., great trouble
etc.
    Tr' of Irish *sean-thriobloid, sean oibir, &c.*
    an obscure and vulgar expression.

He bees there always = He does be there etc
    An attempt to translate the Irish Present Consuetudinal
    into English, perhaps suggested by the similarity of
    sound *Bian se* = He does be pronounced [*sic*] Beean she.

By such long and loving apprenticeship Hyde arrived at the
language of *Beside the Fire,* ' that English idiom of the Irish-

thinking people of the West . . . the only good English spoken by
any large number of Irish people today.'³ As a general rule. Hyde
professes to give the '*ipsissima verba*' of the traditional storyteller, but there is one story in which he admits to a certain
measure of creative writing, as he explains in a note:

> I heard the story of Giollis na gCos Dubh from an old game-
> keeper, Seamas O h-Airt, in Roscommon, near where it joins
> Mayo and Sligo. He had the greatest repertoire of stories of
> any *shanachie* I ever met.⁴ He is, unfortunately, dead, so that
> I have told the story as well as I could recollect it, in my own
> language, since I could not reproduce the *ipsissima verba*. It
> is told, however, nearly as I heard it. . . .

The following extract from the story in question is a good
example of how Hyde could blend his own experience of the
sights and sounds of the countryside, gained from his regular
vigils for wild geese and duck, into the fabric of a traditional
tale:

> Guleesh accordingly went to the old rath when the night
> was darkening, and he stood with his bent elbow leaning on
> a gray old flag, waiting till the middle of the night should
> come. The moon rose slowly, and it was like a knob of fire
> behind him; and there was a white fog which was raised up
> over the fields of grass and all damp places, through the cool-
> ness of the night after a great heat in the day. The night was
> calm as is a lake when there is not a breath of wind to move
> a wave in it, and there was no sound to be heard but the
> cronawn (hum) of the insects that would go by from time to
> time, or the hoarse sudden scream of the wild-geese, as they
> passed from lake to lake, half a mile up in the air over his
> head; or the sharp whistle of the fadogues and flibeens
> (golden and green plover), rising and lying, lying and rising,
> as they do on a calm night. There were a thousand thousand
> bright stars shining over his head, and there was a little frost
> out, which left the grass under his foot white and crisp.
> He stood there for an hour, for two hours, for three hours,
> and the frost increased greatly, so that he heard the breaking
> of the *traneens*⁵ under his foot as often as he moved. He was
> thinking in his own mind, at last, that the sheehogues⁶ would
> not come that night, and that it was as good for him to

return back again, when he heard a sound far away from him, coming towards him, and he recognised what it was at the first moment. The sound increased, and at first it was like the beating of waves on a stony shore, and then it was like the falling of a great waterfall, and at last it was like a loud storm in the tops of the trees, and then the whirlwind burst into the rath of one rout, and the sheeogues were in it.

It all went by him so suddenly that he lost his breath with it, but he came to himself on the spot, and put an ear on himself, listening to what they would say.[7]

Although, as I shall try to show later in this chapter, Hyde had been working for several years on translations of folk poetry, he seems, as late as 1887, to have despaired of ever being able to make a worthy English version of his collection of Gaelic lore. In an article entitled ' Some Words about Unpublished Literature ' in the *Gael*,[8] 7 January 1888, he tells his readers:

> . . . I would willingly go on to give some description of that store of poems, epigrams, and stories, which instead of being enshrined between the leaves of a dead book, are inscribed upon the living page of the hearts of the Irish people, and consequently, wherever Scions of our race are found, be it at home or in the new world, should possess an interest relatively greater than that of anything foreign.
>
> But here I am met by a difficulty which I find insurmountable, for the language in which the unwritten treasures of the golden bygone ages are enshrined, is itself in a dying condition, and the great traditions of the past of necessity must fade away with the framework in which they have been set. I cannot, consequently, venture to produce any of them here; few of the readers of the GAEL would (I regret infinitely to say) understand them, and any attempt at translations so as to give the tone or keep the spirit of the original, would be at once disheartening and impossible.

Instead he presents a selection of folksongs in English ' which have spontaneously sprang [*sic*] up and taken root amongst the peasantry—poor and scanty successors of the noble army of those which they are displacing or have displaced.'

However, even though the native language is dying, the folk-instinct survives:

The lower Irish are born songsters, they make songs upon anything and on the slightest occasion, and no sooner do they lay aside their own language than they attempt versification in English.

He gives an example of some verses composed by a man who, when he was young, never spoke English but who, in his old age, attempted to tell in English verse how he was robbed of the price of a little black pig he had sold at the fair:

I went to the fair like a sporting young buck,
    And I met with a dame,
    Who belonged to the game,
    And up to me came
    To be sure of her luck.
    She tipped me a wink,
    And we went into drink,
    We danced a few reels,
    And wan double jig.
    But in the phweel round
    She slip her hand down,
    And robbed me quite bare of
    The price of me pig.

Hyde more than once apologizes for the vulgarity and coarseness of these pieces; ' when we compare them with the beautiful Irish lyrics . . . which they have so unworthily supplanted, we are tempted to exclaim with Hamlet, " Oh, what a falling off was there " '. Describing them as ' the merest mushroom growth of a late day ', he goes on:

It is as though its own bark had rudely been stripped off the Irish tree, and a new artificial covering wrapped around it, and it is now only that [it] is beginning to absorb the sap and to cling to the trunk like something natural.

These words are significant, implying as they do that Hyde at this time accepts as inevitable the fact that English is to be the new vernacular of the Irish people. Even more explicit are his closing words:

The best we can hope for the future is that as the new language of the peasantry becomes more easy manage, [sic]

113

and begins to fit better the organs and mind of those who use it, the beautiful and pure lyrics of such masters as Moore, Mangan, Davis, and Griffin, as well as the songs from that golden repertoire the 'Spirit of the Nation', and other collections of a similar character, may gradually spring up with it, as it were, a natural growth in the hearts of the young generation, and quietly supersede the semi-barbarous productions which are as yet only too prevalent in the homes and round the hearths of the Irish nation.

There is no doubting the fact that in 1888 Hyde, however reluctantly, accepted English as 'the new language of the peasantry'. Indeed, by 1890 he was prepared to state this belief openly and unequivocally. In the article headed 'Gaelic Folk Songs' in which he introduced the famous series on 'The Songs of Connacht', in the *Nation* of 26 April 1890, he declares:

Now, however, that the force of circumstances, or to speak more truly the example of some of the leaders of the Irish race, have induced men to contemptuously throw aside Gaelic, and seeing that from the centre to the sea English will be the language of the rising generation, it may be possible that a poet may yet spring up amongst us who shall combine in a union of sympathy both the upper and lower classes, not of one province only, but of all Ireland.

On 10 May, in the same series, he returns to the subject:

. . . The discouragement and the apathy of those who have influence, the attitude of our Press, which would as soon think of advising the people to stand by their language, traditions, and customs as they would of exhorting them to buy the London *Times* and stand by the Government— all these have changed Southern and Western Ireland within a couple of decades in a manner which no outsider can realise, and have rendered it impossible now to collect myriads of interesting relics of a self-developed Aryan people, which could have been amassed without trouble fifty years ago. . . .

. . . The leaves are now gone and the tree is bare: they will never grow again, never,—to use the Irish phrase— while grass grows or water runs.

I suppose the people who helped to bring this about are glad of it, but for my part I honestly confess that I am heartily sorry.

I will have occasion to return to this subject later, in the context of the Gaelic League. Here I want to refer back to Hyde's final paragraph in the *Gael,* and consider to what extent the sentiments he expresses there represent his real attitude to Anglo-Irish poetry. I suspect a considerable measure of hyperbole in the phrases 'that golden repertoire "The Spirit of the Nation" '[9] and 'the beautiful and pure lyrics of such masters as Moore, Mangan, Davis and Griffin'.[10] A more sober appraisal of the same poets is found in his review of Sparling's *Irish Minstrelsy*[11] which appeared in the *Irish Monthly*[12] later in the same year 1888. Here we find Hyde expressing interesting views on the subject of Irish verse in English.

. . . And here we may say a word about the value of translations from the Gaelic, for the purpose of interpreting the *perfervidum ingenium Hibernicum.* The truth is that Gaelic songs mostly depend for their effect upon the alliteration and collocation of words, and that this effect is wholly and of necessity lost in any and every attempt to transfer them into another language, so that what in Irish are the most gorgeous and decorative verses imaginable, may become in English poor and bald; while, on the other hand, what in Irish is jejune enough, may become positively glittering with beauty in the hand of a true poetical translator. Thus, for example, the exquisite lines of Mangan (our best poetical translator, though he did not himself understand a word of Irish) given, of course, in this volume :—

> Oh, my dark Rosaleen,
> Do not sigh, do not weep!
> The priests are on the ocean green,
> They march along the deep.
> There's wine . . . from the royal Pope
> Upon the ocean green;
> And Spanish ale shall give you hope,
> My dark Rosaleen!
> My own Rosaleen!

Shall glad your heart, shall give you hope,
Shall give you health and help, and hope,
My dark Rosaleen[13]

correspond to these four undercorative lines of the original:

Oh, Roseen, let there not be grief on you, for all
                    that happened to you,
You have your pardon to get from the Pope, beyond!
The Friars are coming on the brine, advancing on the sea,
Do not spare the Spanish wine on my Roseen Dubh.

The most popular verse in Ireland at this time was that of the *Nation* poets, especially that of Thomas Davis. Of course Davis, in verse or in prose, was a propagandist;[14] even a love-song like ' Annie Dear ' is made to serve the national cause:

For once, when home returning,
            Annie, dear,
I found our cottage burning,
            Annie dear,
Around it were the yeomen,
Of every ill an omen,
The country's bitter foemen,
            Annie, dear.

Hyde shows himself severely critical of such verses, and is particularly annoyed, as one would expect, by Davis's habit of sprinkling what Hyde shows to be meaningless scraps of Gaelic among his English lines to give them an Irish flavour:

As to the selection which Mr Sparling has made from Davis, Ferguson, Mangan, Gerald Griffin, and other poets of note, and the space which he has accorded to them respectively, it would, of course, be easy to find plenty to say, and even to object to, if one were so inclined. We might, for instance, find fault with the insertion of those wretchedly weak lyrics of Davis's, ' Annie Dear ', ' Love's Longings ', and ' Máire Bhán astor ', the last a particularly objectionable effusion, from the really abominable nonsense (it is hard to command one's temper) of the Irish phrases in it.

> ' With her kisses and her song,
> And her loving *maith go leor* '

conveys absolutely no meaning; but his

> ' Fond is Maire Bhan astor
> Fair is Maire Bhan astor,'

etc. is actually nauseous, ' my astor ' being just the same thing
as if a foreigner writing English were to speak of ' my oh
love '. The *a* is a word in itself, the sign of the vocative case,
and means ' oh! ' Still we cannot be angry with Davis, for
his noble and generous treatment of the Irish language contrasts only too favourably with that of some of his followers
of the present day[15]—only we cannot help wishing that Mr
Sparling had omitted the pieces we have mentioned; and,
for that matter, perhaps the ' Flower of Finae ' and ' The
Volunteers ' also, and give us instead his ' Celts and Saxons '
and ' Nationality ', both of which express, as perhaps no other
of his poems has done, the whole life-work and aspiration
of the man himself. . . .[16]

By 1888 Hyde was well qualified to express opinions on Irish
verse. From his early booklists we know that he had read more
or less all that was in print of Gaelic verse and a considerable
amount in manuscript. He had also read most of the verse translated from Gaelic. A later booklist, given at the end of the 1880-
1882 volume of his diary under the heading ' College Prizes ',
shows that he was equally well read in the mainstream of English
poetry. Furthermore, over the preceding ten years he had filled
several notebooks with his own verse: original compositions and
translations from Gaelic, with occasional ventures into German
and French.

His first significant poem in English, written 'one night by the
fire, late, I remember'[17] is a translation of an Irish poem by Tadhg
Gaelach Ó Súilleabháin (' Gaelic Timothy O'Sullivan '), 'A Róis
na h-aoine, a shaoi na féile '.[18]

> Rose of the Universality, holy and heavenly leader
> Thou of thy flock on the mountains the comforter, carer and
> feeder,

Save me, protect me and keep me on mountains a desolate
           wand'rer,
Steer me, preserve me and help me and guard me from Death
           and the Plund'rer.
From Famine, from dread and from darkness, from Death
           and destruction and danger,
Guard me, that ultimate day of the Universe be not a
           stranger.
From scorching and burning and flashing and fervour of
           lightning and thunder,
From war and oppression and tumult, and elements riving
           asunder;
From the bursting and burning and flashing of livid-red
           lightning and thunder,
From war and from tumult of nature, and elements riven
           asunder.

Over a quarter of a century later Hyde published a slightly
amended version of this poem in *Religious Songs of Connacht*
(volume II, page 227).

Another poem written (he thinks) in 1878 and headed simply
'After the Irish' is:

Will you come far away to the wilds of Mayo
    My Ullachán dubh o,
Will you visit that clime for a time to stay oh,
    My Ullachaun dubh o,
Where hues of the heather together blend,
And ocean's commotions the cold rocks rend,
With odour of flowers the hours to spend,
    Oh my Ullachán dubh o[19]

Here it is interesting to note his efforts to reproduce the internal
rhyming and word-music of Gaelic verse, the 'alliteration and
collocation of words' upon which, as he says in his review of *Irish
Minstrelsy,* 'Gaelic songs mostly depend for their effect.' This
was a skill he was to develop with considerable success in his
later verse translations. It should however be noted that Hyde
was not a pioneer in this field. This distinction belongs to J. J.
Callanan (1795-1829), a Corkman who is buried in Portugal
whither he had gone as a private tutor in the vain hope that the
sunny climate would restore him to health. He made some notable

translations from Gaelic, and was the first to endeavour to convey, or at least to succeed in conveying anything of the distinctive rhythm and word patterns of his originals. The best example of his success is 'The Outlaw of Loch Lene', the opening stanza of which runs:

> O many a day have I made good ale in the glen,
> That came not from stream, or malt, like the brewing of men.
> My bed was the ground, my roof, the greenwood above,
> And the wealth that I sought—one far kind glance from my
>   love.

Hyde would have met this and other translations by Callanan in *The Ballad Poetry of Ireland*, edited by Charles Gavan Duffy (Dublin, 1848), which is in his list of ' College Prizes ' at the end of his diary for 1880-1882. He may not have read anything of Callanan's work when he wrote his ' Ullachán dubh o '.

Following close on Callanan is another verse-translator from Gaelic who succeeded in conveying something of the form as well as the matter of the native songs. This is the humble schoolmaster for whom Yeats expressed sympathy and regard, Edward Walsh (1805-1850). In the introduction to his *Irish Popular Songs* Walsh notes ' the pleasing stream of liquid sounds ' which is a feature of Gaelic verse, and

> the beautiful adaptation of the subject of the words to the song measure . . . which seems the natural gait of the subject, whatever that may be, from which it cannot be forced, in a translation, without at once destroying the graceful corres-pondence which gives its most attractive grace to the original. . . . The Irish scholar will perceive that I have embodied the meaning and spirit of each Irish stanza within the com-pass of the same number of lines, each for each; and that I have also preserved, in many of the songs, the caesural and demi-caesural rhymes, the use of which produces such har-monious effect in Irish verse.

Hyde met the work of Edward Walsh very early in his Irish reading. *Jacobite Relics* is fourteenth in his first list. It is interest-ing that in the preface to his own *Love Songs of Connacht* he makes almost the identically same claim as Walsh does above:

. . . I have differed somewhat from yourself [Dr Sigerson, to whom the book is dedicated], Mangan, Ferguson, and other translators, in endeavouring to reproduce the vowel-rhymes as well as the exact metres of the original poems. This may give English readers, if the book ever fall into the hands of any such, some idea of the more ordinary and less intricate metres of the people, and of the system of Irish interlineal rhyming, though I fear that the unaccustomed ear will miss most of it.

The following year, when he was twenty, fierce nationalism was his theme. He wrote a series of 'Ballads of '98' in which he places himself among the rebels with 'The Craoibhín Aoibhinn's Speech', a spirited harangue, and 'The Craoibhín Aoibhinn's Story' in which he invents for himself a rebel grandfather:

> In ninety-eight when a rebel fate
> Drove men unarmed to arms,
> My grandsire then raised many men
> To avenge their burning farms.

This fictitious ancestor went around the country rallying the common people. Naturally, he spoke Irish:

> They spoke in the Gaelic language old,
> The language of the land,
> And many a curse that is best untold
> They gave the English band.
>
> .   .   .   .   .
>
> But English gold, as ever of old,
> Betrayed the rightful cause,
> And English lies and English spies
> And bloody English laws.
>
> And the dungeon's flag was my grandsire's bed,
> Cold and damp and bare,
> And the people were left without a head
> And broken was their war.[20]

Another ballad in the series begins:

It was a rebel pikeman,
Beside the stream he stood,
The point of his pike was crimson,
His hands were red with blood.
He stood beside the water
And shouted clear and high:
Come, Saxons, to the slaughter,
I'm ready here to die.

At this period he has no time for conciliation:

And think upon O'Connall [*sic*]
The confidence he had,
Believing that persuasion
Alone could do us good,
Who curbed us back the hour
Our nation had most power;
A curse upon his scruples
Who shrank from shedding blood.

Up! answer with the answer,
The answer that ye should,
Shout 'not an instant longer',
Shout 'Steel alone, and lead'.
Shout 'Down with them, and down
With Union Jack and Crown,
Their barracks and their bayonets,
Their English blue and red.'

This sustained outburst marks the end of a phase that had begun
in 1877 with 'Graun a' peeca géur'. It is the last time that a call
to arms and physical force is sounded in his verses. Politics, and
the relationship with England, do indeed recur as themes, but
after 1880 his thinking takes a different course, and he shows
concern for national ills of another kind.

It is a relief to find among these bloodthirsty ballads a gentle
translation made in the same month of August 1880:

Oh were you on the mountain or saw you my love,
Or saw you my own one, my queen and my dove,
Or saw you the maiden with the step firm and free,
And oh, is she pining in sorrow like me?

I was upon the mountain and saw there your love,
I saw there your own one, your queen and your dove,
I saw there the maiden with the step firm and free,
And she was not pining in sorrow like thee.[21]

Indicative of a new direction in his political thinking is a poem
written in 1881, an appeal for unity and the re-awakening of a
sense of national identity:

Oh shame upon shame to thee fanatic nation
Who shout for the Orange or cry for the Green,
Whilst Erin your mother in deep desolation
Is bleeding to death—disinherited queen.

My country! Oh when shall the lesson be learned
So cruelly taught thee; for aye should it be
In letters of flame on thy bosom imburned:
Rely on thyself and unite and be free.

The Catholic crawling to social position
The wrongs of his nation refuses to heal,
The Protestant sneers at his petty ambition
Regardless as he of the national weal.

We pray, we adjure thee, thy children adjure thee,
Drop faction and party—drop pander to pelf,
The unborn ages of the Future implore thee
To turn thee from England and look to thyself.

Then trebly condemned, and thrice cursed the nation
Which warned like to thee shall refuse to combine,
And neglects what an age brings but once—an occasion
—Oh God! to be there for the crisis be mine!

Looked at historically, there is a pathetic irony about the last line.

An interesting subject claims his attention in 1887, the idea that
the working classes in England should unite with the Irish people
in opposition to their common oppressor, ' the Ascendancy '. On
this theme he produced one of his longest poems up to then.
The title was ' Through the nation a trump has been sounded ';

the following extracts give an indication of his treatment of the
theme:

Then Brothers of England, ye Many, who eat in the sweat of
your brow
Our rights and your rights go together, oh, befriend us and
look to us now.
We hated and cursed you of old, but we curse you no more,
for we know
Our masters have also been yours, and a class, not a people,
our foe.
For surely the days be approaching when this shall be uttered
no more,
That ' nations arise against nations to slay and oppress as
before ',
For the people are peaceful and loving, nor do workers on
workers make war,
Though the drones in the gate would incite us, and the rulers
of people that are.

.   .   .   .   .

For the band of Humanity binds us and brings us together
as one,
And the knowledge of work and of hunger and the struggle
so hardly begun.
And the love of our children and kin and the fear that is
common to man,
To labour for others for nothing through the whole of his
life's little span:
To toil as we toil—that our bread may be snatched from our
mouths at the last,
And earn—to give up our earnings; to thresh—and surrender
the threshed.
Oh, Brothers of England, look towards us, our hopes and
our fears are the same.
We know you, we love you, we trust you, we are one in
communion of aim,
Then closed be the Book of the Past, with the crimes of your
race against ours;
Not ye, oh not ye were its authors, but the powers that
mastered your powers.
But our love has outlived our hatred, our Present out-blotted
our past,

We greet you, ye Workers of England, for of one same
    mould are we cast.
Then by all that is sacred to man, by the roof-tree, the fire
    on the hearth,
By the great cause of labour itself, by the labour and fruits
    of the earth,
We reach you the right hand of friendship and now—
    but if never again—
We conjure you to meet us as brothers and to stand beside
    us as men.

Another poem written at this period expresses his dejection at the
supine, culturally moribund state of Ireland, in comparison with
the cultural richness of Germany. Hence the title, ' Oh! well for
the poets of Fatherland ',

                     the men who sung
    Their native land in their native tongue

      .   .   .   .   .

But I must sing in an alien tongue
Where once our native bards have sung.
How can I lift an ennobling strain
To slaves who hear—but hear in vain!
How can I touch one freeborn string
When slave among slaves am I who sing?

      .   .   .   .   .

How can a slave a poet be?
And we are slaves from sea to sea;
And every opening germ of song
Is blighted by the Saxon tongue.
Then marvel not that we are now
Sunk so deep and fallen so low.
No bard to make our pulse beat high—
A land unfit for Poetry.
Without a language of its own;
Whose ancient laws, whose rights are gone.
Without a hope of being free;
Oh, Ireland, I pity thee!
Thou land of long-lost liberty,
I can, alas! but pray for thee.

On 1 July of that year, 1887, he wrote one of his best-known translations:

> My grief on the sea,
> How the waves of it roll!
> For they heave between me
> And the love of my soul!
>
> Abandoned, forsaken,
> To grief and to care,
> Will the sea ever waken
> Relief from despair?
>
> My grief, and my trouble!
> Would he and I were
> In the province of Leinster,
> Or county of Clare.
>
> Were I and my darling—
> Oh, heart-bitter wound!—
> On board of the ship
> For America bound.
>
> On a green bed of rushes
> All last night I lay,
> And I flung it abroad
> With the heat of the day.
>
> And my love came behind me—
> He came from the South;
> His breast to my bosom,
> His mouth to my mouth.

The subject for the Vice-Chancellor's prize in English verse that year was ' Déirdre '. Hyde had long been familiar with this tragic heroine; among the books he bought at O'Daly's auction in 1878 was ' Déirdre, or, the Lamentable Fate of The Sons of Usnach, an ancient dramatic Irish tale, one of the three tragic stories of Erin . . .', edited in 1808 by Theophilus O'Flanagan. Hyde not only won the prize but he was tempted to try his hand on the other two tales that make up what have come to be known as

K

'The Three Sorrows of Irish Story-Telling': 'The Fate of the Children of Tuireann' and 'The Fate of the Children of Lir'. At the same time he turned to some old Irish poems attributed to St Columba or Colmcille and printed in Reeves's edition of the life of the saint by Adamnan.

He worked very rapidly, as the following entries in his diary show:

20 January 1888 I read nothing except a few hundred lines of Ovid, but I wrote a long poem of 24 quatrains from the Irish: 'Delightful it is on Binn [sic] Eadair to rest', etc . . .

5 March I began an English poem on The Fate of the Children of Lir, and wrote over a hundred lines of it.

9 March I finished my poem in four and a half days, more than 900 lines. I took a good drink to celebrate. . . .

14 July I went to Seághan na Pighne's house and had a drink and a game of cards with him. I lost nothing. I wrote some of my poem on the Fate of the Children of Tuireann—that is to say, I made a start on it and wrote about a hundred lines. . . .

It was quite by accident, according to Hyde himself, that the fruit of these intensive literary labours appeared in book form some seven years later.[22] In a brief introduction he explains the circumstances:

The first of the following poems, 'Déirdre', was written (successfully) for the Vice-Chancellor's Prize in Dublin University in 1887, about which time, being enamoured of the subject, I also tried to turn the other two 'Sorrows of Story-telling' into orthodox English Iambics. They would however, never have seen the light—at least not in this shape—had they not, in Mr Fisher Unwin's absence, been sent to press in mistake for a volume of the New Irish Library.[23] Hence their appearance now. I have subjoined to them a few ballads on St Columcille, founded on the Latin of Adamnan, or translated from the Irish. The difference between the epic wholeness of Pagan romance and the fragmentary nature of early Christian story is very obvious to any student of Irish literature, and these few pieces, despite their conventional English treatment, may, I think be regarded as, in this respect at least fairly typical.

As things turned out, they were destined to make another appearance some forty years later. Their author was by that time the first President of Ireland, and for his Christmas card for four consecutive years he used the material of his *Three Sorrows,* etc., printed in separate pamphlets by the Talbot Press as follows:

Déirdre	1939
The Children of Lir	1940
The Children of Tuireann	1941
Songs of St Columcille	1942

It is also perhaps worth noting that one of the 'Columcille' poems, 'St Columcille's Farewell', was Hyde's first contribution to the *Boston Pilot*. It appears in the issue for 4 August 1888.[24]

In January 1888 Hyde translated an Irish poem of a different kind from those he had collected from the oral tradition. This was 'Slán Chum Pádraic Sairséal', which appears in *The Poets and Poetry of Munster* (first series) with a verse translation by James Clarence Mangan. Hyde's is a much more literal translation, and conveys more of the simple pathos of the original than Mangan's does:[25]

> Patric Sarsfield the prayers of all with you!
> Prayers from me and from Mary's Son for you!
> Since the ford-pass at Birr you occupied,
> And since Limerick was bethrothed to you,
> >   Och ochon.
>
> Over the mountain I'll go wandering
> Towards the West, if the way be possible,
> Where the camp of the Gael is congregate,
> Broken men who would not amalgamate,
> >   Och ochon.
>
> My farewell to the halls of Limerick,
> And the heroes who kept us company!
> Bonfires lighted and cards and merriment,
> God's own prophecies often read to us,
> >   Och ochon.

London-Derry a murrain fall on you,
Darkness cover you, worse than powder-smoke!
And the number of fine tall gentlemen
Wind-exposed, or with clay for coverlets!

                   Och ochon.

Och, the breaking at Boyne and Limerick,
And the fight that at Moate was broke on us,
But the cruellest back-blow struck on us
Was the Sunday we fought in Augharim,

                   Och och hone.

Patric Sarsfield a long farewell to you
Blessings of sun and moon and stars on you,
Woe's in Limerick, Leinster languishes,
Munster mourns and Connact grieves for you

                   Och och hone.

There they go from us, chiefs of Ireland,
Browns and Dillons and James's gentlemen,
Captain Talbot, the heart of nobleness,
Patric Sarsfield whom women doated on,

                   Och och hone.

On 26 June 1888, 'in the morning', he made a translation 'From the Irish: a folk-song. MS. penes me', which, surprisingly enough, he did not include in the *Love Songs of Connacht*:

The Curlew mountains are fine in winter,
They are not imbedded in ice nor snow
The cuckoo calls from the greenwood's centre,
The thrush and the corncrake sing below.

The hounds are hunting, the rocks resounding,
They follow the faun that flies before,
The torrent comes from the mountain bounding
Salmon are leaping beside the shore.

I think of my mountain late and early
Where blossoms are golden and glad and gay,
Where the wheat springs up and the yellow barley
And birds are piping on every spray.

The tips of the rushes are heavy with honey
There is butter and cream from the silken kine,
No northern snow on its slopes so sunny
Will trouble its coasts or harbours fine.

Where the bee has his home and is wisely working
And women have honey from day to day,
But deep in my bosom a care is lurking,
The love of my heart is far away.

Your fair thin forehead, the wide world's wonder
Your tresses that hang in a golden sheaf,
Have torn the strings of my heart asunder
And covered my heart with a cloud of grief.

I am as a man that is even dying
For lack of the jewel his eyes would see,
Will you not visit me where I am lying
And take God's blessing and comfort me.

Perhaps he rejected it as overall unworthy of a place in his book, but it has lines, and at least one stanza, that could stand comparison with some things he included.

In 'half an hour' on 4 July he translated a song of which he says in the *Love Songs* that 'there are few songs of the great bards themselves that are in my opinion as sweet as it': 'Mala Neifin: The Brow of Nefin' (*Love Songs*, p. 9).

On 28 August he notes: 'Working on Yeats's book, Irish stories'. This, of course, is *Fairy and Folk Tales of the Irish Peasantry,* edited by W. B. Yeats and published by Walter Scott in the autumn of 1888. The collection contains three stories from *Leabhar Sgéulaigheachta* translated by Hyde himself: 'Teig O'Kane and the Corpse', 'The Piper and the Puca' and 'Munachar and Manachar'. In the introduction Yeats thanks Hyde for 'valuable and valued assistance in several ways', and individual notes on Irish words and phrases are acknowledged to be Hyde's. In the same introduction Yeats provides helpful advance notice for Hyde's forthcoming book:

. . . Mr Douglas Hyde is now preparing a volume of folk tales in Gaelic, having taken them down, for the most part, word for word among the Gaelic speakers of Roscommon and Galway. He is, perhaps, most to be trusted of all. He knows the people thoroughly. Others see a phase of Irish life; he understands all its elements. His work is neither humorous nor mournful; it is simply life. I hope he may put some of his gatherings into ballads, for he is the last of our ballad-writers of the school of Walsh and Callanan—men whose work seems fragrant with turf smoke.

Finally, the year 1888 saw the publication of what might be described as the first official anthology of the new literary movement, *Poems and Ballads of Young Ireland,* which is the subject of the following, hitherto unpublished, letter from Ellen O'Leary to Douglas Hyde:

134 Rathgar Road.

Dear Mr Hyde,

'Twas stupid of me to tell you we had only one of your poems in the ballad book. We have the 98 ballad, St Columcille and the Heron, and the little love song translated from the Irish about which W Yeates [*sic*] was always raving. They are all good specimens. . . .

The 'little love song' was 'Oh, were you on the mountain' which I have quoted on page 121. (Ellen O'Leary must have been absentminded. There are two other poems by Hyde in the small collection: 'Death Lament for John O'Mahony' and 'Marching Song of the Gaelic Athletes').

Hyde tended to write his poems in isolated bursts of creative energy. The next notable occasion was September 1892, when in the space of four days he made nine of the verse-translations for his *Love Songs*:

7 September	'O youth whom I have kissed'.	L.S.	108
8 September	'A honey mist on a day of frost'	L.S.	71
	'Star of my sight, you gentle Breedyeen'	L.S.	117
	''Tis my grief I'm not going'	L.S.	121
9 September	'My Una a queen is'	L.S.	123

10 September	'She casts a spell'	L.S.	135
	'I shall not die for thee'	L.S.	139
	'No man's trust let woman claim'	L.S.	143
11 September	'Little child, I call thee fair'	L.S.	141

Around the same time—he does not give the date—he wrote 'Ringleted youth of my love'. (*Love Songs,* p. 41)

In 1890 he had started a weekly column in the *Nation* under the heading, 'Gaelic Folk Songs'. After three introductory articles in English, interspersed with examples of the Gaelic songs and verse translations in English, he changed his title to 'Danta na mBard Connactac' [*sic*], 'Poems of the Connacht Bards'. There was also a change in presentation: the linking text as well as the songs was in Irish, followed by an English translation of the whole. Throughout 1890 he printed what he described as the first three chapters of a single work, 'The Songs of Connacht': 'Songs of Carolan and his Contemporaries'; 'Songs in Praise of Women'; and 'Drinking Songs'.

The fourth chapter, 'Love Songs', appeared in the *Weekly Freeman* in 1892 and early 1893. In his review of 1892 he explains the business arrangement he had with the paper:

> I printed my Connacht songs in the Weekly Freeman, without payment except that they gave me the plates.

In 1893 the *Freeman* plates were used to produce a book:

> I brought out my Love Songs of Connacht, and it was given a wonderful welcome by all the papers and by everybody. I published it at half a crown.

Hyde was fortunate in the timing of his book; the literary climate was favourable. For almost fifty years Anglo-Irish poetry had been weighed down by its burthen of nationalist propaganda. Poets were popular if they bewailed Ireland's wrongs and chanted her virtues. There had been exceptions, of course. Callanan and Walsh had turned to the Gaelic songs of the people, and each had succeeded in a few instances in putting something of the form and flavour of folk song into their English verses. Sir Samuel Ferguson in particular, with his scholarly knowledge of the Irish language and antiquities, had produced not only noble epics[26] but some delicate love-songs translated from the Irish. 'Cashel of Munster', 'The Coolun' and 'Paistin Fionn' anticipated all the simple directness of the *Love Songs of Connacht*. And yet Ferguson declared his bitter disappointment as he looked back at the apathy with which his work had been received:

> At present the cultured criticism of the day is averse to the Irish subject in any form, and the uncultured will not have it save in that form of helotism in which I at least will not present it.[27]

Despite disappointment, Ferguson laboured on. Two years before his death he wrote:

> My business is, regardless of such discouragements, to do what I can in the formation of a characteristic school of letters for my own country.

Although Ferguson himself saw little enough fruit from his literary life-work, his labours were not in vain. The year that he died, 1886, was the year that young W. B. Yeats resolved to turn away for good from Indian subjects, shepherds and fauns and become an Irish poet. Ferguson's example had a strong influence on him at the time, and Ferguson's aim was realized under Yeats's leadership, as Katherine Tynan recalls:

> The Ireland of my young days was terribly unexacting in the matter of poetry. . . . Of course there was always Mangan and Ferguson, Callanan and Edward Walsh, and the best of de Vere; but these were dead or old, and Ireland was placidly accepting for poetry what was merely propagandism or heart-less exercises in unsimple simplicity. These were the things we young ones were reproducing with great satisfaction up to the time when W. B. Yeats brought a new soul into Irish poetry. . . . What I would claim for Mr. Yeats is that he established, or at least re-established, the artistic conscience and the artistic ideal in Irish Poetry.[28]

It was into this new climate that the *Love Songs* were born, a fact that made their welcome all the greater and their influence all the more immediate. Irish poets, their artistic conscience awakened, were looking for new themes and new modes; Hyde provided them with the genuine folk theme and the Gaelic mode. Furthermore, the *Love Songs* came as a timely corrective to what Austin Clarke calls ' that shadowy world of subdued speech and nuance '[29] that was the heyday of the Celtic Twilight. The inevitable reaction to the misty romanticism of those early days was tempered by Hyde's presentation of the genuine emotions of country men and women expressed in the freshness and immediacy of living speech.

Of the forty-five songs in the collection, Hyde gives verse translations for twenty-five. In these latter he makes his task doubly difficult by ' endeavouring to reproduce the vowel-rhymes as well as the exact metres of the original poems ' (Preface). In many cases he achieves his purpose ingeniously as in

> For thee I shall not die,
> Woman high of fame and name;
> Foolish men thou mayest slay
> I and they are not the same.

.   .   .   .   .

> The golden hair, the forehead thin,
> The chaste mien, the gracious ease,
> The rounded heel, the languid tone,
> Fools alone find death from these.

.   .   .   .   .

> Woman, graceful as a swan,
> A wise man did nurture me,
> Little palm, white neck, bright eye,
> I shall not die for ye.

(I should point out that the original in this case is one of ' those pieces which the true bards left after them ', and not a folk song. Hyde gives a few of these formal pieces at the end of his collection).

At other times, however, he has to resort to forced rhymes, inversions and poetic diction which are out of tune with the simple directness of the originals. In such cases one must turn to the literal translation for a reflection of the primitive simplicity

of the Gaelic. Compare, for example, his two translations of the
second stanza of ' The Dark Girl of the Valley ':

Whoever saw my house, with no roof but the rush,
Where the road bends out to the far west,
The bee loves to roam and to build there his home
In the sun and the heat of harvest.
When withered is the root, the bough will bear no fruit
'Tis the young twigs shoot by the river,
O lovely golden fay, who stole my heart away,
Farewell to thee today, and for ever

Whoever would see my house with no roof on it but sedge,
And it made upon the side of the road. Sure the bee comes
and makes the nest With the sun and heat of harvest. When
the rod withers there remains on it no fruit As there be's
upon the youngest sprout, And O beautiful handsome cool,[30]
to which my heart has given love, I send with thee forever
a farewell and a hundred.

It was Hyde's prose that won Yeats's unstinted admiration:
' the prose narrative that flows about his *Love Songs of Connacht* . . . The prose parts of that book were to me, as they were
to many others, the coming of a new power into literature.'[31]

Hyde's later literary work does not fall within the scope of this
volume. In 1906 he published *The Religious Songs of Connacht*
after they had been serialized in the *New Ireland Review* from
June 1895 to June 1905. His *magnum opus,* as regards research
and scholarship, was *A Literary History of Ireland,* first published
in 1899; a new addition appeared in 1967. Of this work Maud
Gonne wrote that it was 'an inspiration to O'Leary's group of
young poets, writers and revolutionists; it supplied the intellectual
background of revolt.'[32]

Hyde also had the distinction of writing the first play in Gaelic,
'Casadh an tSugáin' (The Twisting of the Rope), which was first
performed at the Gaiety Theatre, Dublin, on 21 October 1901 by
members of the Gaelic League Amateur Dramatic Society, with
Hyde himself in the principal part.[33] Although it does not fall
strictly within the limits of this study I feel that the historic
occasion merits brief mention in the present chapter. The play
was written at Coole:[34]

28 August 1900   Yeats set me writing a play on 'The Twisting of the Rope', and I wrote a good part of it from the scenario he drew up for me.

29 August   Finishing 'The Twisting of the Rope'. Tired and a little unwell. Lady Gregory gave me a bottle of champagne at dinner.

30 August   Martyn came to dinner. I read 'The Twisting of the Rope' to him yesterday and he was very pleased with it.

31 August   Yesterday and today I read 'The Twisting of the Rope' to Lady Gregory and she typed it in English from my dictation. A fine day. I wrote part of another little play.

The play was put on with 'Diarmuid and Gráinne'[35] which was acted by Mr F. R. Benson's Shakespearean Company. Hyde records the excitement of the first night:

21 October 1901   The great day came at last. This morning I went to see the Bensons rehearsing 'Diarmuid and Gráinne'. Chatted with them and with Yeats. In the evening at about 9.30 I collected my group. Benson's men made up our male actors and their make-up woman prepared our girls. I got the costumes[36] from a man named Trevanion?, a Jew, [sic] I believe, for £4.0.0; the boys themselves provided báiníns[37] and the girls made their own costumes. When the curtain went up at 10.45 we could see nothing, but we went gaily through our piece without a trace of nervousness and the audience loved it. The house was packed to the doors, and they all said that they preferred 'Casadh an tSugáin' to 'Diarmuid and Gráinne'. Home around 12.30. O'Connell came to dinner with us.

The contrast between the natural spontaneity of the Gaelic amateurs portraying an Irish folk-comedy and the incongruity of English professionals trying to bring an Irish legend to life was not lost on Yeats or Lady Gregory. The point was hammered home by Frank Fay in a review of the evening's programme in the *United Irishman* (26 October 1901):

Monday evening was a memorable one for Dublin and for Ireland. The Irish language has been heard on the stage of the principal metropolitan theatre, and 'A Nation Once Again' has been sung within its walls, and hope is strong within us once more.

Of 'Diarmuid and Gráinne' Fay wrote:

> To my mind the greatest triumph of the authors lies in their having written in English a play in which English actors are intolerable. . . . All through the play the English voice grated on one's ear, and the stolid English temperament was equally at variance with what we wanted.

'Casadh an tSugáin' had been produced by William Fay who, with his brother Frank, 'had been in the habit of playing little farces in coffee palaces and such like.'[38] At the beginning of 1902 Yeats and Lady Gregory joined forces with the Fays and the original Irish Literary Theatre became The Irish National Dramatic Company and finally The Irish National Theatre Society. Henceforth Yeats, Lady Gregory, Synge and George Russell had their plays performed by Irish actors.

Hyde wrote a few more plays in Irish which were popular in those early days of national resurgence,[39] but the Gaelic League took up more and more of his time. From 1893 until 1915, when he resigned from the movement, he gave himself almost entirely to the work of organizing and propaganda. Ceaseless travel, speechmaking and pamphleteering made it impossible for him to find time, as Yeats would have him do, 'for the making of translations, loving and leisurely, like those in *Beside the Fire* and the *Love Songs of Connacht*.'[40] Henceforth, for Yeats, he was 'the great poet who died in his youth'.[41]

Be that as it may, Douglas Hyde left a decisive mark on Anglo-Irish literature. The day after his death a distinguished Irish poet wrote of him:

> We need not claim that in quantity and quality of achievement he was great as a writer; but we surely can say that he did write well, that he did help others to write greatly— that he did help Irish letters, in all its branches, to be native, continuous, rooted, branching and fruitful.[42]

VI

1890-1893: National Literary Society and the Gaelic League

Hyde found remarkably little to record in the first eight months of 1890. Then, in September, an unexpected turn of events brought a major change in his life:

On September 10, 1890, in consequence of an arrangement with Willie Stockley, who had asked a young woman in Fredericton to marry him and she refused, so that he didn't wish to be in her presence any longer, I sailed for Liverpool, spent a day there and embarked on the Polynesia, Allen line, for Montreal. Had a very stormy passage, the hatches having sometimes to be battened down, but I wasn't seasick. Sighted icebergs and whales and porpoises. On board I met two young women, Misses Ede and Nicholls, and became very friendly with them. I believe the former fell in love with me. A couple of months later, from Vancouver, she sent me her portrait, and I returned the compliment, but because I did not wish to prolong the acquaintance I did not write to her any more.

There was a man named Bond, plenipotentiary of New-foundland, with whom I consumed some cocktails, a German generally drunk who had been a slave-dealer in Constanti-nople and who finding I spoke German unbosomed himself to me, and told awful lies; an old English general (& his daughter) who used to boss the smoking room; a fool of a young conceited idiot who made a butt for us; and generally the consensus of opinion was that each man of us ' never struck a pleasanter crowd'. We spent our time playing quoits, reading, smoking and playing cards; we also had a concert at which I gave them an Irish song. We got to Quebec on the 21st and to Montreal at midday on the 22nd, where I put up at the Windsor, an hotel equal to Metropole [*sic*] or the Grand, with a curious couple brother and sister named Tayleur, great friends of Miss Gonne. Saw several of my friends off by rail and spent the rest of the evening in celebrating our arrival and drinking that most insidious but excellent drink, the cocktail.

Left Montreal on 23rd at 7.30 p.m. and got to Fredericton 430 miles away at 2 p.m. next day and went to stay with Col. Maunsell, commandant of the military school, who was a relative of Stockley's, a Home Ruler and a Co. Limerick man, to whom I had been introduced in Ireland. I spent three weeks or more with him, experiencing the greatest [sic] from him and every one else and then changed into the University to Stockley's rooms which were nice and comfortable. I make my own breakfast and lunch and go for dinner at 6.30 to a house 10 minutes from the College. The praepositus Harrison received me very kindly. I got to work on the 1st of October, and with only a few holidays at intervals remained till Xmas. 3 lectures each day from 9 in the morning to 12 or 1: French, German and English. I did not find any great difficulty in that.

This account was written at the end of 1890. Immediately after it he writes:

The most important events of the past year were: the honour of M.R.I.A. to be conferred on me, thanks to Maxwell Close who paid the cost, £26 or more.[1] The publication in The Nation of my *Danta na mBard Connachtach,* and my journey to Canada and acceptance of Stockley's professorship. Not to mention the lecture on modern literature which I gave at the College and which was printed in the papers.

He enjoyed the outdoor life in New Brunswick:

Jan 1891.   Fredericton, N.B.

Spent the last three months very pleasantly, as I said above. The best things were the shooting, the skating and the parties. I shot 11 woodcock one day to my own gun, and went on many expeditions with a Mr Forester, an Englishman who had been a banker and who is now an officer. A good, decent man; he doesn't know much about literature but he is an expert at the hunt. The officers made me a member of their mess, the only place where I can get a drink of whiskey, for the Scott Act prohibiting the sale of drink is rigorously enforced here.

The river froze on Nov. 25 and gave us a week's skating before the snow fell. The depth of the snow varies from 1 to 2 feet, but in drifts it is sometimes 3 or 4 feet deep. There comes a fall of snow once or twice a month, but it often ends in rain which melts the upper snow which then hardens as ice on the top of the under snow and forms a strong crust. About one day in twenty the thermometer may be above freezing point. During the other nineteen it varies from 10 below to 25 above zero, but this has been an exceptionally cold year.

On St Stephen's day I started for a hunting expedition with two wealthy young traders from the town, Cheshunt and Randolph, (the latter is going to marry the Premier's daughter) and three Indians or half breeds, for a place called Guspereaux between forty and fifty miles from Fredericton where there were said to be lots of caribou. We brought with us a tent and lots of provisions and toboggans. We drove with a team of horses on a big sleigh forty-two miles and though we started at 8 in the morning we only got to the last house in the settlement at midnight. The man of the house, D'Arcy or William O Dorchuidh, an old Irishman from Co. Kilkenny, came out and he stark naked without a screed on him. We invaded the house, hunted the daughters who were sleeping in the kitchen round the stove, and passed the night there. Next day we started in a snow storm for a point some miles farther in among the woods. We were hauled in by another team, and pitched our tent. We left a couple of inches of snow on the floor of the tent and covered this thick with spruce branches, spread our blankets, coats, skins, etc. over this and heating the tent with a light stove we slept comfortably. Unfortunately there was such a crust upon the snow that the noise of our snow-shoes could be heard for half a mile, and during the 12 days I remained in camp there never came a fall of snow to cover the crust and deaden the sound. The consequence was that though I put up a fine herd of caribou from behind a thicket I was unable to creep on them to get a shot. I walked 25 or 30 miles on snow-shoes on this occasion. We did little in camp except to eat too much. I shot a couple of partridge, a tufted grouse and three large porcupines weighing 25 or 30 pounds each with rifle bullets, but that was all.

We used to spend the evenings smoking and telling stories.

I got many stories from the Indians and told them many, and learned a couple of hundred Milicete words, but did not get far enough to reduce the language to any kind of grammar, or even learn the conjugation of verbs. I paid a dollar and a quarter per day to the Indian who was with me, and the whole trip cost me forty-five dollars. I left the others behind me and came home for the opening of the college on January 8th.

Apart from this major expedition, he found a full and varied social life at Fredericton, into which he entered with gusto: dances and card parties, sleigh drives, snow-shoe parties and in the spring, when the ice cleared, canoeing. One evening he delivered a lecture on folklore at the Presbyterian kirk; on another occasion he entertained the town Literary Society with readings from Katherine Tynan, Rolleston, etc. On 10 February he wrote a letter to the College magazine putting forth some views on the study of Greek. Finally the time came for farewell speeches:

28 May 1891   The Encaenia or commencements. Sir Leonard Tilly and all Fredericton there. Twelve graduates. Proceedings lasted from 3 till 6. Harison [sic] made me make the graduating speech malgré moi, but it went off well. I drew tears, I was told, from the girls! Dinner at the Alumni Society at Queen's Hotel at 9.30, I on the left of the chairman. Two members of government and some 50 more there. Drank healths in water! . . .

29 May   The Students of the Lit. & Deb. Society invited me to be present at their last meeting. I went unsuspiciously [sic] and found the whole college, ladies and all, there and they made me a presentation of pipes and stems and case and strong a stick [sic]. Returned thanks as best I could. All crowded round me afterwards and shook hands and said good-bye most cordially.

In his typically methodical manner he records the substance of his courses at the university:

15 May 1891   During the 2 terms of less than 3 & less than 5 months I read with the 4th and 3rd year Hamlet, As You

Like It; Milton, 2 books; about ¼ of the Golden Treasury; Hales longer English poems (Spenser, Dryden, Milton, Pope, Gray, Keats, Shelley, Coleridge, Wordsworth); some of Math. Arnold's poems. All of Carlyle's Past and Present & a very little of Green's history.

With the sophomores I read Macbeth, 12th Night, Hen IV (both), Henry V. Merchant of Venice, 12th Night [*sic*]. Shorter poems of Milton and Dryden. A whole volume of Emerson, 12 essays & J. S. Mills Inaugural Address.

With the Freshmen I read Julius Caesar & the same plays I read with the Sophomores, some of Palgrave, Aylmer's Field, Enoch Arden. Sesame & Lillies (not all) & a little Tennyson.

In addition to this I gave several open lectures on various things & branched off to lecture on Socialism, Booth's Movement, Proportional representation, Henry George's Land system, J. S. Mill's life & works, George Sand, etc., etc.

In French I read with the Sen. & Jun. during the last term Le Bourgeois Gentilhomme, Le Malade Imaginaire, Bertrand et Raton, & L'Avare.

With the Sophomores L'Abbe Constantin & Extracts from Turrel.

With the Freshmen Le voyage de M. Perrichon, Le Siege de Berlin et d'autres contes de Daudet, Le voyage de Christophe Colombe par Chateaubriand.

In German Grimm, a couple of German comedies & the Grammar were all, German being unknown as Sanscrit here. The number of students in each class varied from 5 to 38.

On the way home he visited Boston and New York:

3 June 1891   Left Fredericton at 7.45 in the morning. Got to Boston for nine dollars at 9.30 at night, passing through Maine. Put up at the Crawford House, a comfortable hotel in Court Street, on the European plan; a dollar a night for my room, voilà tout. I had a drink or two when I arrived.

4 June   . . . Hunted up Roche of the Pilot, O'Reilly's[2] successor, who took me to the St Botolphe Club there; nice quiet intelligent men all, & had much drink, eating & talking, chiefly about O'Reilly's statue; did not get away till 12 or 1, or even later. Roche was kindness itself, & Browne, a barister [*sic*] to whom I talked much was excessively polite and intelligent.

141

5 June   Went to Harvard Cambridge by electric car, just outside Boston. Hunted up Ganong [?] and his wife & Raymond [?]. Was shown all over that mass of luxury, Harvard College. Went home & had supper with them & afterwards went to a Mr Newell, a great folklorist who showed me my last book, not knowing the author. Home after an interesting day at 10 p.m.

6 June   . . . Roche dined with me in the evening & we took a long walk round Back Bay won from the sea. Home early.

7 June   Sunday. Went with Fraulein[3] to hear Phillip Brooks. He speaks like a torrent for speed. Nichts besonderes. Afterwards went out to Miss Conway & was introduced to her whole family & above all to Miss Guiney who was there and whom I went to see.[4] Had a long talk. Stayed for tea & remained talking till near ten.

8 June—Talk & drink with Roche. Fraulein met me & lunched with me at the hotel. Went with her to the New Library & Museum; the pictures were worth nothing, all daubs. I took my leave of her without tears on either side. Went home to Roche to his brother in law's. Tea there, beer and cigars afterwards. Did not get away till 12. Far out of town.

9 June—Went out to Miss Guiney some dozen miles out of Boston. Spent 3 or 4 hours with her & lunched. She is a pleasant girl, full of talk and enthusiasm. We spoke mostly of people of her acquaintance. I enjoyed my visit to her, except that she is a bit deaf. Took a parlor [sic, American style] car to Fall river, a couple of hours journey, & there got at 8 in the evening on board an enormous floating palace of a steamer which brought me to New York at 7 next morning for 4 dollars.

10 June   Went to the Everett House, Union Square, near the centre of New York. Met a man from Ohio & went out in a steamer with him to see the statue of Liberty, presented to America by France, & so large that 12 men could stand round the torch held in the right hand. Went to Central Park on the elevated railway and saw tens of thousands of people riding high in their carriages. When I got back I found Russell and Patrick awaiting me. They brought me to the Irish Society and I stayed with them until midnight and drank a little. Russell was delighted to see me.[5]

11 June   Russell breakfasted with me & I spent most of the day with him at the Gaelic Society and hunted in vain for O'Donovan Rossa and another man. Spent the evening very pleasantly with Patrick, drinking and talking. Home at midnight.

12 June   Hunted up Bliss Carman & Gregg & asked them to breakfast with me. Went over Brooklyn Bridge, looked at rifles & stores. Turned into the Irish Society later on. Tea with Russell and a long discussion with him and the other people until nightfall.

13 June   This morning I went to O'Donovan Rossa and had a long talk and drinks with him. He brought me to Patrick Forde in his office[6] and I spent a long time talking to him. Then I went to Haarlem to see a baseball game but I did not stay long there. The glass was 90 in the shade. I went to the Gaelic Society where I had a drink with Walsh and dinner with Russell, after which we went to a concert of Irish music by McGilvrey's band in the Madison Hall, the biggest hall I have ever been in. The music was very good. Home at 11.

14 June   Sunday. Russell, Gregg and Bliss Carman breakfasted with me. Great talk with them until 12.30, when I went with Russell to meet Patrick and we went together to Tailtinn where the Irish Society have a house in the country. Home to tea with Russell and another drink or two, and in bed by midnight after a pleasant day. The glass was over 90 in the shade.

15 June   A terribly hot day—the glass 113 in the sun and 95 in the shade. I bought a Colt revolver and bullets for 20 dollars and a return ticket for Niagara for 16 dollars. I wrote a speech on the state of the Irish language etc. This evening I went to the Gaelic Society where they put on a feis in my honour. Fifteen or twenty people there. Speaking Irish. A good supper. Iced wine and plenty of punch; we drank a fair amount. There were six speeches in Irish and as many or more in English, and all in praise of me. We stayed talking and drinking until 3 in the morning. I wasn't drunk, but I had had enough. Six of them came back to the hotel with me at 4 a.m.

16 June   Russell came for me and brought me, before I had eaten a bite, to Mlle. Carusi. I spoke to her and she squeezed

my hand warmly and gave me a rose. At midday I sat on my bed with the glass 100 in the shade. Then a storm broke. A big meeting of the Gaelic Society this evening. I spoke in Irish and in English. Colman in the chair. There was one person there who kissed my hand, and all shook hands with me. Home at midnight. Drinks.

The next three days were taken up with his visit to the falls.

21 June   Sunday. I went to Brooklyn to hear Talmage. There were 4,000 people there. He gave an able sermon. I came back and went with Patrick and Russell to the Irish school in the Bowery. There were 30 people there, all Irish speakers. I made a speech, and spoke very well, I believe. . . .

23 June   I went out to O'Donovan Rossa, had a drink and a talk with him, and he brought me to the top of the Herald building from which I had a view of the whole city. Then I went to the British Consul about my gun and my books, but without success. I spent a couple of hours talking to Augustine Forde, Patrick's brother. I invited Gregg to come and have a drink with me; he came at 6.30 and we had a good drink. Patrick and O'Hanlon then arrived and brought me to the Gaelic Society where I found that the womenfolk had prepared a feast in my honour : food and wine of every kind. There were thirty or more people present. I spoke in Irish and in English, and two lawyers (Gough? and?) [sic] spoke after me. We then had a small dance, like the dances in Canada. There was a French girl with whom I spoke in French. The ladies left at 2.30, but I stayed on with a man named Lynch and Boland, O'Mahoney (a bookseller), McCrystal, Dr Coughlan and Ward. We talked about Parnell, etc., until 6 in the morning.[7] They came home with me.

On 25 June he sailed for home, laden with presents including several bottles of whiskey.

His diary for the summer of 1891 illustrates an interesting facet of Hyde's character. As a youth in the first flush of discovery of the native language and culture he gloried in his Irish ancestry, and even invented a ' grandsire ' who rallied the peasant pikemen in 1798. Now, at the age of thirty-one, he shows himself very ready to play the role of country gentleman. As a Protestant rector's son he was born into what was regarded in the Ireland of the time as minor Ascendancy; as a graduate of Trinity College, a Doctor of Laws and a Member of the Royal Irish Academy he had considerably enhanced his social standing. He could mingle at ease with the aristocracy:

14 July 1891 A tennis party at Frenchpark [Lord and Lady de Freyne's]. We went and played a good deal.

15 July A very warm day. A dance at Boyle. Tennis and dinner at Ratra. We didn't go to the dance.

16 July I drove Annette to the tennis tournament at Boyle. We were there until 8.30; home by 11.

17 July To the tennis tournament again. After a few good games Annette and Fagan lost to Miss White and Smith. Dinner with Dr Hamilton, drinks with Dick French, etc. It was after 11 when we got home. I was tired, and had taken a fair amount of drink.

20 July Cricket at Frenchpark. Annette and I went . . . A fair amount of people there.

21 July We went to Boyle to finish the tennis. The day turned very wet. I had a bad partner, a lady named Miss Marsh, and I was beaten. A terrible day. Dinner and drinks with Dr Hamilton; home at 9.

27 July Cricket match at Frenchpark: Castlerea versus the garrison. I fielded fairly well but got only one or two runs. Lunch at the Big House.

3 August I went by train to Castlerea, from there to Athlone and Athenry, where I had a few hours delay. Then to Ennis and on to Limerick, passing through Gort, Ardrahan and Cratloe. I reached Limerick at 9.30 and booked in at the George Hotel.

4 August I spent the night in the hotel and this morning I met Sellors and we had a couple of drinks together. Then I took the train to Foynes, 24 miles from Limerick, and arrived at Ard-an-oir, the home of Charlotte Grace O'Brien. She and Miss Spring Rice, the sister of Lord Monteagle, were there,[8] and Stockley and Miss Osbourne came in the afternoon. A very wet day.

145

5 August Miss Spring Rice left. We went to Mount Trenchard, the home of Lord Monteagle. Had a long talk with his wife. A beautiful place.

6 August Out with my gun. A Miss Knox was here. Talking on my fingers to Grace. Took a boat to Foynes Island, to the home of Stephen de Vere. I killed a white rabbit at forty yards, and a crow.[9]

7 August Dined with Lord Monteagle and had a long talk with Miss Butcher, his wife's sister. Home at 12. Walked a couple of miles.[10]

This contrast between Hyde the crusader for all things Gaelic and Hyde the Anglo-Irish country gentleman was to continue all through his life. Even when, a few years later, as President of the Gaelic League, he became, in Yeats's words, ' the cajoler of crowds and of individual men and women ', he himself was never one of the crowd. However passionately and sincerely he might campaign to save the remnants of the popular Gaelic culture (and his passionate sincerity is, needless to say, beyond all doubt), in private life his preference was for the aristocratic and urbane. This strange blend of popularity and aloofness is accurately conveyed in Yeats's appeal to the ' Dear Craoibhin Aoibhinn ' to share with him the secret of humouring the public:

> You've dandled them and fed them from the book
> And know them to the bone; impart to us—We'll
> keep the secret—a new trick to please.
> Is there a bridle for this Proteus
> That turns and changes like his draughty seas?
> Or is there none, most popular of men,
> But when they mock us, that we mock again?[11]

In September 1891 Hyde took up the study of Anglo-Saxon, and by the end of October he had finished Sweetman's Prose Extracts. He was evidently bent on improving his qualification for a university teaching post. This seems to be confirmed by an entry on 16 December 1891:

> Writing letters to every one about the post in Belfast and the one in Chicago.

18 December   Still writing letters about Belfast. . . .

19 December   Having my papers printed. Terrible work with them. Fowler in Crow Street was the printer. Six pages, twenty copies, for 19 shillings. Sheehan was hurrying me all day; it was heavy work. Went out to Sells [his old German professor] and persuaded him to give me a reference. Everything was ready just as the last post bag was being closed, and I threw it in. I was exhausted; drank a couple of glasses of champagne and went to bed early.

The following is the text of his application for the post in Belfast:

To His Excellency The Right Hon. Lawrence Earl of Zetland.

May it please your Excellency,

I have the honour to offer myself as a Candidate for the Professorship of History and English Literature now vacant in the Queen's College, Belfast.

I beg to enclose a list of degrees and honours which I obtained in Trinity College, Dublin, both in English, Celtic, and Foreign Literature.

I am not ignorant of University teaching, having lectured during the year '90 '91 on English and Modern Literature in the State University of New Brunswick.

A presentation was made to me by the Students when leaving, and I enclose the testimonial of the President of the University.

Although I have chiefly worked at English and Modern Literature I am also fairly acquainted with the Greek and Latin Classics, with Anglo-Saxon, and with the Language and Literature of the Gaels of Scotland, and have some knowledge of Hebrew.

Praying that this Memorial may receive your Excellency's favourable consideration,

I have the honour to be your Excellency's most obedient servant.

DOUGLAS HYDE, LLD., M.R.I.A.

His application was backed by the following impressive references:—

Provost's House, Trinity College,
Dublin, December 28th, 1891.

No one is more competent to judge or had more opportunities of judging of Dr Douglas Hyde's ability and attainments than Dr Dowden our Professor of English Literature. I shall think it scarcely necessary to add anything to what he has written, yet I cannot refuse to give my testimony both as head of this College and as having had Dr Hyde in my class when I was Regius Professor of Divinity. I found him a good linguist, a man of minute and various reading, and a very diligent Student. His publications show that he has not been idle since the termination of his college course, and the satisfactory manner in which he temporarily discharged the duties of Professor of English Literature in New Brunswick gives me confidence in recommending him as one who may be advantageously entrusted with other duties of the same kind.

GEORGE SALMON, D.D
Provost of Trinity College, Dublin.

December 10th 1891.

Dr Douglas Hyde is one of our most brilliant and distinguished scholars of recent years. I leave it to himself to recite his long and varied series of University distinctions. English, French, German, Italian, Celtic, History, Law, Literature, Theology—in all the wide range included by what these names imply he has proved his ability and attainments. He is also of course acquainted with Greek and Latin and he has made some study of Anglo-Saxon and I believe of Hebrew. Already his scholarship has produced fruit in works which are widely and favourably known to Celtic students. To those who can deal with them, these speak for themselves. With his abundance of learning Dr Hyde has retained his brightness and freshness of intellect and his geniality of temper, he has not lost touch with actual life and reality. He has successfully acted as ' locum tenens ' for Professor Stockley of the University of New Brunswick, and there gained the high esteem both of the students and the President.

Dr Hyde informs me of a possible vacancy in the New

University of Chicago, a Professorship of Belles Lettres or a Professorship of English and Anglo-Saxon, for which he may be a candidate. I venture very earnestly to commend his claims to those who made the appointment. I believe that Dr Hyde would make an admirable Professor, and I am sure he would augment his present roll of distinctions by works of scholarship which would do credit to the great Institution with which he would be connected.

EDWARD DOWDEN, LL.D,

D.Lit. (Dat). Hon. L.L.D. (Edinburgh)
Professor of Eng. Lit., in the University of Dublin.

University Club, Dublin.
December 19th 1891.

Dear Dr Hyde,

Understanding that you are a candidate for a Professorship in English Literature, I have much pleasure in testifying to my belief that you are eminently well qualified for such a post. I have had opportunity of being acquainted with your literary faculty and attainments, and I should fully expect that from your intellectual capacity and cultured taste you would be specially able to impart efficiently the results to others. Your power of acquiring Languages must give you great advantage in dealing with the genius and individual character of the English.

Though we should miss greatly your assistance in the collection and illustration of the folk lore of this country, I sincerely wish you always every success in any other part of the globe if it should be your lot to be called thither.

Believe me to remain
Yours very truly,
M. H. CLOSE
Treasurer of the Royal Irish Academy.

It is a curious fact that there is no mention of any reaction from Belfast, or any sequel whatever to this application. Neither is there any further mention of the post in Chicago.

On his next visit to Dublin he met a man who was to become one of his closest friends, Fr Eugene O'Growney.

11 February 1892   Reading in the library. I met O'Growney for the first time. A young man with a large head, thick-lipped, pleasant without being handsome or well-groomed; kindly, slow-speaking; perhaps the only learned man in Ireland today who speaks Irish correctly. I had a long talk with him and I am to visit him in Maynooth.[12]

Just then, however, Hyde was on his way to London. He crossed that night, and next day he went to see David Nutt who had published Hyde's *Beside the Fire*. He found Nutt ' alert, with a very English accent, même prononcé ', but courteous. He does not record the subject of their discussion. Next day, by the merest chance, he found himself at a meeting of the Irish Literary Society :

13 February   . . . I met Crook [a friend and contemporary at Trinity College] in the Strand and he brought me to a meeting of the new Irish society they are establishing. Barry O'Brien, Rolleston and Yeats were there. They chose twelve Vice-Presidents, myself among them. . . .

The Irish Literary Society had developed out of a meeting at Yeats's house in Chiswick on 28 December 1891. Yeats, Rolleston and Dr Todhunter were among the founder members, as was W. P. Ryan, who gives an account of the meeting and of the development of the Society, and of the National Literary Society founded in Dublin some months later, in his book *The Irish Literary Revival,* published by the author in London, 1894.

17 February   I went to lunch at a restaurant with Yeats and a man named Garnett, a pleasant young man who is a reader for Fisher Unwin. He urged me to make translations of Irish stories and that he would publish them for me in four or six volumes.

This interesting entry bears out a statement in a letter from Yeats to John O'Leary :[13]

Did I tell you about the ' Irish Saga Series ' that Unwin is thinking of? Douglas Hyde who is now in London came with me to see Garnett the other day who thinks Unwin will take it up. It is to give standard translations by Hyde of the old Epic Tales and will consist of 8 or 9 volumes. Hyde is to send in a scheme for the first three or four in a couple of weeks.

Hyde took the idea seriously. On 30 March 1892 he records that he was 'making a list of the Irish stories for Garnett.' The scheme, however, never came to fruition. It probably got submerged in the storm of controversy that broke out some months later between Yeats and Sir Charles Gavan Duffy concerning the purpose and scope of 'The New Irish Library', under the auspices of The Irish Literary Society in London and the National Literary Society in Dublin, with Fisher Unwin as publisher. Later in this chapter I shall quote Hyde's account of the row.

On the evening of the lunch with Garnett Yeats brought Hyde home to Bedford Park, Chiswick, to meet his neighbour Dr Todhunter. Hyde records a few impressions:

A thin, distinguished looking man, of medium build, with finely-chiselled features. His wife is one of the Digbys; I know her sister. We had a long talk, and Dr Todhunter told me a Norse tale, and told it very well.

On the way home he called to the National Liberal Club where he met his friend Crooke:

I had a cigar and a glass of punch with him, in the company of the scoundrel Tim Healy, but without speaking to him.[14] Home at 12.30 or 1 a.m. Very cold.

A few days later he went to Cambridge, where he spent three days. The following week his friend Miss Butcher brought him to meet Burne Jones, the painter:

4 March 1892 . . . I had a long talk with him. An old, grey-haired man, kindly, child-like, with a faraway look in his eyes as if he did [not?] belong to this world. He has an extraordinary interest in Ireland and in Irish literature. He had my books; he told me he had almost every Irish book that was in print, and everything that Jubainville had written. He was remarkably well informed [on Irish literature].

On 10 March he returned to Dublin, and a few days later he fulfilled his promise to visit Fr O'Growney at Maynooth:

14 March 1892   I went to Maynooth on the 9.16 train. O'Grow-ney was at the station to meet me. He showed me around the college and afterwards we had an excellent lunch with champagne. Clancy, the professor of English and Ancient Classics, was there, and Maguire. There were about 500 students in the place. They have three lectures a day, and study for another 5½ hours. They are not allowed to speak to one another except for 2 or 3 hours in the day. They have no fires in their rooms; they are not allowed to smoke, or visit one another in their rooms, or speak at meals or in the quadrangles. They are required to attend O'Growney's [Irish] lectures and lectures in English literature for the first three years of their course. They all speak Latin very well. Shakespeare and Milton is read with them, and especially Macaulay. O'Growney says that at least 200 of them have some knowledge of Irish.
The annual income of the college is about £15,000, but they buy only £20 worth of books in the year. Three sheep are killed every day, and the students are well fed.

One more visit made around this time deserves mention:

24 March 1892   I did not go anywhere until evening when, about 8.30, I went to call on Standish O'Grady. His wife was there, and someone by the name of O'Clery, and the conversation was excellent. They [Standish and O'Clery] went about midnight, but I stayed with Mrs O'Grady and she was reading my hand and discussing it until Standish came back. I left eventually at about 2 a.m., with the curlews crying over my head all the way home.
She said that among the hundreds of hands she had read she had never seen a hand more interesting or more extra-ordinary than mine. She took an impression of it with ink on paper, and she earnestly urged me to have great courage and self-confidence for, she said, I had it in me to do great things.
I drank the most of a bottle of wine, and I was a little tipsy on the way home.

Mrs Standish O'Grady's predictions were amply fulfilled, early and late. Within six months Hyde was President of the National Literary Society, in another twelve months he was President of the Gaelic League, and finally, forty-five years later, he was President of his country, by then a sovereign, democratic state.

In his summing up of the year 1892 Hyde wrote:

> The most significant events of this year for me were that I was elected President of the National Literary Society and that I delivered a lecture to its members.

The National Literary Society, founded in Dublin in the summer of 1892 was a development of the Irish Literary Society established in London some months earlier. W. B. Yeats was the prime mover in the formation of both societies.

Hyde gives a fairly long account of the first meeting he attended. It also happened to be the meeting at which Sir Charles Gavan Duffy propounded his views on book publishing which were to cause a bitter split in the society from the start:

30 July Writing at the Academy and doing some shopping. At 8 o'clock this evening I went to the Mansion House[15] to a meeting of the Irish [*sic*] Literary Society. A young man named O'Kelly was the secretary, Sigerson in the chair. King, Rolleston, Quinn of the Land League, McGrath of *United Ireland* and above all Sir Charles Gavan Duffy were there. Sir Charles pressed business through in a thoroughly practical manner. He said many interesting things. Amongst them that he himself edited and saw through the press every vol. of the Irish National Library series of the 48 men.[16] He got £1,000 himself for the Eng. edition of his 'Young Ireland',[17] twice as much as all the Young Ireland writers got for all theirs put together. They only got £25 a vol. from Duffy the publisher. Sir Charles gave Ireland a 2/0 edition of his Young Ireland but never made a red cent out of it. The scheme which was debated was the starting of an Irish publishing company, capital £3,000 or so, to disseminate Irish books—to be written—amongst the Irish people through the means of publishers & news agencies. A lot of sub-committees were appointed.[18]

Almost exactly a month later he casually mentions his position in the new organization:

29 August ... To the Mansion House for a meeting of the new
   National Society of which I am president. Duffy (Charles
   Gavan) in the chair. Home by 11.20.[19]

The raising of literary standards in Ireland was Yeats's immediate aim, and here he came into a head-on collision with Gavan
Duffy.[20]

> I had definite plans; I wanted to create an Irish Theatre;
> I was finishing my *Countess Cathleen* in its first meagre
> version, and thought of a travelling company to visit our
> country branches; but before that there must be a popular
> imaginative literature. I arranged with Mr Fisher Unwin
> and his reader, Mr Edward Garnett—a personal friend of
> mine—that when our organization was complete Mr Fisher
> Unwin was to publish for it a series of books at a shilling
> each. I told only one man of this arrangement, for after I
> had made my plans I heard an alarming rumour. Old Sir
> Charles Gavan Duffy was coming from Australia to start an
> Irish publishing-house, and publish a series of books, and
> I did not expect to agree with him, but knew I must not seek
> a quarrel.

But a quarrel was inevitable. Sir Charles in 1892 was ' Oisín i
ndiaidh na Féinne '[21] living in the past, too old to change. In his
view, what was good for the people in the forties, in the days of
his prime, was good for them still. Yeats, on the other hand,
was passionately committed to the establishment of a new literature in Ireland, and had already laid the foundations for it by
his own writings and by his influence on the young writers of
the day. ' In the persons of Duffy and Yeats the two schools, the
two eras, met and clashed in 1892.'[22]
   Hyde presided at some stormy sessions:

27 January 1893 ... To a meeting of the committee of the
   National Literary Society. There was a terrible row between
   Taylor and Yeats, between O'Leary and Sigerson. We broke
   up at about 11. I never saw anything like it, but I escaped
   without a blow, thank God.[23] Afterwards I retired to Corless
   with Yeats and Coffey and we had a few badly-needed drinks.

2 February ... A meeting of the committee. Uproar again,

154

though not as bad as the last night, about the publishing of books by Fisher Unwin. I was in the chair and I had a hopeless task of trying to keep order: Taylor against Yeats and Sigerson against O'Leary.[24] To James Coffey's place where I had a drink and a chat. Home at 1.30.

Peace was restored at a special meeting held some three weeks later:

27 February 1893 . . . To a special meeting of the committee of the society this evening. They agreed on the following motion without dissension:

> That the Council of the Irish National Literary Society approves of the arrangement by which Sir C. H. [*sic*] Duffy is editor & an Rolstunach & D. de h-Ide[25] sub-editors of a series of Irish books. That so long as this arrangement is maintained the Council will loyally and cordially promote the Circulation of the series. That the Council hereby authorize the President to make this resolution known to all whom it may concern. That Dr D. de h-Ide be instructed to act on the Society's behalf as such sub-editor & that he is to communicate with the Council regarding the books which are to be edited.

The first volume in the *New Irish Library* was *The Patriot Parliament of 1689,* by Thomas Davis, edited with an introduction by Sir Charles Gavan Duffy. It was a reprint of a series of articles which had appeared in the *Dublin Monthly Magazine* in 1843. In other words, it was exactly the type of publication which Yeats feared might appear if Sir Charles had his way: a harking back to Young Ireland of fifty years before. The book sold well; it was soon out of print, but Yeats was not impressed. In a letter to the editor of *United Ireland* (a letter which seems to have escaped the notice of Alan Wade, and which I therefore think worth quoting here in full) he writes:

September 1, 1894.

Dear Sir,

It is no manner of use our deceiving ourselves about the sale of the 'Patriot Parliament'. It is perfectly well known

155

that the first volume of any much talked of series is certain of a large sale, quite independent of its merits, and the ten or fifteen thousand sold is not exceptional. The question is whether it did or did not help the other volumes, and I have reason to know that numbers of the peasantry refused to buy 'The Bog of Stars'[26] because of the dulness of its predecessor. Believing, as I do, that literature is almost the most profound influence that ever comes into a nation, I recognise with deep regret, and not a little anger, that the 'New Irish Library' is so far the most serious difficulty in the way of our movement, and that it drives from us those very educated classes we desire to enlist, and supplies our opponents with what looks like evidence of our lack of any fine education, of any admirable procession and balance of mind, of the very qualities which make literature possible. Perhaps honest criticism, with as little of the 'great day for Ireland' ritual as may be, can yet save the series from ebbing out in a tide of irrelevant dulness, and keep the best opportunity there has been these many decades from being squandered by pamphleteer and amateur. We require books by competent men of letters upon subjects of living national interest, romances by writers of acknowledged power, anthologies selected from men like de Vere, and Allingham, and Ferguson, and impartial picturesque lives of Emmet, Wolfe Tone, Mitchell and perhaps O'Connell, and if they are not to be obtained, let us bow our heads in silence and talk no more of a literary renaissance, for we can, at least, cease to be imposters.

If you re-read my remarks in the *Bookman* upon 'The Patriot Parliament' you will find that instead of criticising its historical merits I assumed them and called it a good book for the proceedings of a learned society. I made no other criticism than that it was 'dull', whereas, you prefer the words 'not brilliant' or 'particularly readable'. I accept your amendations with pleasure, and we are one again.

Yours sincerely,

W. B. Yeats.

Next to providing 'a popular imaginative literature' Yeats intended his new societies to provide a platform for public lectures:

The two societies were necessary because their lectures must take the place of an educated popular Press, which we had not, and have not now, and create a standard of criticism.[27]

The inaugural lecture of the Dublin Society was delivered by Dr Sigerson, who spoke on 'Irish Literature: Its origin, environment, and influence'. Then, on 25 November 1892 Douglas Hyde delivered his presidential address:

> 25 November   Working all day at the Academy preparing my lecture. I DELIVERED MY LECTURE [*sic*] at the Leinster Hall in Molesworth Street. Over 100 people present; a shilling a ticket. 'On the necessity for de-Anglicising the Irish People'. Miss Purser and the Gwynnes, Henry French, Mrs Rowley etc and Miss L'Estrange there listening to me. It lasted about an hour and twenty minutes. It was good, I believe. I was highly praised. To the Hibernian [Hotel] with Sheehan for punch. Afterwards to Sigerson; I stayed until 1.30 and drank two more glasses. Home by 2.[28]

In this great speech Hyde was clearly conscious of addressing not merely the hundred or so who sat in front of him but the Irish people as a whole. He took great care over the preparation of it,[29] and the result was a well-argued challenge to his fellow-countrymen to make up their minds to be Irish or English, but to end the anomaly of apeing England and hating her at the same time:

> It has always been very curious to me how Irish sentiment sticks in this half-way house—how it continues to apparently hate the English, and at the same time continues to imitate them; how it continues to clamour for recognition as a distinct nationality, and at the same time throws away with both hands what would make it so.
> If Irishmen only went a little farther they would become good Englishmen in sentiment also. But—illogical as it appears—there seems not the slightest sign or probability of their taking that step. . . . It is just because there appears no earthly chance of their becoming good members of the Empire that I urge that they should not remain in the anomalous position they are in, but since they absolutely

refuse to become the one thing, that they should become the other; cultivate what they have rejected, and build up an Irish nation on Irish lines.

The reason why Irishmen cannot settle down contentedly and form part of the British Empire is that

do what they may the race of to-day cannot wholly divest itself from the mantle of its own past. . . . The dim consciousness of this is one of those things which are at the back of Irish national sentiment, and our business, whether we be Unionists or Nationalists, should be to make this dim consciousness an active and potent feeling, and thus increase our sense of self-respect and of honour.

Hyde points to the irony of the fact that just when Home Rule seemed in sight, the Irish people were abandoning ' the language, traditions, music, genius, and ideas ' that had survived centuries of persecution and oppression:

What the battleaxe of the Dane, the sword of the Norman, the wile of the Saxon were unable to perform, we have accomplished ourselves. We have at last broken the continuity of Irish life, and just at the moment when the Celtic race is presumably about to largely recover possession of its own country, it finds itself deprived and stript of its Celtic characteristics, cut off from the past, yet scarcely in touch with the present.

Having thus made his diagnosis of Ireland's ills, he goes on to propose a definite remedy:

In order to de-Anglicise ourselves we must at once arrest the decay of the language. We must bring pressure upon our politicians not to snuff it out by their tacit discouragement merely because they do not happen themselves to understand it. We must arouse some spark of patriotic inspiration among the peasantry who still use the language, and put an end to the shameful state of feeling—a thousand-tongued reproach to our leaders and statesmen—which makes young men and women blush and hang their heads when overheard speaking their own language.

He goes on to deplore the decay of traditional Irish surnames and Christian names, place-names,[30] music and games. Then, in the last couple of minutes of his speech, as if suddenly realizing the platform from which he spoke, he turns to ' perhaps the principal point of all ' which, he says, he has taken for granted:

> That is the necessity for encouraging the use of Anglo-Irish literature instead of English books, especially instead of English periodicals. We must set our face sternly against penny dreadfuls, shilling shockers, and still more, the garbage of vulgar English weeklies like *Bow Bells* and the *Police Intelligence*. Every house should have a copy of Moore and Davis.

He ends with an appeal for united effort, calling, in effect, for a cultural, non-political ' Sinn Féin ' (Ourselves, i.e. national self-reliance) revolution:

> In conclusion, I would earnestly appeal to every one, whether Unionist or Nationalist, who wishes to see the Irish nation produce its best—and surely whatever our politics are we all wish that—to set his face against this constant running to England for our books, literature, music, games, fashions, and ideas. I appeal to every one whatever his politics—for this is no political matter—to do his best to help the Irish race to develop in future upon Irish lines, even at the risk of encouraging national aspirations, because upon Irish lines alone can the Irish race once more become what it was of yore—one of the most original, artistic, literary, and charming peoples of Europe.

Hyde was disappointed with the immediate reaction to his appeal,[31] but there can be no doubt about its long-term results. It was published in a booklet with other speeches[32] and, as he says himself, it set some people thinking. Among these was a young civil servant in the Accountant General's office at the Four Courts, Eoin Mac Neill from County Antrim, who conceived a plan to put into effect the ideas that Hyde had propounded. But that was several months later.

In the meantime Hyde was busy promoting the interests of the National Literary Society. Early in the new year he went to Cork for an important meeting:

23 January 1893   I went to Cork with Yeats on the 9.15 coach
[train?]. Count Plunkett and O'Mahoney were there before
us. We went to the Victoria Hotel where we had dinner
and I had two good glasses of punch. Then we went to the
meeting organised to promote the National Literary Society.
Denny Lane was in the chair and made the first speech,
reading from a script.[33] I then spoke, and I was in top form.
Yeats spoke after me, and Count Plunkett after him. There
were about 150 people present, including representatives of
every literary society in Cork. Sheehan's brother was there.
We went back to Lane's house and had drinks. He has two
attractive young daughters. Hartog and others were there.
Home in good form about 12.30.

24 January   Hartog showed us the Royal College; then we went
to Sheehan's house. Talk and drinks. To a big dinner of
the Philharmonic Society as guests of Denny Lane. Much
drinking and smoking. Left at 12 with young Sheehan and
went to Dr Ryan's house where there were more drinks.
Home by 1.10.

Next day he returned to Dublin where, a fortnight later, he
met the most shy and self-effacing figure of the literary revival:

8 February   ... I went with Miss Purser to a pleasant little party
with the great 'incognita', Miss Barlow.[34] I had a long talk
with her and with Mistress O'Mahoney, and walked home
with the latter. I had dinner with the Coffeys, and with
Coffey's help I wrote part of my lecture for tomorrow night.
Home by 11.

The lecture, to the Literary Society, was on Irish books published
in the previous year. A week later, on 16 February, he presided
at an excellent lecture by Standish O'Grady. On the last day
of the month he went to London.

1 March 1893   Spent the morning in the hotel writing, not feeling too well. This evening I went to a meeting of the London
[sic] Literary Society. Graves in the chair. We had a lecture
by Stopford Brooke on the English language as a medium
for the Irish people. It was well done. I was the first speaker
after the lecture; I didn't do too well or too badly. Mrs
Bryant spoke after me, and then W. Wilde and Crooke.

Afterwards we went to the National Liberal Club with Crooke and spent a good while there eating and drinking. I went home with Rolleston about 1 a.m.[35]

3 March Lunch with Fisher Unwin and Garnett, and a good lunch it was. Home, and this evening to dinner at Stopford Brooke's house with Rolleston. Interesting and amusing conversation. I liked the Brookes very much.[36]

4 March Went to lunch with Crooke at the National Liberal Club and had a great talk with him until 5 o'clock. Then to the rooms of the Society for a meeting of the Council at which I was in the chair. Dinner with Rolleston at a German eating-house. Home about 11.

5 March Walking on Wimbeldon Common. I didn't go to church. A beautiful day. In to London for a talk on Morocco by Rolleston's brother, and from there to dinner with the Todhunters at Bedford Park. Home by 12.30. Mrs Emmery? [*sic*] there.

6 March A visit to the British Museum. From there to Hewetson who is now sleek and prosperous since he married a wealthy American. Then I went to Bader[37] who gave me new stuff to put on my eyes. Went back and dressed for dinner with Fisher Unwin. Miss Amy Manders was there; the man who wrote ' How to be happy though married '; a minister and a ' Jahu ' [?] from Bermuda; two Americans named Perrin or something like that; Mrs Fisher Unwin, who is a daughter of the great Cobden, M.P., and others. An elegant meal; good conversation. Home by midnight.

On 10 March he made another visit to Bader who told him that his eye-trouble was ' ophthalmia granulosa ' and changed the prescription for his glasses. That evening:

> I went with Rolleston to a meeting of the Rhymers Club. There were about ten present, and almost every one of them had a poem. I took part, and drank a good deal. Afterwards I had dinner at the ' Cheshire Cheese '.

Next day he looked up his friend Thomas Flannery and had a Gaelic session:

11 March   I went to Flannery and had a long journey to get to him. He sent for McSweeney from county Cork and we spent the greater part of the day talking Irish, drinking and smoking, and McSweeney sang a few songs for us. There was another man there, half-English, to whom I did not take very well. Home about 10.

As always on these visits to London, he went to see a play:

15 March   . . . I went to the Lyceum Theatre to see Irving and Miss Terry in Tennyson's 'Becket'. The mise en scene was good, but the play itself was a poor piece. I got the last train home.

He also managed to drown the shamrock:

17 March   St Patrick's Day. I went with Rolleston to the Literary Society rooms where I met Miss Matthews (the judge's daughter), Miss Eccles, Miss Hickey, etc. I then went to Miss Rowley's hotel and had a talk with her. There was a Miss Palmer, an Englishwoman, with her and they invited me to stay for dinner. Coneybeare the M.P. also came to dinner, and we had a lively conversation. Miss Palmer's talk didn't make much sense; she praised the Irish people a tort et a travers. I didn't care much for Conneybeare [sic]. We drowned the shamrock in champagne. Home around 11.30.

18 March   I went to see Miss Butcher but she wasn't at home. Then I went to call on Lady Wilde and talked with her and her company. I had to introduce myself to her because Miss Rowley wasn't there as she had promised to be. This evening I went to St James's Theatre to see 'Liberty Hall'; it was good. Home around midnight; punch.

21 March   Visited Miss Butcher. Augusta and Mrs Prothero were there also. Long talk with them. Then to the Grafton Galleries to see the Impressionists' paintings. Home and to a party at the Lawrences at Wimbledon. The host is a son of Sir Henry Lawrence who fell at Lucknow.

22 March   To Herdman but he wasn't at home. To Francis Fahy; a long talk with him.[38] Then to Parliament. John Redmond brought me in and I talked with him for a long

time. From there I went to see Burne Jones's pictures. Called to see Miss Palmer and Miss Rowley but I did not find them at home. Rolleston and I went to a meeting of the National League in Chancery Lane.[39] Only a dozen people there; Lynch was lecturing. Rolleston and I spoke. Talked Irish to Mark Ryan and his brother.

Next evening he crossed to Dublin, and a fortnight later he was back home in Frenchpark, preparing his *Love Songs of Connacht* for the press and in his spare time tidying up the place in preparation for an important visitor, Lucy Cometina Kurtz.

He had first met Miss Kurtz five months previously:

20 October 1892 I went to Dublin. The old man was not too well when I was leaving home. I went to Morrisons' Hotel and from there to Stillorgan where the Oldfields had a big party. I walked to the station with F.C. and with Fraulein Kurtz, a girl whom Annette picked up in Kerry.[40] Home about 10.30.

F.C. is Frances Crofton, with whom Hyde had maintained a very special friendship over the years since they first met in May 1882. Indeed, by 1886 he was seriously considering marrying her:

23 June 1886 . . . We began to talk of marriage etc. She told me that an officer had once proposed to her, but that she had turned him down, and that she never wished to marry but would die an old maid.

Miss Crofton was musical and artistic. She brought Hyde around the galleries in Dublin, and tried in vain to teach him to sing. Over the years they had been honest and frank with one another, and their relationship had developed into a relaxed friendship from which the idea of marriage was excluded by mutual agreement.

Now he met Fraulein Kurtz, daughter of a research chemist from Wurtemberg who had graduated at Trinity College Dublin, and was immediately attracted to her. In May 1893 she came to stay at Frenchpark for a fortnight; she was back again at the end of June. Perhaps because of his emotional involvement, Hyde's diary is unusually erratic at this period. There is only one entry for June:

25 [June 1893] ANNETTE AND MISS KURTZ CAME
HOME and I went to the station to meet them. Annette
came directly from England and Lucy from Lucan, where
she had stayed at the Spa Hotel since she left this house.
They are both well.

Next he gives a review of the month of July:

I do not remember rightly what we did for the following
month. However, things took their course, between hope
and despair, certainty and uncertainty, doubt and assurance,
anxiety and confidence, but each day the net was closing
about my neck until we decided firmly and finally that we
were going to get married, and we were publicly engaged.
One day we went with the Parkers to Lough Key and had
lunch on Trinity Island; another day the Peeles came on a
visit; another day Mrs Lloyd came and Annette told her that
we were engaged. Another day we went to the Big Castle,
and finally we settled with John French to take Ratra from
the beginning of the new year at a rent of £50 a year. That
was a great move.[41]
Around the 21 July Lucy and I went by train to Athenry
to the Roches' house near Monivea and we spent eight
happy days there, in a large pleasant house, receiving every
kindness from them. I wrote a lot of Irish from the lips of
an old man, stories and songs, and I spoke a lot of Irish
there. We also met a number of the county people: Dalys,
Frenchs, Blakes, etc.
On Saturday 29 July we left Roches' and came to Dublin;
she to Tarpey's Hotel and I to the Hibernian.

30 July   Sunday. I went to church on my own and after lunch
we went out to Stillorgan. Dr Cuppy was there. A long talk
with them, and home. Afterwards I spent the evening with
Dr Sigerson, and O'Neill Russell who had returned to Ireland
the previous day.

31 July   Lucy and I went from shop to shop. We were photo-
graphed together by Werner. We went out to the Cliffes'
house in Dun Laoghaire. I came back and we established
'THE GAELIC LEAGUE' to keep the language alive
among the people. Mac Neill, O'Neill Russell, Hogan,
O'Kelly, Fr Hayden, Quinn and several others present, about

10 to 12. I was in the chair. I spoke at length in Irish and in English, and everything went well. Dinner with Lucy. I slept at the Hibernian.

Next morning Hyde was out shopping for furniture with his fiancée; that evening she left to visit relatives in England. Two days later he used his influence as president of the National Literary Society to get the use of their room for the new Gaelic League for one night per week.

Next day,

4 August 1893   I sent five books to people,[42] wrote several letters and had lunch with Sheehan. I went to the Gaelic League and they elected me president. I spoke in Irish and in English. I gave drinks to Sigerson and Russell. I spent the evening in the dingy ill-furnished [?][43] rooms of McCall in Patrick Street, drawing up an account of the activities of our Literary Society over the past year.

A few days later Hyde returned to Frenchpark, in good time for the opening of the shooting season. On 3 October he was back in Dublin, and on 9 October he crossed to Liverpool to rejoin Lucy. She brought him to the home of the Danish Consul, at Blundell Sands, who was evidently a friend of her family. There he stayed on the eve of his wedding

10 October 1893   MY WEDDING DAY. After breakfast with the Caroes a carriage arrived to take me to the church with Miss Green, a sister-in-law of old Caroe and a very nice woman. We went together, and the carriage went back for Lucy. The priest's name was Winslow. He married us straight out of the book, without omitting any part of the service, although I asked him to. I got my own back on him when I signed my name in Irish in the register.

The honeymoon—over a month—was spent in Paris, on the Riviera[44] and in London; they arrived back in Ireland on 17 November. On 22 November Hyde went to a Gaelic League meeting and recited 'Monachar and Manachar'.[45] Next day he went with Yeats to a Council meeting of the Literary Society of which he was still president.[46] He was to have read a paper to the Gaelic League on 29 November but he had to cancel it because of a cold.

On 1 December he bought a brougham for £33, and on 3 December he and his bride arrived home in Frenchpark to a rousing welcome:

> 3 December 1893 WE CAME HOME after being away exactly two months. When we came out from Ballagh to Taobh-na-craoibhe there were a hundred or a couple of hundred people at the cross roads to welcome us. There was music, and a big arch across the road covered with ivy and a green banner with 'Fáilte' [welcome] written on it. When we came to Ratra there was another big arch across the road, and as many people. They took the horse from under the carriage and drew us home from the Ratra road until they arrived into the yard, and such shouting and hullabaloo you never heard. I sent three half-barrels of porter out to them: one to the cross-roads, one to Rathkerry and the third to Moran's house where there was another big green arch. They drank their fill and were well satisfied.
> The old man is poorly, keeping to the bed most of the time, with a swollen hand and a touch of eczema.

His summing up of the year 1893 is significant. He begins:

> The greatest thing I did in the past year—indeed, the greatest thing I ever did in my life—was that I got married.

He then goes on to give the customary review of the year's events. The extraordinary thing about this is that he notes his arrival in Dublin with Lucy at the end of July, her leaving for England and his return home, but makes no reference at all to the founding of the Gaelic League. At the very end of the review he adds, almost as a postscript:

> 30 June [sic] We established the Gaelic League and I was made president of it. MacNeill and Lloyd, Gordon and O'Neill Russell were the people who did most of the work. I didn't do much.

It is clear then that Hyde had no part at all in the planning of the new movement. Neither did he recognize its coming into existence as an event of very great significance. On the other hand, the fact that he was invited to take the chair at that first meeting, and that three days later he was elected president of the League, was an acknowledgement of his unique part in preparing the ground in which such a movement could take root and flourish.

Equally certain is it that the development of the Gaelic League over the next two decades during which it became the most dynamic force in Irish life was due in a very large measure to the personal qualities of its president, who gave himself heart and soul to its leadership.

His life up to this point had been a curious mixture of dilettantism in his formal studies and immense concentration and drive in the things that engaged his real interest: his general reading, his writing and, above all, his efforts to preserve the remnants of Gaelic culture. At last, in the Gaelic League he found an outlet for the enormous energy of which he was capable, and for twenty-two years that energy was sustained in a campaign that swept the country like a whirlwind, whipping up enthusiasm where there had been apathy and idealism where, after the Parnell split, there had been disenchantment and bitter division.

The extraordinary impact of the Gaelic League on every aspect of Irish life is attested to by the following contemporary account:

> It began and encouraged a general national examination of conscience; every institution in the land was shown how it had sinned against itself and the soul and vitality of the nation by its neglect of the national language. Political leaders, on the whole, heard the plainest truths, mainly on the subject of the distinction between politics and nationality and on the flowery phrase-making they had substituted for serious thinking.[47]

This is how a Frenchman described the League in 1907:

> The Gaelic League is not a society of scholars, and leaves to others all that concerns literature and philology, pure and simple. It is occupied with propaganda, the application of its doctrine of a national renaissance on the basis of the

national language. It intends to confer anew upon the country a psychological education, and, by means of the national language, by the revival of national art and literature, and the reconstitution of a national social system, to regenerate its soul from within and teach Ireland how she may again be a nation. . . .

This French historian puts his finger on the key point of the League's organization:

From the start the League has had the good sense officially to declare that it was both necessary and desirable that it should stand apart from all political and religious struggles; such has been its line of conduct, and now within it are found representatives of every party, from the strongest Orangemen to the fiercest Separatists.[48]

For a brief period at the beginning of the century Irishmen of every shade of opinion found themselves able to put aside centuries-old differences in their enthusiasm for an ideal that transcended religion and politics, the ideal of a Gaelic Ireland.[49] One of the staunchest supporters of the League was Dr Kane, a leading Belfast Orangeman who declared that though he was a Unionist and a Protestant he did not forget that he was an O'Cahán (Gaelic form of Kane).[50]

But the very enthusiasm and force of nationalist feeling which the League generated flowed inevitably towards political as well as cultural independence. Hyde strove manfully to steer the League clear of direct association with either the parliamentarians or the proponents of physical force, but as early as 1907 his friend James Hannay (better known as 'George Birmingham', the novelist) warned him of the inevitability of a collision:

I take the Sinn Fein position to be the natural & inevitable development of the League principles. They couldn't lead to anything else. . . . I do not myself believe that you will be able to stride the fence for very much longer. You have, in my humble opinion, the chance now of becoming a great Irish leader, with the alternative of relapsing into the position of a John Dillon. It will be intensely interesting to see which you choose. Either way I think the movement you started will go on, whether you lead it or take the part of poor Frankenstein who created a monster he could not control.[51]

Hyde was not ' striding the fence '. On the contrary, his feet were firmly planted on the side of neutrality, and he declared his position in decisive and unmistakeable terms. In 1913 things moved rapidly to a climax in Irish politics. The Liberal government at Westminster, maintained in office only by support of the Irish members, committed themselves to granting Home Rule to Ireland, and the bill passed through the Commons in January 1913. The move was warmly welcomed by the majority of the Irish people, but the Protestant majority in the four north-eastern counties, alarmed by the prospect of ' Rome Rule ', created a Gilbertian situation by proclaiming that they would defy the British government, by arms if necessary, in their determination to remain British. Under Sir Edward Carson, and with the open support of prominent British Conservatives, they formed, drilled and armed an Ulster Volunteer Force to resist Home Rule.

Ironically, it was Eoin MacNeill, from whose fertile brain the concept of the Gaelic League had sprung, who provided the south's answer to this northern militarism. Even more ironically, it was in the pages of *An Claidheamh Soluis,* the official organ of the Gaelic League, on 1 November 1913, that MacNeill wrote an article under the heading ' The North Began ', in which he proposed the founding of a National Volunteer Force. It was he also who chaired a meeting in the Rotunda Rink in Dublin at which three thousand young Irishmen, many of them Gaelic Leaguers, signed on as Volunteers pledged to take up arms ' to secure and maintain the rights and liberties of the Irish people.'

MacNeill's conduct seriously undermined the position of Douglas Hyde. Here was his righthand man, the man who had travelled the length and breadth of Ireland over the previous twenty years as secretary of the Gaelic League, now advocating armed rebellion.

Even more embarrassing to Hyde's position as president were the inflammatory speeches and writings of Patrick Pearse, the most gifted and influential of the younger Gaelic Leaguers. Speaking at the grave of Wolfe Tone in June 1913 he declared that in Tone's stated aim 'to break the connection with England' he, Pearse, found implicit 'all the teaching of the Gaelic League and the later prophets.' At the Emmet Commemoration in Brooklyn, New York, in March 1914, he made even more explicit the link between the League and armed revolution:

> A new junction has been made with the past; into the movement that has never wholly died since '67 have come the young men of the Gaelic League. Having renewed communion with its origins, Irish Nationalism is today a more virile thing than ever before in our time. Of that be sure.

> I have said again and again that when the Gaelic League was founded in 1893 the Irish Revolution began.

Again in January 1914, writing on the prospects of success for the young men of Ireland, 'learning again the noble trade of arms':

> In the third place, the young men of Ireland have been to school to the Gaelic League. Herein it seems to me lies the fact which chiefly distinguishes this generation from the other revolutionary generations of the last century and a half. . . . We have known the Gaelic League, and
> 'Lo, a clearness of vision has followed, lo, a purification of sight'.

Hyde never wavered in his conviction that the League, as such, must preserve its total independence of all political movements. In June 1913 he delivered an extraordinary address to the Coisde Gnótha, the executive of the Gaelic League, in which he defended his policy of the previous twenty years and attacked those who were seeking to change that policy. He ended with a solemn warning:

> Árduighim mo ghuth go láidir anocht anaghaidh poilitidheachta i gConnradh na Gaedhilge, agus anaghaidh na ndroch-rudaí leanas go ró mhinic do'n phoilitidheacht so, mar is léir daoibh féin. . . . Bheirim rabhadh daoibh (rabhadh óm chroídhe amach) anocht—má leantar do phoilitidheacht taobh istigh de'n Chonnradh . . . go

dtiomáinfear amach as an gConnradh na daoine is fearr, duine ar dhuine . . . agus béidh cead ag an bhfuaighleach a rádh ann sin (an rud atá uatha b'éidir) gurab iad-san amháin na fíor-patriots, agus nach bhfuil ins an gcuid eile dínn acht daoine gan mhaith agus lucht beag-is-fiú.

I raise my voice strongly tonight against politics in the Gaelic League, and against the evils which all too often result from such politics, as you yourselves know. . . . I give you a warning tonight, a warning straight from my heart—if politics continue within the League that, one by one, the best people will be driven out of it . . . and those who are left will then be able to say (as perhaps they want to say) that they are the true patriots, and that the rest of us are only useless good-for-nothings.

In 1914 the Great War broke out, and John Redmond, the leader of the Irish Party at Westminster, urged the Volunteers to enlist ' in defence of right, of freedom and religion in this war.' His speech split the Volunteer movement in two, and Hyde was quick to seize on this example of how politics brought only discord and division. In a speech in English at Cork in December 1914 he began by declaring his belief that the rise of the Volunteers could not but turn in the long run to the benefit of the language movement ' since nationality divorced from language is an absurd and impossible doctrine.' He then went on to make a reasonable distinction between the official policy of the League and the rights of individual members:

But, mark my words, we, who consider the revival of the national language as of paramount importance to the Irish soul, can only keep the good will of the public by eschewing the politics of the moment, namely, these things which split up that public into sections as a log is split with an axe. Of course the Gaelic League has always kept politics out of its councils, but each individual Gaelic Leaguer has a perfect right outside of the Gaelic League to take part in any politics he wishes.

At the same time, however, people who held high places in the League (as, of course, MacNeill and Pearse did, though he did not mention them) should be doubly circumspect in their words and actions:

> When any man holds a prominent position, even though a voluntary and unpaid position, in the League, I would urge him, except in very special instances, for the good of what we all have at heart, to allow other people (and indeed there is no lack of them!) as far as possible to do the fighting and the talking in the political parties.

He went on to make a categorical statement of his own position:

> So strongly do I feel in this matter that when I was asked the other day whether in the event of a special Ardfheis being called to consider if the Gaelic League might not now become a political body, whether, I say, in the event of it so deciding, I myself would wish to continue as President of it under those circumstances, I most unhesitatingly said No.

A few months later precisely what Hyde had envisaged did in fact take place. At an Árd-Fheis in Dundalk in 1915 the constitution of the Gaelic League was amended to declare that its aim in future would be the realization of 'a free, Gaelic-speaking Ireland.' When the result of the vote was announced Hyde immediately vacated the chair and left the meeting, and the Gaelic League, forever.

Hyde's resolute stand on this fateful issue, though much criticized at the time and afterwards, was finally vindicated by no less an authority than Eoin MacNeill himself. Almost twenty years later he recalls his own reaction to Carson's militarism:

> I felt that a crisis had arrived in Irish affairs that was likely to determine in the event, the whole future interest of Ireland, and with all the importance I attached to the Gaelic League movement and its underlying principles, I felt that it was hardly possible for any Irishman to stand aside in the coming political struggle. While I still hold this view, I accuse myself of one serious mistake. Though Irishmen as Irishmen might be obliged to do their part in the political struggle, that did not imply that every organisation or asso-

ciation to which they belong should also be brought into
political activity. . . .

I now think that the Gaelic League should have adhered to
its own programme and should have kept entirely clear of
politics, and that its failure to do so, for which I am in part
responsible, has been bad for the objects of the League and
has had other bad results in the time that followed.

'How the Volunteers Began', in *The Irish
Volunteers 1913-1915*, p. 71.

This is almost exactly what Hyde said in 1914.

Until a definitive biography of Douglas Hyde is available there
will be a hiatus in modern Irish historical writing. His influence
on the past eighty years of Irish history has been immense and
profound, and although the actual course of events was not what
he would have chosen, his ideology was the mainspring which
set these events in motion. It was he who created the ground-
swell on which the Volunteer movement was launched; his
students and disciples were the officers and men of the insurrection. With the zeal of a convert he opened the eyes of Irish
men and women to the source of their identity as a nation.
Because he was neither soldier nor politician, Douglas Hyde finds
no ready niche in Ireland's hall of fame; yet few of the soldiers or
politicians influenced the course of modern Irish history as
fundamentally as he did.

Whatever is rooted, traditional, distinctively Gaelic in Irish life
today owes its survival in whole or in part to him. The saying
he adopted for his friend Euseby Cleaver is eminently true of
himself: 'nihil Hibernicum a me alienum puto'. His character
and personality are reflected in one sentence of Lady Gregory's
which might be written on his tombstone:

He has done his work by methods of peace, by keeping
quarrels out of his life, with all but entire success.

N

Appendix I

Hyde's booklist as given at the end of volume three of his diaries (see chapter II). Most of the Irish books are listed in *Bibliography of Irish Philology and of Printed Irish Literature* compiled by Richard Irvine Best (Dublin, 1913). Many of them appear also in *Clár Litridheacht na Nua-Ghaedhilge (1850–1936)*, a bibliography of Irish Gaelic books compiled by Risteárd de Hae and Brighid Ní Dhonnchadha (Dublin, 1938). There are several books in Scottish Gaelic in the first list; these are identified in *Typographia Scoto-Gadelica or Books Printed in the Gaelic of Scotland from the year 1567 to the year 1914* by the Reverend Donald Maclean (Edinburgh, 1915).

References are given in brackets after Hyde's titles: B. followed by the number of the page in Best's work; de Hae and the number of the paragraph in *Clár Litridheacht na Nua-Ghaedhilge*; Maclean and the number of the page in Scottish bibliography.

Particularly in the case of Anglo-Irish books in Hyde's second list there are several titles not found in the bibliographies. There are one or two items I failed to identify.

At the top of the first list Hyde notes: ' Taid na leabhair seo uile san reim & ordughad ann a bhfuair me iad ' (All these books are listed in the order in which I acquired them). Otherwise there are no headings. In the first list he inadvertently omits the number 49, and numbers 47 and 97 are in capitals.

First List

1 An Tiomnadh Nuadh in English Characters [The New Testament] two copies.
   also one in Irish characters.   (B.243)
2 Irish Primer. Irish Society.
3 Foleys foclóir [dictionary].   (B.12)
4 Masons Irish Grammar.   (B.46)
5 Neilsons Grammar.   (B.45)
6 Moores Melodies translated by McHale.   (de Hae 871)
7 An Teagasg Criosdaighe [The Cathechism]
   McHale.   (B.247)

8 Stáir eaglaise na hEirionn [History of the
   Church of Ireland] King.   (de Hae 587)
9 An Biobla Naomhtha [The Holy Bible]
   a small & a large copy.   (B.243)
10 De Vere Coney's foclóir [dictionary].   (B.11)
11 Cara an pheacuidhe.
12 Abhráin spioradálta.
13 Munster poets. 2d series. Eirionnach.   (B.196)
14 Jacobite Relics. 2 copies.   (B.196)
15 Céud leabar Gaedheilge. Soc' for Preservation &c.   (B.47)
16 Wrights Grammar.   (B.47)
17 O'Donovan's Grammar.   (B.46)
18 Tadgh Gaolach O Suilliobáin's Poems.   (B.219)
19 Homers Iliad translated into Irish by McHale.
20 Miss Brookes Relics of Irish Poetry.   (B.187 and 195)
21 An dara leabhar Gaedheilge. Soc' for Preservation &c.   (B.47)
22 The Book of Fenagh. edited by O Kelly   (B.81 and 236)
23 Eachtra Diarmaid & Ghrainne &c. Ossianic
   Society.   (B.103)
24 Laoithe Fiannuigheachta. Ossianic Society. (de Hae 898)
25 Irish Poems collected & edited by O Daly.   (de Hae 897)
26 Echtra [sic] bodaigh an chóta lachtna.
   A Fenian tale & Grammar &c. O'Daly.   (B.46)
27 Dr. Gallagher's sermons & a translation. Bourke. (B.249)
28 Imteacht na trom-dáimhe [proceedings of
   the Bardic Institution] &c. Ossianic Society. (B.114)
29 Ancient Prophecies of Irish bards, with
   translation. O Kearney.   (B.171)
30 Donleavy's Teagasg Criosdaighe [Catechism
   Irish & English].   (B.246)
31 Hardiman's Irish Minstrelsy 2 vol.   (B.196)
32 Foras Feasa air Éirinn [Keating's History
   of Ireland] & translation by Haliday.   (B.255)
33 Leabhar na g-Ceart [The Book of Rights].
   Edited by O Donavan [sic] Celtic Soc.   (B.170)
34 Oidche clainne Usneach [sic] [The Fate

175

	of the Sons of Uisneach] & Gaelic Soc's translations 1808	(B.92)
35	O Cathán s testiment [*sic*] in the Munster Irish	(B.243)
36	Miscellany of Celtic Soc' Gilla Brighde Mac Coinmhidhe &c.	(B.78)
37	O'Reilly's Dictionary with O Donavans [*sic*] supplement.	(B.12)
38	Gaelic Poetry. old version collated with new &c. Dean of Lismore	(Maclean 106; B.188)
39	O Mulloy's 'Lucerna Fidelium'. printed in Rome 1687.	(B.246)
40	An Teagasg Criosdaighe & dánta le hO Eodhasa [Catechism and poems] Rome 1707.	(B.245)
41	O'Brien's Irish Grammar.	(B.45)
42	Principal Anglo-Irish songs in Irish verse by McCoy	(de Hae 857)
43	Pilgrim's Progress translated into Irish.	
44	Searc-leanmhúin Criosd, or Imitation of Christ from the Latin.	(B.248)
45	Leabhar na cnoc. Scotch Gaelic.	(Maclean 269)
46	Duain le Uilliam Livingstone. Scotch Gaelic.	(Maclean 165)
47	LAOITHE FIANNUIGHEACHTA Fenian or Ossianic Lays Ossianic Society.	(de Hae 898)
48	Irish Prayer Book.	
50	The Satires of Aonghus Ua Dálaigh or the Bárd ruagh.	(B.200)
51	The Adventures of Donncadh ruadh Mach [*sic*] Cónmara.	(B.210)
52	Catechism in Connacht Irish written phonetically. Most barbarous.	(B.247)
53	Moore's Melodies &c. translated by McHale edited & corrected by Bourke.	(de Hae 871)
54	Dán-diadhga air Chriosd. 540 lines	
55	Midnight Court or Cúirt an Mheadhon-Oidhche, 1800.	(B.212)

56 Poems on the Clann Dhomhnail by the
Munster bards. Edited by O'Looney.   (B.197)
57 A couple of Miss Edgeworth's stories in
Irish. 1834. Ulster Gaelic Society.
58 Cath Muige Léana, or The Battle of Moy
Léna. Celtic Society   (B.104)
59 Original edition of 'Irish Jacobite Poetry',
interlinear trans.   (B.196)
60 First Series of Munster Poets. O Daly,
a.d. 1850.   (B.196)
61 Crioch déighionach an duine. 55 ranna.
ad 1818.
62 Féin Theagasg Gaedeilge, i.e. a good many
poems. O Daly 1846. & Introduction to a general
Irish Grammar.   (B.46)
63 Laoi na mná móire & tagra na muice & an
Cleire.
64 Grammar & Teagasg Criosdaighe by Hugh
McCurtin ad 1733.   (B.45)
65 McLeod's Gaelic Dictionary   (Maclean 271)
66 Sgéla na heiséirighe from the lebor na
hUidre.   (B.232)
67 Tria fragmenta annalium Iberniae.
O Donavan Archaeological Society 1860.   (B.254)
68 Irish glosses. Whitley Stokes. Archaeolocical
[sic] Society 1860.   (B.8)
69 Kurgefasste irische Grammatik mit Lesestucken.
Ernst Windisch.   (B.35)
70 Cambells 'Scéalta na n árdalbanach' [Stories of
the Scottish Highlands] IV volumes.   (Maclean 60)
71 Joyce's Irish Grammar.   (B.47)
72 Toras na croice. McHale.
73 Craobh Urnaighthe Cráibhighthe. Archbishop
McHale.
74 Cannon Bourkes [sic] Irish Grammar. 1879.   (B.47)
75 Poems in Scotch Gaelic translated into English
verse by Munro. 1843   (Maclean 300)
76 Barron's Ancient Ireland, bound with other Irish
tracts   (B.1)

101	Beatha agus dánta Dughail Buchanan.	(Maclean 39)
102	Dánta le Mac Colla. 1839.	(Maclean 182)
103	Dánta leis an Dochtúir Mc Dómhnal.	(Maclean 198)
104	Mary McKellar's Gaelic Poems. 1879.	(Maclean 242)
105	Mac Cheyne's Life & Sermons in S. Gaelic.	
106	Macghniomhartha Fhinn. Gaelic Union. 1881.	(B.102)
107	Laoidh Oisín ar Thír na n-óg. id.	
108	An Eaglais Choitchionn. S. Gaelic. 1847.	
109	Dánta air Thomás Dubh, Iarla Úrmhúmhan.	(B.199)
110	Beatha gearr Naoimh Phádruig. o'n mBeurla.	

Second List

1 O'Mahony's translation of Keatings History of
   Ireland.   (B.255)
2 O'Sullevani Bhearri Historia Iberniae.
3 O'Reilly's ' Irish Writers '. Celtic Soc'.   (B.74)
4 O'Curry's Lectures on the MSS of Ireland, &c.   (B. 63, 74)
5 Wrights history of Ireland. 3 vols.
6 Vita Sancti Columcille, by Adamnan. Archael. Soc.   (B.67)
7 Joyce's Names of Irish places.   (B.20)
8 Apologia pro Hibernia. Stefanus Vitus.   (B.186)
9 Cambrensus Eversus. Celtic Society. an ceud
   leabhar de.   (B.186)
10 O'Brennan's Antiquities.   (B.152)
11 O'Brennan's ' History of Ireland '.
12 Mitchel's Life of Aodh O'Neill.
13 The spirit of the Nation.
14 McCarthys book of Irish ballads.
15 Duffy's Irish Ballads.
16 Mitchel's Last Conquest of Ireland (Perhaps).
17 Meehan's Confederation of Kilkenny & Davis' Essays.
18 Blackies's Language & Literature of the Scotish [sic]
   Highlands.
19 Anderson's ' Native Irish '.
20 ' The Geraldines ', translated by Meehan.
21 Mitchel's Jail Journal.
22 Lyrics of Ireland, edited by Lover.
23 Davis Poems.
24 Father Prout's relics.

1   A MS of ' Cáth Chnoca ' 33 large pages. O Daly's writing.
2   MS. 'Cath Muighe Mochruime'. 30 large pages. A very old MS.
3   'Dánta diadha'. 8 large pages. written by Michael O Longan. a.d. 1798.
4   A MS of about 36 songs beautifully written on good paper. old. About half by Carolan.
5   A poem of 98 quatrains by Eoghan O Dubhtaigh on Maolmuire McCraith archbishop of Cashel. 13 pages. O Daly's writing.
6   Preface to Dr. Keating's ' Key to the Mass ' 33 large pages. O Daly's writing.
7   A collection of 32 songs & poems, by Connacht writers.
8   ' Eactra Toirealbha Mc Stairn '. 38 close middlesized pages.
9   ' Eactra triúr mic Toirealbha Mc Stairn '. 33 large close pages.
10 Oidhidh Cloinne Lir. 18 close pages middlesized, old.
11 Eachtra Cearbhaill Ua Dálaigh mac na miochómhairle. 44 pages, close.
12 A fragment of 81 88 [sic] pages very old & small of ' Eachtra 3 mic righ na hIorraidh '.
13 About half of the ' Bruighean Caortainn '. 10 pages.
14 A splendid MS of the first two books of Dr. Keatings ' Trí Biorgaethe an Báis'. 120 large pages. red & black ink. Bound and interleaved.
15 A magnificent copy from the Leabar Breac of ' Teagasg Cormaic Mc Airt da mac Cairbre Lifeachair '. 23 large pages.
16 A very fine copy of an old MS made for O'Donavan [sic] in 1837, by Mark Prendergast 23 immense pages.
17 Two copies of the ' Cúirt an Meadhon Oidhche ' by O Daly with notes & additions etc by other scribes & Wolfes metrical translation of it in English verse.
18 A beautiful volume of poetry transcribed by O'Donavan & O'Curry on thick paper nicely bound consisting of eighty four poems by such bards as Muireadach Albanach, Fearfas an Cainthe, Dómhnal O Dalaigh, ad 1404, Maoileachlainn na n-úirsgéul O Huiginn, Donncadh Mór O Dálaigh, 1244, Philip bocht Ua Huiginn etc! There are altogether 1200 stanzas or ranns or 4800 lines most beautifully written in the book.

Appendix II

Title-page or catalogue description of the books listed at the end of volume three of Hyde's diaries. After his death, Hyde's library was auctioned at 'Ratra', Phoenix Park, Dublin (his residence after he had retired from the Presidency) on 10 October 1949 and following days.

First List

1 An Tiomna Nuadh ar dTighearna agus ar Slanuightheora Iosa Criosd ar na tharruigh go firinneach as an nGreigis ughdarach ris an tAthair is onoruighthe a nDia Uilliam O'Domhnuill, Aird Easpug Thuaim. 1830.
   Tiomna Nuadh ar dTigearna . . . ris an tAthair is onoruighthe a nDia Huilliam O Domhnuill. London : (for the British and Foreign Bible Society), 1816.

2 Irish-English Primer, or spelling-book, intended for the use of schools; containing about four thousand Irish monosyllables, with their corresponding explanation in English; together with extracts from the Proverbs of Solomon. Dublin : printed for the Irish Society by M. Goodwin, 1823.

3 Foley, Daniel, B.D. An English-Irish Dictionary; intended for the use of students of the Irish language, and for those who wish to translate their English thoughts, or the works of others, into language intelligible to the present Irish-speaking inhabitants of Ireland. Dublin : Wm. Curry, 1855.

4 Mason, Henry Joseph Monck. A grammar of the Irish language, compiled from the best authorities. Dublin : printed by M. Goodwin, 1830.

5 Neilson, Rev. Wm., D.D. An introduction to the Irish Language in three parts. i. An original and Comprehensive Grammar. ii. Familiar phrases and dialogues. iii. Extracts from Irish books and Manuscripts, in the original character. With copious tables of contractions. Achill : printed at the 'Mission Press', 1843.

6 Moore, Thomas. A selection of Moore's melodies, trans-

lated into the Irish language by the Most Rev. John MacHale, Archbishop of Tuam. Dublin: James Duffy, 1827.

7 MacHale, John. An Teagasg Criosdaighe, De réir comhairle Ard-Easboig Thuama, agus Easbog na cúice sin. Atha-Cliath, Clobhuailte T. Coldamhell, 1839.

8 King, Robert. Ceachtanna sóthuigsiona air stair eagluise na h-Éirionn, chum úsáide tosuightheóiridhe. Dublin: printed by Goodwin, 1850.

9 An Biobla Naomhtha air na tharruing ó na teangthaibh bunadhúsacha go Gaoighilig . . . tre cúram agus sáothar an Doctúr Uilliam Bhedel, Roimhe seo Easpog Chillemóire a nEirinn. (very many editions).

10 De Vere Coneys, Thomas. Focloir Gaoidhilge-Sacs-Bearla, or An Irish-English Dictionary, intended for the use of students and teachers of Irish. Dublin: published for the Irish society by Hodges and Smith, 1849.

11 Cara an Pheachaidhe (a pamphlet of the Irish Society). Dublin: William Ridings (late George Herbert), n.d.

12 Abhrain Spioradalta le h-aghaidh usaide na h-eagluise chriosdaighe ann Eirin. Achill, 1843. An chlóidh cheath-ramadh. Air na meadughadh go mór. Acuil, 1846.

13 The Poets and Poetry of Munster: a selection of Irish songs by the poets of the last century, with metrical translations by Erionnach. Second series. Dublin: John O'Daly, 1860.

14 Reliques of Irish Jacobite Poetry with Biographical Sketches of the Authors, interlinear literal translations, and Historical Illustrative Notes by John O'Daly; together with Metrical Versions by Edward Walsh. Dublin: John O'Daly, 1866.

15 Ceud Leabhar Gaedhilge. First Irish Book. Dublin: Society for the Preservation of the Irish Language, 1877.

16 Wright, Rev. Charles H. H. A grammer of the Modern Irish Language, designed for the use of the classes in the University. With a preface by the Rev. Daniel Foley. Dublin: Hodges and Smith, 1855.

17 O'Donovan, John. A grammer of the Irish Language, published for the use of the senior classes in the College of St. Columba. Dublin: Hodges and Figgis, 1845.

18 Timothy O'Sullivan's (commonly called Tadg Gaelach)

Pious Miscellany; containing also a collection of Poems on Religious Subjects, by Aenghus O'Daly the divine, Tadhg Mac Daire Mac Brody, John Hore; together with Patrick Denn's Appendix. Edited by John O'Daly. Dublin: J. O'Daly, 1858.

19 An t-Iliad. Air Chogadh na Tróighe ro chan Homear, aisdríghthe o Ghreag-bhearla go ran Gaoidhilge le Seághan, ard-easbog Thúama. (An chead—an t-ochtmhadh leabhar). i mBaile Atha-cliath, clobhuailte le Gudman agus a chomh-chuideacht. John Cumming, 1844.

20 Brooke, Charlotte. Reliques of Irish Poetry, consisting of Heroic Poems, odes, elegies, and songs, translated into English verse, with notes, explanatory and historical, and the originals in the Irish character, to which is subjoined an Irish tale. Bonham, 1789.

21 An Dara Leabhar Gaidhilge. Second Irish Book. Dublin: Society for the Preservation of the Irish Language, 1878.

22 The Book of Fenagh in Irish and English originally compiled by St. Caillin, Archbishop, Abbott and Founder of Fenagh, alias Dunbally of Moy-rein, tempore S. Patricii, with the contractions resolved, and, (as far as possible), the original text restored. The whole carefully revised, indexed, and copiously annotated, by W. M. Hennessy, M.R.I.A. Dublin, 1875.

23 Toruigheacht Dhiarmuda agus Ghrainne; or, the pursuit after Diarmuid O'Duibhne, and Grainne the daughter of Cormac Mac Airt . . . edited (with translation) by Standish O'Grady. Dublin: Transactions of the Ossianic Society, Vol. III, 1857.

24 Laoithe Fiannuigheachta; or, Fenian poems, edited (with translation) by John O'Daly. Dublin: Transactions of the Ossianic Society, Vol. IV, 1859.

25 The Irish Language Miscellany: being A Selection of Poems by the Munster Bards of the Last Century. Collected and edited by John O'Daly. Dublin: J. O'Daly, 1876.

26 Eachdra agus imtheachta bhodaig an chota lachtna, in Fein-Teagasc Gaoidheilge, Fourth edition. Dublin: J. O'Daly, 1871.

27 Sermons in Irish-Gaelic by the Most Rev. James O'Gal-

lagher, Bishop of Raphoe, with literal idiomatic English translation on opposite pages, and Irish-Gaelic vocabulary, also a Memoir of the Bishop and his times, by the Rev. Canon Ulick J. Bourke, M.R.I.A., President of St. Jarlath's College, Tuam. Dublin: Gill, 1877.

28 Imtheacht na Tromdaimhe; or, the proceedings of the great Bardic Institution, edited (with translation) by Professor Connellan. Dublin: Transactions of the Ossianic Society, Vol. V, 1860.

29 The Prophecies of SS. Columbkille, Maeltamlacht, Ultan, Seadna, Coireall, Beorcan, &c. Together with the prophetic collectanea, or gleanings of several writers who have preserved portions of the now lost prophecies of our saints, with literal translation and notes. Dublin: J. O'Daly; London: J. R. Smith, 1856.

30 An Teagasc Criosduidhe de réir ceasda agus freagartha, air na tharruing go bunudhasach as bréithir shoilléir Dé agus as toibreacaibh fíorghlana oile. The Catechism, or Christian Doctrine by way of question and answer, drawn chiefly from the express Word of God, and other pure sources. Irish and English. Paris: James Guerin, 1742. Re Cead an Rígh, agus re Déightheisd na nOllamhun re Diaghacht. Third edition, Dublin: James Duffy, 1848.

31 Hardiman, James. Irish Minstrelsy, or Bardic Remains of Ireland; with English Poetical translations. Collected and edited, with notes and illustrations by James Hardiman. Two volumes. London: Robins, 1831.

32 Forus Feasa air Eirinn, mar a nochtar príomhdala na hinnse o Phartalon go Gabhaltus Gall, ar na chnuasach, & air na tiomsughadh o phriomhlebhraibh Shenchusa Eirenn, agas o iliomad d'ughdaraibh barantamhla coigcríche le Seathrun Ceitin, ollamh-diadhachta. An 1 chuid. (Irish text with translation, edited by William Halliday. Only volume 1 appeared.) Dublin: printed by J. Barlow, Bolton Street, 1811.

33 O'Donovan, John. Leabhar na gCeart, or, The Book of Rights, now for the first time edited, with translation and notes. Dublin: Celtic Society, 1847.

34 O'Flanagan, Theophilus. Deirdri, or, the Lamentable Fate

of The Sons of Usnach, an ancient dramatic Irish tale, one
of the three tragic stories of Erin; literally translated with
notes and observations: to which is annexed the old historic facts on which the story is founded. Transactions of
the Gaelic Society, Vol. 1. Dublin, 1808.

35 Tiomna Nuadh ar dTighearna agus ár slanuightheora Íosa
Críosd: do tarraingíoch roime-seo go fírinneach as an
ngreigis go gaodhailge chonachdach; agus anois ata ais-
drigthe de réir na greigise ceadna go gaodhailge chúige
mumhan: le Riobeard O Catháin o Chontae Chláir
Baile-atha-Cliath: Hodges, Smith and Co.; Lunduin:
Samuel Bagster agus a mhic, 1858.

36 O'Donovan, John. Miscellany of the Celtic Society. . . .
Poem on the Battle of Dun by Gilla-Brighde mac Con-
mhidhe. Dublin, 1847.

37 O'Reilly, Edward. An Irish-English Dictionary with
copious quotations from the most esteemed ancient and
modern writers, to elucidate the meaning of obscure words,
and numerous comparisons of Irish words with those of
similar orthography, sense or sound in the Welsh or
Hebrew languages. A New Edition with a Supplement,
containing many thousand Irish words, with their inter-
pretations in English, collected throughout Ireland, and
amongst ancient unpublished manuscripts. By John
O'Donovan, LL.D., M.R.I.A., the profoundly learned
editor of the 'Annals of the Four Masters' and other
great works of native Irish history and grammar. Dublin
and London, 1864.

38 The Dean of Lismore's Book, a selection of ancient Gaelic
Poetry, from a manuscript collection made by Sir James
M'Gregor, Dean of Lismore. . . . Edited with a translation
and notes by the Rev. Thomas M'Lachlan and an intro-
duction and additional notes by William F. Skene.
Edinburgh: Edmonston, 1862.

39 Lochrann na gcreidmneach .i. Diosgan dioghlomhtha, as na
priomhúghdaruibh lea ttrachdarar leigheann na bethaidh,
rannta a ttri ccodchuibh; a ttrachdarar leigheann criosduidhe, á miniúghadh na nairtegal, fa mbi lucht ainbhfis
dheasbhaidh á ttuigsiona, ag tabhthann na ccreidmheach;

& á ccomhradh ghearr shimplidhe, lea cclaoidhter gach sort eithrice go hurasda, & lea ndaingnither na catoilici go leir uile san ccreidemh choir. Ar na chur a cclo san Romh, maille re ugdarras San Phropaganda, le brathair bocht dord Froinsias. Froinsias o Maolmhuaidh, 1676.

40 An Teagasc Criosdaidhe ann so, arna chuma do Bonabhentura oeodhasa brathair bocht Dord San Proinsias a ccolaisde S. Antoin a Lobhain. Secunda aeditio. Romae, Typis Sacrae Congreg. de Propag. Fide. Anno M. DCC. VII.

41 O'Brien, Reverend Paul. A practical Grammar of the Irish Language. Dublin: printed by H. Fitzpatrick, 1809.

42 MacCoy, Reverend Edward. Miscellaneous Poems Translated into Gaelic. By the Rev. Edward MacCoy. Dublin, 1869. Another edition, Dublin: Traynor, 1878.

43 Gluaseachd an Oilithrigh no Turus an Chriosduighe o'n t-Saoghal so chum an t-Saoghal le teacht fa amhlughadh aisling. Aistrithghe o mBearla Eoin Bhunian. (By Christopher Anderson). Part 1 only issued. Dublin: John Robertson and company, 1837.

44 Kempis, Thomas à. Searc-leanmhain Chriosd. A gceithre leabhraibh le Tomas A Cempis. Aisdrighthe ua'n Laidion mbunudhasach & comheasta go duthrachdach leis na mac-leabhraibh is fearr teisd & is airde ceim a bhFraincis & a Sagsbheurla, leis an Athair Domhnall O'Suilliobhain. Dublin; 1822.

45 Leabhar nan cnoc: comh-chruinneachadh do nithibh sean agus nuadh: airson oilean agus leas nan Gaidheal. (The edition in the National Library is dated 1898 and is called a 'New Edition'.)

46 Livingston, William. Duain agus orain le Uilleam Mac Dhunleibhe. . . ar na cur amach air iarrtus agus fo iuil Chomuinn Ilich. (Edited by R. Blair). Glasgow: Sinclair, 1882.

47 O'Daly, John. Laoithe Fiannuigheachta; or, Fenian Poems, Second Series. Seilg Sleibhe na mBan. The Chase of Sliabh na mBan. Dublin: Transactions of the Ossianic Society Vol. VI, 1861.

48 Leabhar na hUrnuighe chomhchoitcine (The Book of Common Prayer). London, 1856. (Presentation copy from the Church of England Book Society).

50 O'Donovan, John. The Tribes of Ireland: A Satire by Aenghus O'Daly; with poetical translation by the late James Clarence Mangan; together with an historical account of the family of O'Daly; and an introduction to the history of satire in Ireland by John O'Donovan, LL.D., M.R.I.A.. Dublin: John O'Daly, 1852.

51 Mac Conmara, Donncadh Ruadh. Adventures of Donncadh Ruadh Mac Con Mara, a slave of Adversity. Written by himself. Now for the first time edited, from an original manuscript, with metrical translation, notes, and a biographical sketch of the author, by S. Hayes. Dublin: John O'Daly, 1853.

52 Dr. Kirwan's Irish Catechism, published under the sanction of The Most Rev. Oliver O'Kelly, Archbishop of Tuam. Fifth edition, Dublin: Richard Grace, 1852. Another edition, Galway: printed for James Davis, 1845.

*53 Moore, Thomas. A selection of Moore's melodies, translated into the Irish language by the Most Rev. John MacHale, Archbishop of Tuam. Dublin: James Duffy, 1827. Another edition 1871.

54 I was unable to identify this item.

55 Merriman, Brian. Mediae Noctis Consilium (Cuirt an Mheadhoin Oidhche). A heroic comic poem in Irish-Gaelic. Dublin: Gill, 1879.

56 O'Looney, Brian. A collection of poems, written on different occasions, by the Clare bards, in honour of the Macdonnells of Kilkee and Killone . . . collected and edited by B. O'L. Dublin: John O'Daly, 1863.

57 Edgeworth, Maria. Forgive and Forget. A tale of Maria Edgeworth. Rosanna, by the same. Translated into Irish for the Ulster Gaelic Society, by Thomas Feenachty. Maith agus Dearmad, sgeul beag d'ar b'ughdar Maria Edgeworth. Rosanna on ughdar cheadna. Air na d-tarraing go firinneach o Bheurla go Gaoidheilg, air iarratas & fa thearmonn na Cuideachta Gaoidheilge Uladh a m-Beul-Fearsaide le Tomas

---

*In Hyde's list are the words 'edited & corrected by Bourke'. This no doubt would be Canon Ulick J. Bourke. I have been unable to find an edition to suit this description.

o Fiannachtaigh Oide Gaoidheilge a m-Beul-Fearsaide. Belfast: Archer; Dublin: Curry, Jun, 1833.

58 Curry, Eugene. Cath mhuighe Leana, or the Battle of Magh Leana, together with Tochmarc Moimera, or the courtship of Momera. . . . Edited with translation and notes by Eugene Curry. (Annual Report of the Celtic Society, 1854). Dublin, 1855.

59 O'Daly, John and Walsh, Edward. Reliques of Irish Jacobite Poetry with Biographical Sketches of the Authors, interlinear literal translations, and Historical Illustrative Notes by John O'Daly; together with Metrical Versions by Edward Walsh. Dublin: Part 1, Samuel J. Machen; Part 2, John Cumming, 1844.

60 O'Daly, John and Mangan, James Clarence. Poets and Poetry of Munster: a selection of Irish Songs by the poets of the last century, with poetical translations by the late James Clarence Mangan, now for the first time published with the original music, and Biographical Sketches of the Authors by John O'Daly. Dublin: John O'Daly, 1849.

61 Crioch Deigheanach don duine. Dan diadha. A mbaile Atha-cliath Duibhlinne, san bhliadhain d'aois ar Ttigearna 1818.

62 O'Daly, John. Fein-Teagasc Gaoidheilge. Self-instruction in Irish: or, the rudiments of that language brought within the comprehension of the English reader, without the aid of a teacher. Contains some pieces for reading, prose and verse. Dublin: John O'Daly, 1846.

63 I was unable to identify this item.

64 MacCurtin, Hugh. The Elements of the Irish Language, Gramatically explained in English, in 14 chapters. By H. Mac Curtin. Suim bhunudhasach an teaguisc chriosdaidhe a bpros agus a ndan. Printed at Louvain, Anno 1728.

65 MacLeod, Norman and Dewar, Daniel. A dictionary of the Gaelic language in two parts, i. Gaelic and English; ii. English and Gaelic. Bohn, 1845.

66 Scéla na Esergi: a treatise on the Resurrection. Now printed for the first time, from the original Irish in Lebor na h-Uidre. . . . With a literal translation. By J. O Beirne Crowe. Printed for the editor, Dublin, 1865.

67 Mac Firbisigh, Dubhaltach. Annals of Ireland. . . . Three fragments, copied from ancient sources by D. Mac Firbisigh, and edited with a translation by J. O'Donovan. (Irish Archaeological and Celtic Society). Dublin, 1860.

68 Stokes, Whitley. Irish glosses. A medieval tract on Latin declension, with examples explained in Irish. To which are added the Lorica of Gildas, with the gloss thereon, and a selection of glosses from the Book of Armagh. (Irish Archaeological and Celtic Society). Dublin, 1860.

69 Windisch, Ernst. Kurzgefasste irische Grammatik mit Lesestucken. Leipzig: Hirzel, 1879.

70 Campbell, J. F. Popular Tales of the West Highlands. Four volumes. 1860-62.

71 Joyce, Patrick Weston. A Grammar of the Irish Language. Dublin, 1878.

72 Toras na croiche. Aistrighth [sic] le Seaghan mac Hale. A m-Baile Atha-Cliath: Seamus O Duibhthe, 1855. Other editions 1859, 1861.

73 Mac Hale, John. Craobh urnaighe craibhthige tiomsuighthe as an Sgriobhain dhiadha, agus ranta toghtha na h-Eaglaise. Le Seaghan mac Hale. Baile Atha Cliath: Seamus O Duibhthe, 1853. Another edition, 1857.

74 Bourke, Reverend Ulick J. The College Irish Grammar, containing besides the usual subject of Grammar, some remarks in the form of dissertation on the orthography of the language; how it became fixed; on the number of declensions, and number of conjugations, etc., compiled chiefly with a view to aid the students of St. Patrick's College, Maynooth, and of the Catholic University of Ireland, in the study of the national language. Dublin: John O'Daly, 1856. Fifth edition, 1868.

75 Munro, R. Minor Poems and Translations. Edinburgh, 1843.

76 Barron, Philip P. Ancient Ireland: a weekly (afterwards monthly) magazine. Established for the purpose of reviving the cultivation of the Irish language, and originating an earnest investigation into the ancient history of Ireland. By Philip P. Barron, Esq., of the county of Waterford. (Issues of 1, 10 and 31 January; April; May) Dublin, 1835.

o

77 Compananch an Chriosdaigh; no tiomsugh d'urnaighibh craibhtheacha, oireamhnach chum gach dualgais do bhaineas le creideamh, do chomhlionadh. Dublin: D. Tegg, 1842.

78 O'Brennan, Martin A. Antiquities. Dublin: printed for and published by the author, n.d., but dedication to John MacHale dated April 1858. Tuireadh na h-Eireann, The Dirge of Ireland, by the Most Rev. John O'Connell, Bishop of Kerry (d. 1704), is a long poem on the sorrows of Irish history. It occupies pages 64 to 177 of the volume.

79 An Treas Leabhar Gaedheilge. The Third Irish Book. Dublin: Society for the Preservation of the Irish Language, 1879.

80 O'Kearney, Nicholas. The Battle of Gabhra: Garristown in the County of Dublin, fought A.D. 283. For the first time edited from an Original Irish manuscript, with introduction, literal translation, and notes. Dublin: Transactions of the Ossianic Society, Vol. I, 1853.

81 O'Kearney, Nicholas. Feis Tighe chonain chinn-Sleibhe; or The Festivities at the House of Conan of Ceann-Sleibhe, in the County of Clare. Edited (with translation) by N. O'K. Dublin: Transactions of the Ossianic Society, Vol. II, 1855.

82 M'Lauchlan, T. (editor). The Poems of Ossian. Edinburgh, 1859.

83 MacKenzie, John. Eachdraidh A' Phrionnsa, na Bliadhna Thearlaic le Iain Mac-Choinnich. Duneideann [Edinburgh], Thornton agus Collie, 1844.

84 MacKenzie, Angus. Eachdraigh na h-Alba, anns am bheil gearr-iomradh air na nithibh is cudthromaich' a thachair 'san rioghachd o na ceud linnibh, gu meadhon an naoidheamh linn deug. Le Aonghus MacCoinnich. Glascho [Glasgow]: Mac-na-Ceardadh; Oban: Muilleir, 1867.

85 Macintyre, Duncan Ban. Songs and Poems in Gaelic. Edinburgh, 1848. Sixth edition, 1858.

86 M'Donald, Alexander. Eiseirigh na Seann Chanain Albannaich; no, an Nuadh Oranaiche Gaidhealach. Le Alastair Donullach (Mac Mhaighistir Alastair). An Seachdamh Clobhualadh. Edinburgh: Maclachlan and Stewart, 1874.

87 Doubtful.

88 Mackintosh's Collection of Gaelic Proverbs and Familiar Phrases. Englished a-new. Edinburgh, William Stewart, 1819.

89 Doubtful.

90 Jerram, Charles Stanger. Dan an Deirg, agus Tiomna Ghuill (Dargo and Gaul). Two poems from Dr. Smith's collection, entitled the Sean Dana. Newly translated, with a revised Gaelic text, notes, and introduction, by C. S. Jerram, M.A., Scholar of Trinity College, Oxon. Edinburgh, Machlachlan and Stuart, 1874.

91 Am Filidh Gaidhealach or the Highland Minstrel. A collection of the most popular ancient and modern songs of the Gael of Scotland. Inverness, 1873.

92 MacNeill, Reverend Nigel, LL.D. Neniae. Cian Dhain. Le Danaibh eile. Neniae, with other poems. Edinburgh, Glasgow, etc. MDCCCLXXII.

93 The Gael. A monthly magazine. (Started in Toronto in 1871 by Angus Nicholson, then editor of the *Canadian Scotsman*.)

94 Calder, Rob Donn. Songs and Poems in the Gaelic Language by Rob Donn, the celebrated Reay country poet.

95 Forbes, Reverend John. Long Geal: Dan Spioradail. The White Ship, a spiritual poem. Edinburgh, n.d.

96 O'Suilliobhain, Seamas. Seanmoirigh Gairid agus Abharain Diaga do leanbhuighe. Curta le ceile a gcomhair gach Domnach san mbliaghan le Teagasgtoir Sgoil Domhnaidh. Aisdridhethe o'n Sags-bheurla go Gaoidhilge le Seumus O'Suilliobhain. Dublin: printed by Goodwin and Nethercott, 1847.

97 Todd, Reverend James H. Cogadh Gaedhel re Gallaibh. The Wars of the Gaedhil with the Gaill, or the Invasions of Ireland by the Danes and other Norsemen. The original Irish text, edited, with Translation and Introduction. London: Rolls Series, 1867.

98 MacKenzie, John. Sar-Obair nam Bard Gaelach. Edinburgh. (National Library copy—Edinburgh: John Grant, 1907).

99 Mac-Choinnich, Iain. Orain Gae'lach le Uilleam Ros, air an co'-chruinneachadh ri ceile le Iain Mac-Choinnich ann an Inbhiriue. An Dara clo-bualadh. Glasgow, Edinburgh and London, 1834.

100 Sinclair, Arch., Jun. An t-Oranaiche. The Gaelic Songster. Glasgow, 1879.

101 Maclean, Reverend Donald, (ed.) The Spiritual Songs of Dugald Buchanan. First edited 1767; several editions. (That in the National Library of Ireland is Edinburgh, 1913).

102 Mac-Colla, E. Clarsach nam Beann, no Dain agus Orain, ann an Gaelic, le Eobhan Mac-Colla. An Dara Clodh-bhualadh, meudaichte agus ath-leasaichte. Dun-Eidin/Edinburgh, 1839.

103 Doubtful, but could be Maclean 198.

104 MacKellar, M. Poems and Songs. Gaelic and English, Edinburgh, 1880.

105 Sinclair, Ailean. Iomradh air Beatha agus Ministreileachd an Urramaich R. M. McCheyne, maille ri Litrichean, sear-moinean, agus laoidhean leis. Edinburgh: Religious Tract Society of Scotland, 1879.

106 Comyn, David. Mac-ghniomhartha Fhinn (Sliocht Saltrach Caisil). The youthful exploits of Fionn. . . . Re-issued for the use of Schools. The ancient text, modern Irish version, new literal translation, vocabulary, notes, and a map. Dublin: The Gaelic Union, 1881.

107 Laoidh Oisin ar Thir na n-Og (The Lay of Oisin on the Land of the Young). Carefully revised and edited with a new literal translation, and copious vocabulary. By members of the Council of the Society for the Preservation of the Irish Language. Dublin: Gaelic Union Publications, 1880.

108 I was unable to identify this item.

109 MacCraith, Flann. Panegyric on Thomas Butler, the tenth Earl of Ormonde, by Flann, son of Eoghan MacCraith, a Munster Poet who flourished circa 1580, now for the first time translated from an original Irish manuscript, by John O'Daly; the notes by John O'Donovan, LL.D., M.R.I.A. Reprinted from the Transactions of the Kilkenny Archaeological Society for 1851. Dublin: John O'Daly, 1853. (Only fifty copies printed).

110 Wordsworth, Christopher. Naomh Padruig, a bheatha, agus a aimsir. St. Patrick, his life and times. . . . Translated into Irish by Thaddeus O'Mahony. Dublin, University Press (M. H. Gill), 1854.

1 Foras Feasa ar Eirinn. . . The History of Ireland, from the earliest period to the English Invasion. Translated . . . and annotated by John O'Mahony. New York: 1866.

2 Historiae Catholicae Iberniae compendium, Domino Philippo Austriaco, Hispanarum, Indiarum, aliorum regnorum atque multarum ditionum regi catholico monarchaeque potentissimo dicatum a D. Philippo O'Sullevano Bearro, Iberno, cum facultate S. Inquisitionis, ordinario et regis, Ulyssipone excusum a Petro Crasbeeckio Regio Typographo, anno Domini 1621. Edidit, notulisque ac indicibus illustravit Matthaeus Kelly, in Collegio S. Patricii apud Maynooth Professor, etc. Dublinii, apud Johannem O'Daly, 1850.

3 Transactions of the Iberno-Celtic Society for 1820. Vol. I, Part 1, containing a chronological account of nearly four hundred Irish Writers commencing with the earliest account of Irish history, and carried down to the year of Our Lord 1750; with a Descriptive Catalogue of such of their work as are still extant in verse or prose, consisting of upwards of one thousand separate tracts. By Edward O'Reilly, Esq. Author of the Irish-English Dictionary and Grammar, &c, &c, &c. Dublin: Printed for the Society, by A. O'Neil, at the Minerva Printing-Office, Chancery-Lane. 1820.

4 Lectures on the manuscript materials of ancient Irish history. Delivered at the Catholic University of Ireland, during the sessions of 1855 and 1856. Dublin, 1861.

5 The History of Ireland from the earliest period of the Irish Annals to the present time by Thomas Wright. London and New York, 1854.

6 Life of Saint Columba, Founder of Hy. Written by Adamnan, ninth abbot of that monastery. Edited by William Reeves, D.D., M.R.I.A., Rector of Tynan, and Canon of Armagh. (The Historians of Scotland, Vol. VI. English and Latin.) Edinburgh, 1874.

7 The Origin and History of Irish Names of Places, by Patrick Weston Joyce. Dublin, London, and Edinburgh, 1874.

8 White, Stephen. Apologia pro Hibernia. Edited by M. Kelly. Dublin, 1849.

9 Cambrensis refuted or rather Historic Credit in the Affairs of Ireland taken from Geraldus Cambrensis, who is proved to abound in most of the blemishes, while destitute of most of the qualifications, of a legitimate historian. By Gratianus Lucius, a Native Irishman. Translated from the original Latin . . . by Theophilus O'Flanagan, A.B., some time scholar of Trin. Col. Dublin. Dublin: printed by Joseph Hill, No. 36, Denmark-Street. M. DCC. XCV.

10 See number 78 in the first list.

11 Ancient Ireland: her Milesian Chiefs, her Kings and Princes—her Great Men. Her struggles for liberty. Her Apostle, St. Patrick. Her Religion. By Martin A. O'Brennan, LL.D., Principal of the Collegiate Seminary, 57, Bolton-street, Dublin. Dublin: John Mullany, 1855.

12 Mitchel, John. The life and times of Aodh O'Neill, Prince of Ulster; called by the English, Hugh, Earl of Tyrone. With some account of his predecessors, Don, Shane, and Tirlough. Dublin: Duffy's Library of Ireland, 1876.

13 The Spirit of the Nation: by writers of the Nation Newspaper: Political Songs and National Ballads. Dublin: James Duffy, 1876.

14 M'Carthy, Denis Florence. The Book of Irish Ballads. Dublin: Duffy's Library of Ireland, 1846. New edition, 1869.

15 Duffy, Sir Charles Gavan. The Ballad Poetry of Ireland. Dublin: James Duffy, 1845. Fortieth edition, 1869. (Hyde's edition, according to the auction catalogue, was 1847.)

16 Mitchel, John. The Last Conquest of Ireland (Perhaps). Dublin, 1861.

17 Meehan, Reverend Charles Patrick. The Confederation of Kilkenny. Dublin: Duffy's Library of Ireland, 1846. Bound with this: Davis, Thomas. Literary and Historical Essays. Dublin, 1846.

18 Blackie, John Stuart. The Language and Literature of the Scottish Highlands. Edinburgh, 1876.

19 Anderson, Christopher. Historical sketches of the ancient native Irish and their descendants, illustrative of their past

and present state with regard to literature, education, and oral instruction. Edinburgh and London, 1828. Third edition, 1846. (This, according to the auction catalogue, was the edition in Hyde's library.)

20 O'Daly, Dominic de Rosario. The Geraldines, Earls of Desmond, and the persecution of the Irish Catholics. Translated from the original Latin, with notes and illustrations, by the Rev. C. P. Meehan. Dublin: Duffy's Library of Ireland, 1847.

21 Mitchel, John. Jail Journal; or, Five Years in British Prisons. New York, 1854; Dublin, 1864; Glasgow, 1876.

22 Lover, Samuel. The Lyrics of Ireland, edited and annotated by S. Lover. Houlston and Wright, 1858.

23 Davis, Thomas. National and historical ballads, songs and poems. Dublin 1869.

24 The reliques of Fr. Prout late P.P. of Watergrasshill, in the county of Cork . . . collected and arranged by Oliver Yorke, Esq. Illustrated by Alfred Croquis, Esq. Bohn, 1836.

Notes

INTRODUCTION

1 Doncha Ó hAodha, Assistant Secretary of the Gaelic League, quoted in the *Irish Independent*, 10 July 1963, p. 6.
(The grave was cleaned up in 1968 and is now well kept.)

2 Cecily was Hyde's cousin.

3 See Dónal McCartney, 'Hyde, D. P. Moran. and Irish Ireland' in *Leaders and Men of the Easter Rising; Dublin : 1916,* edited by F. X. Martin, O.S.A. London, 1967, p. 50.

4 Austin Clarke recalls Hyde the professor: ' As an undergraduate I escaped at one step from the snobbery of school life and discovered the Love Songs of Connacht, those poems and translations which had started our Literary Revival. Their poet-translator was on the rostrum, and, though I could not always follow the swift rush of Dr Hyde's western Irish, I knew from his gestures that he was speaking a living language. When the future President of Éire enacted Casadh an tSúgáin for us, he took the parts of all the characters, jumping up and down from the rostrum in his excitement, and, as he unwound an imaginary straw rope at the end of the play, found himself outside the lecture room.' (From ' On Learning Irish ' in *The Irish Times,* 10 April, 1943.)

5 His brother Arthur who died of tuberculosis in May 1879.

6 F. X. Martin, O.S.A., ' The Origins of the Irish Rising of 1916 ', in *The Irish Struggle 1916-1926,* edited by Desmond Williams. London, Routledge and Kegan Paul, 1967.

7 Donnchadh Ó Floinn, *The Integral Irish Tradition,* Dublin, 1968, p. 3.

CHAPTER 1

1 This prayerful opening sounds quite natural in Irish; it is an example of how Hyde has adopted the ready piety of the native Gaelic speaker.

2 Arthur French, Whig M.P. for County Roscommon from 1821 to 1832, was created Baron de Freyne in 1839. Charles, third Baron de Freyne of Coolavin, is the person here referred to. He died in 1868 and was succeeded by his son Arthur.

3 The Hydes of Drumkilla were cousins.

4 The spelling varies.

5 The meaning is clear although the verb forms are hopelessly incorrect (semblance of future tenses for the present which he apparently intended):
' A very fine day. I went to Ratra looking for rabbits. I wasn't able to kill a rabbit—[French] because Morris had fired several shots. . . .'

6 The quotation marks are his own. The Irish means:
' and I rode the horse, a fine day [note ' beau ' for the Irish equivalent ' breá '], it is not raining yet.'

7 ' Since I was born I never saw such a sheen on the surface of the lake, or water so calm or a sight so pleasing. The water and the air were as one, and I saw every single island in the water so plainly that I could not tell which

was island and which was water. A heavy mist came down as we were coming home, but we steered by the one star that was visible. But there was great danger there.'

8   William Connolly was the farm hand. His wife was Hyde's instructor in Irish after James Hart's death.

9   Neilson's Irish Grammar is among the books of which details are given in the appendix.

10 His cousins on the maternal side, the Oldfields, were then living in Blackrock, a suburb on the south side of Dublin.

11 Four Greek letters. Probably a mistake for diarrhoea, mentioned elsewhere.

12 ' acht go raibh mo cumhacht-dearcadh ro-bheag.'

13 This could either be an inadvertent follow-through from the previous paragraph or it may refer to eye teeth.

14 Inadvertently for 18.

15 A verse from a Gaelic lament. (tr. ' All we have left to us now, alas/In the place of the wise man [who has died] is weeping and mourning/Tears and wailing and lamentation/Is our lot for the future, and heartache.'

16 Miss Gowring was his landlady for this visit.

17 I myself wrote this poem.

18 ' Graun of the Sharp Pike '.

19 With cold iron Ireland will be free.

20 For by God we swear it.

21 My Graun of the sharp pike.

22 ' Said Graun of the sharp pike '.

23 ' There is more in it, I believe, but I did not get it.'

24 ' I got this from an old woman back at Baile na Locha.'

25 The translation is given in chapter V.

26 Possibly the same as that mentioned in the diary, 23 March 1875. [Translation] : An extraordinary thing happened today. While the Lloyds were in the room a ghost came in, like young Arthur, and opened the door, and the next minute he was gone again. Annette was—?—and the Mistress. The ghost was seen often before this. Emily saw it twice, and the Mistress twice, and Jane saw it once. And when the workmen were here the painter saw a ghost going down the stone steps and he nearly fell in a faint. [The Lloyds were friends who had come on a visit; Emily was a cousin. Jane was probably a maid.]

CHAPTER II

1   Appendix I and II.

2   James Henthorn Todd (1805-1869) was the founder of the Archaeological Society. In 1852 he was appointed Librarian at Trinity College, and it is largely due to his efforts that the Library of TCD now ranks among the great libraries of Europe. With the assistance of John O'Donovan and Eugene O'Curry he classified and arranged the rich collection of Irish manuscripts; he also edited some of them.

3   Sir Thomas Larcom was director of the Ordnance Survey from 1828 until the British Government stopped the grant and brought the survey to an abrupt halt in 1845. In his team he had an extraordinary group of Irish scholars—George Petrie, John O'Donovan, Eugene O'Curry, Edward O'Reilly

—whose work was the prelude to the literary revival of the late nineteenth century.

John O'Donovan was, of course, the editor of that monumental work, the seven volume *Annals of the Four Masters*. In his introduction to the work O'Donovan pays tribute to Larcom: 'The Editor has also been assisted by various others, but more especially by his friend, Captain Larcom, R.E., who had been the active promoter of Irish literature, antiquities, and statistics, ever since the summer of 1825 and who, during his connexion with the Ordnance Survey, exerted himself most laudably to illustrate and preserve the monuments of ancient Irish history and topography.'

4 *Transactions of the Ossianic Society for the year 1856*, Vol. IV Supplement.

5 *Transactions of the Ossianic Society for the year 1853*. Vol. I, p. 5.

6 'This cycle of romance may be called the "Fenian" Cycle, as dealing to some extent with Finn Mac Cumhail and his Fenian militia, or the "Ossianic" Cycle since Ossian, Finn's son, is supposed to have been the author of many of the poems which belong to it.'
Douglas Hyde, *A Literary History of Ireland*, p. 364.

7 Douglas Hyde, *Mise agus an Connradh*, p. 20.

8 See Máirín Ní Mhuiríosa, *Réamhchonraitheoirí*, Baile Átha Cliath. Clódhanna Teoranta, 1963, p. 6.

9 Kingstown is of course the present Dún Laoghaire. The Mansfields were family friends.

10 The Royal Irish Academy.

11 Thomas O'Neill Russell (1826-1908), a native of County Westmeath, spent many years in America as a 'jolly pedlar', 'bagman' or 'drummer'. At home and abroad he was a tireless worker for the Irish language. Hyde describes him as 'rather obstinate'; a correspondent of Hyde's called him 'that Prince of Cranks', while Tim Healy, in a letter to his brother Maurice, says of him: 'I think Russell the most delightful human animal I have ever known: his honesty, sincerity, enthusiasm and love for Ireland and Celtic things, in a man of his years and Protestant training, are marvellous.' (*Mise agus an Connradh*, p. 162 ff.)

12 J. J. MacSweeney was Assistant Librarian at the Royal Irish Academy from 1869 to 1908. He was Secretary of the Society for the Preservation of the Irish Language.

13 Preface, p. v.

14 Frank O'Connor, *The Backward Look*. London, Macmillan, 1966, p. 131.

15 Miss Brooke's preface.

16 In 1939 Hyde wrote (*Mise agus an Connradh*, p. 11): 'This book [i.e., Hardiman's] has not yet been excelled as a rich treasury of the poetry of Ireland.'
Hardiman's Introduction and notes provide much interesting anecdote and information on the background of the poetry. He gives the following example of the pride of ancestry which was characteristic of the Gaelic poets and harpers: 'The late Arthur O'Neill, a northern harper, always expected and received an extraordinary degree of attention, on account of the antiquity and respectability of his *tribe*. He generally sat at table with the gentlemen, whose houses he visited, and once at a public dinner in Belfast, where Lord ——— presided, his lordship made a kind of apology to O'Neill, and expressed regret at his being seated so low at the festive

board. "Oh, my Lord", answered the harper, "apology is quite un-
necessary, for wherever an O'Neill sits, there is the head of the table." '

This is a remnant of the pride of place which the bardic order enjoyed
before the days of Cromwell. 'They were, indeed, until the fall of the old
Irish order an intellectual aristocracy, with all the privileges and, no doubt,
many of the prejudices of a caste.' (Robin Flower, *The Irish Tradition*.
Oxford, 1947, p. 142.)

This was an aspect of Gaelic culture which appealed especially to W. B.
Yeats; he made it the subject of *The King's Threshold* ('Die, Seanchan,
and proclaim the right of the poets.')

17 Edward Walsh (1805-1850) was a schoolmaster. Most of his short life was a
hard grind, teaching convicts in the prison school on Spike Island in Cork
Harbour. John Mitchel, on his way to penal servitude in the Bermudas, met
him there, 'a tall gentleman-like person in black but rather overworn
clothes. . . . Edward Walsh, author of "Mo Craoibhín Cnó" and other
sweet songs, and of some very musical translations from old Irish ballads.'
Most of his original compositions are simple love-songs, with a musical
quality borrowed from Gaelic. 'There is a peculiar melody in his verses, as
hard to be defined as the indistinctly heard murmurings of a far-off brook.
It is as if he had "Heard a weird woman chant what the fairy choir
taught her " [a line from one of his poems] and had learned the charmed
secret from her.' (*The Celt*, No. 19. Vol. 1, 5 December 1857.)

Besides the 'Jacobite Relics' he published *Irish Popular Songs*, with
translation and notes, in 1847.

W. B. Yeats had a particular sympathy for Walsh, and admired his simple
verses. (See *The Leisure Hour*, November 1889; *The Bookman*, July 1895.)
He numbers Walsh among the Irish poets who influenced him in his early
days: 'I took from Allingham and Walsh their passion for country
spiritism, and from Ferguson his pleasure in heroic legend. . .' (*The Cutting
of An Agate*, [1912], reprinted in *Essays and Introductions*. Macmillan,
1961, p. 248.)

18 James Clarence Mangan (1803-1849). A bizarre, erratic genius, whose poetry
is of wildly uneven quality. Lionel Johnson wrote of 'the radiance of his
"Dark Rosaleen", its adoring, flashing, flying, laughing rapture of patriotic
passion. It is among the great lyrics of the world, one of the fairest and
fiercest in its perfection of imagery and rhythm. . . .' He spent much of his
time on hack translations, but his finest work is 'in its marvellous moments
of entire success, greater than anything that Ireland has yet produced in
English verse, from Goldsmith to Mr Yeats.' (From an essay by Lionel
Johnson in *The Prose Writings of James Clarence Mangan*, edited by D. J.
O'Donoghue. Dublin and London, 1904, pp. xiii, xiv.)

Yeats called him 'that strange visionary, ruined by drink and narcotics,
who wrote some half-dozen lyrics of indescribable beauty.' (*The Bookman*,
July 1895, p. 106. See also *The Irish Fireside*, March 1887.)

19 'Éiríonnach' was the pseudonym of Dr George Sigerson, whose friendship
and collaboration with Hyde will be discussed in a later chapter.

20 *Mise agus an Connradh*, p. 17.

21 Hyde gives the impression that it was as a student at Trinity that he used
to call in at O'Daly's shop. 'When I first came to Dublin I used to go into
his bookshop.' In fact, O'Daly died two years before Hyde enrolled at TCD.

It was only on his infrequent visits to Dublin, such as that of June 1877, that he could have met the old man.

22 This contradicts a statement in *Mise agus an Connradh,* p. 17. Writing of the auction Hyde says: 'I went to the auction of his books after his death. He had many manuscripts and they were sold for a few shillings each. I spent every penny I had buying Irish books at bargain prices, but I was not able to read manuscripts at the time, and I did not buy any. This is something which I have regretted ever since.'

23 In his *Literary History of Ireland* Hyde describes this treatise as ' one of the most remarkable prose tracts of ancient Ireland with which I am acquainted.' (pp. 246 ff.)

24 Turlough O'Carolan (1670-1737), known as 'the last of the bards', was a blind harper who composed some two hundred tunes, to many of which he put words. See Hyde, *Literary History,* p. 598, and the curious note on the following page: 'The late bookseller, John O'Daly, of Anglesea Street, had, I believe, a number of poems of Carolan in his possession. . . .'

25 Two well-known traditional songs of which Sir Samuel Ferguson made excellent translations.

26 'Eachtra an Bháis' (The adventure of death).

27 'Eochair-sciath an Aifrinn', a devotional treatise by Geoffrey Keating, circa 1630.

28 'The Midnight Court ' a long poem in an Irish variation of the rhyming couplet, in which the women of Munster plead their case against celibacy, particularly clerical celibacy, before the Queen of the Fairies.

29 Denis Woulfe (Donocha Ulf), a schoolmaster from Sixmilebridge, County Clare, who flourished in the twenties of the last century. See note by T. P. O'Rahilly in *Gadelica,* p. 202.

30 A famous battle of the Fenian Cycle in which Cumhal the father of Finn made war on the high king Conn of the Hundred Battles.
   In his 'Literary History' Hyde translates a passage from a manuscript referring to the battle, and adds a footnote: 'I translated this from manuscript in my possession made by one Patrick O'Pronty (an ancestor, I think, of Charlotte Brontë) in 1763.'

31 Another famous saga of the Fenian Cycle.

32 Canon Ulick J. Bourke was born in County Galway in 1829. He was educated at St Jarlath's Seminary, Tuam, and at Maynooth. As a priest he returned to St Jarlath's where he was professor of Irish for many years. He was a regular contributor of items in Irish to the local newspaper, the *Tuam News,* and had a special fount of Irish type cast for his use. He was a founder member of The Society for the Preservation of the Irish Language and helped in the preparation of the three 'Irish Books' for learners issued by the society. He also published an Irish grammar (number 74 in Hyde's main list).

33 This point is developed in chapter V.

34 Máirín Ní Mhuiríosa: *Réamhchonraitheoirí.* Dublin, 1968, pp. 7 ff.

35 It is difficult to say whether or not this was the occasion when Hyde first became a member of the Society for the Preservation of the Irish Language. About three weeks after his first contact with the society in June 1877 the following entries occur in the diary:
   9 July Yesterday I had a letter from Mr Russell, the gentleman I met

in Dublin. He said he would be grateful if I could get money for the society. The letter was written in Irish, and in Irish characters. 10 July I answered Mr Russell's letter as well as I could in Irish likewise. Russell's appeal was evidently for members and subscriptions. It is unclear whether or not Hyde himself joined at that time.

36 *The Green Book, or Gleanings From The Writing-Desk of A Literary Agitator,* by John Cornelius O'Callaghan. (Dublin, T. O'Gorman, 35 Upper Ormond Quay; London, C. Dolman, 1841).

37 The *Irishman* and the *Shamrock* were two of the English-language weeklies in which David Comyn succeeded in having a Gaelic corner established; he himself undertook to provide the material. Hyde contributed over a hundred poems in Irish to those columns, mainly between the years 1872 and 1884. For details see ' Aguisín le Clár Saothair an Chraoibhín ' by Professor Tomás de Bhaldraithe in *Galvia,* Vols. I-IV (1954-57) pp. 18-24.

CHAPTER III

1 Cambrett O'Kane was a neighbour and a friend of the family. Some years later he married Douglas's only sister, Annette.

2 ' Farewell, farewell to you, County Mayo '. It is interesting to note that Hyde was aware of his inadequacy as a singer. Mary O'Neill, writing in the *Irish Independent,* 19 July 1949, recalls some memories of Hyde as Professor of Irish at University College, Dublin: '. . . I remember the shock to my fresh-from-a-convent musically attuned ear of that tuneless lilting, and the horror of realisation that the Professor had " no ear ".'

3 A drinking song, ' Let us clink glasses. . . .'

4 Oldfield was now an officer in the Royal Irish Constabulary.

5 Miss Frances Crofton was Hyde's first sweetheart. He courted her all through his student days, but eventually they decided quite amicably not to get married. She appears throughout the diaries as ' F.C.'

6 This was one of the stories in *Leabhar Sgéulaigheachta,* Hyde's first book published by Gill in Dublin, 1889. He gives his source as: ' from a spealadóir [mower] named Máirtín Ó Brianáin '. A translation of the story was among Hyde's contributions to Yeats's *Fairy and Folk Tales of the Irish Peasantry* (1888).

7 *English Literature,* Vol. II (listed at the end of the year).

8 ' The Irish Society for Promoting the Education of the Native Irish, through the medium of their own Language ', commonly known as ' The Irish Society ', was established in 1818. The need for the Society arose from the fact that the Irish country people treated with distaste and suspicion the English-language publications of earlier proselytising groups. Indeed, the Irish Society played unashamedly on the naïve devotion of the countryman to his native language: '. . . when the English language is rejected, and its Scriptures are denounced as heretical, we are compelled to offer them instruction in the language which they so enthusiastically love that they refuse—they suspect—nothing that is offered to them in it; a language so hallowed in their eyes, that it is supposed to be incapable of conveying either heresy or error.'

The Society kept up relentless pressure to have Irish recognized as a subject at Trinity College and to ensure that students of Divinity should be encouraged to acquire a knowledge of the language for use in their ministry among the Irish-speaking population. In *1838* the Society jubilantly announced that the desired change had taken place: ' It has been often reasonably demanded, why has there hitherto been no Professorship in the University. It is indeed with the greatest pleasure that we can now announce, that the College has obliterated that reproach, and the Board has unanimously acquiesced in a memorial presented to them, for the establishing in it of a Professorship of the Irish tongue.'

See *History of the Origin and Progress of the Irish Society* by Henry Joseph Monck Mason, LL.D. Second edition, Dublin, Goodwin, Son & Nethercott, printers, 1846; also *Reasons and Authorities and Facts afforded by the history of the Irish Society, respecting the duty of employing the Irish language as a more general medium for conveying Scriptural Instruction to the native peasantry of Ireland*. Fourth edition, Goodwin, Son & Nethercott, 1838.

9 On 17 January he writes: ' My birthday. Alas and alack, how quickly the time passes. My eyes were very painful and I could not read much.'

10 James Sheehan from Cork, who later became a barrister.

11 It is interesting to note that Hyde had begun to frequent the Young Ireland Society in York Street as early as the spring of 1884, twelve months before John O'Leary returned to Dublin from his exile in Paris. This is, of course, the society to which W. B. Yeats refers in *Autobiographies* (1966, pp. 99 ff.).

An unpublished (and hitherto, I believe, unnoticed) minute-book of the society is in Captain McGlinchey's invaluable collection of historical and literary manuscripts. At the weekly meetings papers were read and discussed. Typical subjects were ' Means to Freedom ' (' pointing out the very important part education plays in the re-generation of a country and the effects it would inevitably produce on the minds of a people struggling to be free '); ' Writers and Writing ' (' principally as applied to our own country, and advocating the formation of local clubs to foster a taste for national literature '); ' Edmund Burke, Irishman '; ' Nationalism and Internationalism '; ' Emmet's Legacy to Ireland '; ' The Parliaments of Ireland ' (by J. F. Taylor) and ' Thoughts on Modern National Movement ' (by T. W. Rolleston).

Opposite the minutes of the meeting on 30 October 1885, the following list of names and addresses occurs—presumably those of new members:

C. H. Oldham	17 Waterloo Road
R. I. Lipmann	70 Marlboro "
F. I. Gregg	60 Eccles Street
W. B. Yeats	10 Ashfield Terrace
John R. Eyre	8 Holles Street
W. Stockley	79 Palmerston Road
J. Stockley	"

The six names surrounding that of Yeats are those of Trinity men, all close friends of Douglas Hyde.

Another interesting point from the minute-book is that W. B. Yeats and John McBride were present at meetings in 1885; this was probably the first time they met.

12 Charles Hubert Oldham, B.A. (1860-1926) was the best man of his year at Trinity College, Dublin. He graduated with a senior moderatorship and large gold medal in experimental physics and a senior moderatorship and gold medal in mathematics. In 1886 he founded the Protestant Home Rule Association, and was a frequent speaker at political meetings. He was called to the Irish Bar and went on the northern circuit; later, on the establishment of the Rathmines School of Commerce he was appointed principal. In 1909 he became the first professor of Commerce in the National University of Ireland, and in 1916 he was promoted to the Chair of National Economics in the University, a position he held until his death. His published work includes *Economic Development in Ireland* and *Finances in Ireland*.

He also established the Contemporary Club which will be considered in chapter IV. In 1890 he collaborated with Maud Gonne in the publication of Ellen O'Leary's posthumous volume of verse, *Lays of Country, Home and Friends.*

13 The *Review* had, as Katherine Tynan puts it, ' the crowning glory of introducing W. B. Yeats to the world ', while Oldham had the distinction of introducing Yeats to Miss Tynan: ' Sometime in the Spring of 1885 I had a letter from Mr Charles Hubert Oldham, a young Trinity College man who was about to start the *Dublin University Review,* asking me to help him. Such a request gave me great pleasure in those days. I contributed a poem to an early number, after which Mr Oldham came to see me and told me about Willie Yeats and his father, showing me the *Island of Statues,* Willie Yeats's first considerable poem, which he had acquired for the new magazine. Presently Mr Oldham came to see me accompanied by Willie Yeats. . . .'

(Katherine Tynan, *Memories.* London, 1924, p. 276, and *Twenty-Five Years,* London, 1918, pp. 140-43).

14 T. W. Rolleston was another notable Protestant nationalist. With Stopford A. Brooke he edited *A Treasury of Irish Poetry* (1900). His other published works include *Ueber Wordsworth und Walt Whitman* (1883), *The Teaching of Epictetus* (1886), *A Life of lessing* (1889) and *Grashalme, von Walt Whitman,* translated in collaboration with Karl Knorts (1899). Yeats described his ' Dead at Clonmacnoise ', a translation from an old Gaelic original, as ' an example of the Gaelic lyric come close to perfection '. See also Yeats's remarkable description of Rolleston in *Autobiographies* (1966), p. 170.

15 Stephen Gwynn, whose father was Archbishop King's Lecturer in Divinity at TCD, second to Dr Salmon the Regius Professor. Gwynn himself recalls (*Irish Literature and Drama,* London, 1936, p. 117) such evenings at Dowden's: ' Dowden, of old Protestant stock among the business community of Cork City, was by tradition and conviction strongly Unionist; indeed he took a more prominent political part than any of the other professors. Nevertheless he became a chief rallying point for the new literary movement, whose movers were all strongly nationalist in sympathy. At his house Yeats, then a youth of eighteen to twenty, was a constant guest on Sunday afternoons—often with his father, most brilliant of talkers; [Douglas] Hyde was often present, a former pupil of Dowden's in Trinity, as was also another of the group, T. W. Rolleston. These men

were five or six years older than Yeats; so also was Charles Hubert Oldham, a student of economics in whose rooms opposite the front gate of College the " Contemporary Club " met every Monday night. . . .'

16 O'Grady's description of democracy itself, 'this waste, dark, howling mass of colliding interests, mad about the main chance—the pence-counting shopkeeper, the publican . . .' etc., may well have been some-where in Yeats's memory when he wrote years later of 'Paudeen's pence' and 'Biddy's halfpennies', and the hucksters who 'fumble in a greasy till'.

17 W. B. Yeats, *Poems,* London, 1895, [Notes]. Reprinted in *Collected Poems,* London, Macmillan, 1965, p. 523.

18 See Yeats's Introduction to his *Book of Irish Verse,* where he describes these Gaelic poets of Munster as 'poor wastrels who put the troubles of their native land, or their own happy or unhappy loves, into songs of an extreme beauty. But in the midst of this beauty is a flitting incoherence, a fitful dying out of the sense. . . .'

19 Hyde gives, in each case, the actual Gaelic lines, followed by his own translation.

20 See W. B. Yeats, 'The Secret Rose' (*Collected Poems,* 1965, p. 76):
    A woman of so shining loveliness
    That men threshed corn at midnight by a tress,
    A little stolen tress.

21 The editor by this time was T. W. Rolleston, while C. H. Oldham con-tinued as Managing Director.

22 In the preface to his *Literary History of Ireland* (1899), p. xxxviii, Hyde refers to the neglect of Irish studies at Trinity College: '. . . had the unique manuscript treasures now shut up in cases in the underground room of Trinity College Library, been deposited in any other seat of learning in Europe, in Paris, Rome, Vienna, or Berlin, there would long ago have been trained up scholars to read them, a catalogue of them would have been published, and funds would have been found to edit them. At present the Celticists of Europe are placed under the great dis-advantage of having to come over to Dublin University to do the work that it is not doing for itself.'

23 From his booklist we know that Hyde had firsthand knowledge of almost all the authors mentioned here. He is inaccurate, however, in including Petrie among those who spoke Irish naturally from the cradle.

24 Apart from these two long articles he contributed a couple of poems in Irish. In the August 1885 number 'Smaointe Bhron' [*sic*]. i.e. 'Sad Thoughts', appeared, on the depopulation of the countryside through emigration; and, in May 1886, 'Riaghail Éireannach in Éirinn', in praise of Home Rule as a deliverance from English misrule.

25 On 30 January 1886, at the end of a long report on discussions at the club (on landlordism, free trade, etc.; no mention of education), Hyde adds the following note:
    'I now believe there is no better solution to the question of the colleges in Ireland than that the Romans should have their own college for the sciences and that this college [Trinity] should remain in the hands of the Protestants, but that the professional schools, medicine, engineering, law, etc., should be common to the two faiths. That should satisfy the Romans.'

26 Michael Davitt was co-founder, with Charles Stewart Parnell, of the Land

League in 1879, and one of the prime movers in what was known as 'the new departure' in Irish politics, the coming together of revolutionaries and constitutionalists for the common goal of national independence. See *The Life of Charles Stewart Parnell* by R. Barry O'Brien (London; Thomas Nelson and Sons, 1910), p. 140.

27   Probably Lord Russell of Killowen (1832-1900), the Irish Catholic lawyer who became Lord Chief Justice of England. He was a brother of Fr Matthew Russell, editor of the *Irish Monthly*.

28   Charles Bradlaugh (1833-1891), elected M.P. for Northampton in 1880, declined to take the oath on the grounds that he was a professed atheist; he asked to be allowed to make an affirmation of allegiance instead. The legal wrangle that ensued lasted ten years. At one stage he stood for election at Finsbury. See *Charles Bradlaugh : a record of his life and work*, by his daughter Hypathia Bradlaugh Bonner. (London, T. Fisher Unwin, 1894).

29   Alfred Webb, M.P. compiler of *A Compendium of Irish Biography* (Dublin, 1878) and *The Opinions of Some Protestants regarding their Irish Catholic Fellow-Countrymen*. Second enlarged edition, Dublin, 1886.

30   Pledge number two is evidently a combination of the second and third.

31   'Standish James O'Grady', *Colby Library Quarterly*, Series IV, November 1958. See also George Moore's picture of O'Grady in *Ave* (London, 1911), p. 143.

32   See Lady Gregory, 'Ireland Real and Ideal' in *The Nineteenth Century* (November 1898): 'Dignity and power of expression were to a great extent lost with the tongue that, like all other tongues, expressed the spirit of the race. It went out of fashion. Priests ceased to preach in it and peasants to pray in it.'

33   This pessimistic note was struck seven years before the founding of the Gaelic League.

CHAPTER IV

1   Hyde's introduction to a selection of Sigerson's poems in *A Treasury of Irish Poetry in the English tongue* edited by Stopford A. Brooke and T. W. Rolleston. London, 1900.

2   'Gael' is the Irish word for the native race; 'Gall' means 'a foreigner'.

3   Friedrich Lipmann, a Russian, was a student with Hyde at Trinity, and was at this time living at the Russell Hotel, Stephen's Green. Katherine Tynan describes him as 'a little Russian with a small, wistful Calmuck face'. (*Twenty-five Years*, p. 245). He was also a devotee of William Morris. His subsequent history has the ingredients of a novel: he borrowed money from Morris and others, went to New York where he was accepted in the most exclusive social circles as Count Zubov, a Russian nobleman, and was about to marry a millionairess when he was recognized and exposed, whereupon he committed suicide. Yeats writes of him to Miss Tynan, 27 February 1890: 'I don't understand that poor wretch Lippman, there was little real bad at the heart of him in the days we knew him— It must be a kind of mania—some queer thing awry in his imagination.' (*Letters*, p. 149).

4   George Coffey (1857-1916) was a very close friend of Hyde's at TCD. His
    subject was archaeology and later he became Keeper of Antiquities in the
    National Museum. He published several papers in *Transactions of the
    Royal Irish Academy,* and in the *Journal of the Society of Antiquaries.*

5   Charles Johnston of Ballykilbeg, County Down. Although his father was
    head of the Orangemen in Ulster, Charles and his brother and sister (see
    7 December entry) were quite at home among the young Dublin nation-
    alists. He is, of course, the young man with whom Yeats explored the
    mysteries of Odic Force and Esoteric Buddhism (Yeats, *Autobiographies,*
    1966, pp. 90 ff.)

6   John F. Taylor was a barrister, called to both Irish and English bars. He
    wrote a biography of Owen Roe O'Neill which was published in the
    'New Irish Library' Series (1896). Yeats has many references to Taylor's
    exceptional powers as an orator, but there was an instinctive hostility
    between the two men, while Hyde had a great affection for Taylor. ' Rí-
    fhear ', ' a king among men ', he calls him.

7   James Sheehan, another very close friend of Hyde's College days, also
    became a barrister.

8   *United Ireland,* the official organ of the Land League, was edited by
    William O'Brien. The paper was suppressed and the editor imprisoned
    during the Land War.

9   When Cardinal Newman's attempt to found a Catholic University failed,
    mainly for want of endowment, the bishops of Ireland eventually called
    upon the Jesuits to take over the management of a new University College
    in the same buildings in Stephen's Green. [See *A Page of Irish History :
    Story of University College Dublin 1883-1909.* Compiled by Fathers of
    the Society of Jesus. Dublin and Cork, Talbot Press, 1930. On page 120
    one finds the following interesting recollections of the first students:

    ' Professor Donovan adds there was not at this time so much association
    with the Medical School as came in later years. But he and some of his
    friends were brought into touch with Trinity College through the kindly
    offices of Dr Douglas Hyde, who had rooms there, and used to invite
    Catholic University students to tea and introduce them to some of the
    undergraduates.']

10 Archbishop William Walsh (1841-1921), by his speeches and writings, had
    a powerful influence on the two great controversies in Anglo-Irish politics
    at this time: the land question (tenants' rights and fair rents) and
    education for Catholics. The reference here is probably to an interview he
    gave to the *Pall Mall Gazette,* 2 December 1886, which became a talking
    point on both sides of the Irish sea. The archbishop expressed qualified
    approval of the ' Plan of Campaign ', according to which tenants, having
    made reasonable but unsuccessful overtures to their landlord for reduction
    of rent because of general depression, would withhold such rents and pay
    what they considered a fair rent into the ' Campaign Fund ', to be given
    to the landlord if he agreed or else used as a fighting fund.

11 John O'Mahony (1815-1877) was one of the outstanding figures of the
    Young Ireland movement and of the Fenian organization which succeeded
    it. He spent the last twenty-four years of his life in America where he
    died in poverty. Hyde's special regard for O'Mahony was due in large
    measure to the latter's keen interest in the Irish language. At the top of
    Hyde's list of Anglo-Irish books is O'Mahony's translation of Keating's

History of Ireland, a scholarly work which brought its translator little but ill-health and disappointment. Because of a technical breach of copyright (O'Mahony had used, and fully acknowledged, notes from John O'Donovan's *Annals of the Four Masters*) the sale of the book in Ireland was prohibited.

The poem is printed in *Poems and Ballads of Young Ireland,* (1888) and in *Dublin Verses by Members of Trinity College,* edited by H. A. Hinkson (who married Katherine Tynan) and published in 1895:

In a foreign land, in a lonesome city,
With few to pity, or know, or care,
I sleep each night while my heart is burning
And wake each morning to new despair.

Let no one venture to ask my story
Who believes in glory or trusts to fame;
Yes! I have within me such demons in keeping
As are better sleeping without a name.

From many a day of blood and horror
And night of terror and work of dread,
I have rescued nought but my honour only,
And this aged, lonely, and whitening head.

Not a single hope have I seen fulfilled
For the blood we spilled when we cast the die,
And the future I painted in brightness and pride
Has the present belied, and shall still belie.

In this far-off country, this city dreary,
I languished weary, and sad, and sore.
Till the flower of youth in glooms o'ershaded
Grew seared, and faded for evermore.

Oh my land! from thee driven—our old flag furled—
I renounced the world when I went from thee;
My heart lingers on its native strand
And American land holds nought for me.

Through a long life contriving, hoping, striving,
Driven and driving, leading and led,
I have rescued nought but my honour only
And this aged, lonely, and whitening head.

In *The Middle Years* Katherine Tynan refers to ' Douglas Hyde's fine poem on John O'Mahony the Fenian which I have heard John O'Leary say exactly mirrored the mind of him whom Douglas Hyde had never known.' (p. 22)

12 Yeats by this time had had several poems published in the *Dublin University Review.*

13 It is interesting to compare Katherine Tynan's account of what was probably the same visit, although she says her companion was Rose Kavanagh. Miss Tynan was writing many years after the event, and her reminiscences are not always accurate:
'There was a day when we had tea with Douglas Hyde in Trinity College. Perhaps Craoibhin Aoibhin (pronounced Creeveen Eeveen—i.e. the dear little nut-branch) was at his least inspiring within the walls of his Alma Mater, which was no more motherly to the future lighter of the Gaelic torch in Ireland than she had been to any other of her great sons. I recall the event without any glow of pleasure. It seems to have been a somewhat conventional entertainment, which was not often the case with anything in which Douglas Hyde took a hand.' (*Twenty-five Years*, London, 1913, p. 207.)

14 Preface to 'Cuchulain of Muirthemne' (1902), reprinted in *Explorations*, London, 1962, p. 13.

15 John O'Leary's speech in Cork, quoted by Hyde in *Mise agus an Connradh*, p. 29.

16 W. B. Yeats, 'Popular Ballad Poetry of Ireland', in *The Leisure Hour*, November 1889. The article was written in 1887; see Yeats's *Letters* (Wade), p. 48.

17 See, for example, Yeats's preface to his *A Book of Irish Verse* (1895) and his introduction to the *Oxford Book of Modern Verse* (1936), p. xiv.

18 'Yeats annsin gur bhain se an ceann diom beag nach len a chaint.' Literally: 'Yeats there; he nearly took the head off me with his talk.'

19 French *frac*, a dress-coat.

20 This, of course, is AE, George Russell (1867-1935).

21 At the end of 1888 Hyde has in his booklist 'Hannah Lynch's Defeated' which is probably the novel referred to. It is not in the catalogue of the National Library but under the name Lynch (Hannah) appear *Autobiography of a Child* (1899) *French Life in Town and Country* (1901) and *Toledo* (1898).

22 The capitals and punctuation are as given. It looks as if the last sentence was written first.
William Larminie (1850-1900), another pioneer of the literary revival. He published *Glanlua and other poems* (1889), *Fand and Moytura* (1892), *West Irish Folk-Tales* (1894). A peculiarity of his verse is his use of Gaelic assonance; he hoped to see the practice adopted by writers of English verse. He also had original ideas on Gaelic spelling.

23 There is no suggestion in the diary that Miss Hull ever disliked Hyde. He may mean that he has got to know her better, which is something he would wish for, Miss Hull being, as he says elsewhere, 'the most intelligent and best educated girl in Dublin' (20 March 1889).
Miss Eleanor Hull was daughter of Professor Edward Hull. She was born in Manchester and was for some years a member of the London Irish Literary Society. She became an outstanding Irish scholar; among her best known works are *The Cuchullin Saga* (1898), *A Textbook of Irish History* (1906), *The Poem Book of the Gael* (1912), *A History of Ireland and her People,* 2 vols. (1926-31).

24 M. H. Gill and Son, printers and publishers, who produced Hyde's *Leabhar Sgéulaigheachta* the following year. An indication that the

manuscript was not yet complete is the fact that when the book did appear it was a volume of vii + 261 pages.

25 John Boyle O'Reilly (1844-1890). Arrested in 1860 for his part in the Fenian movement, he was transported to western Australia. He escaped and made his way to the United States where he became a naturalized American citizen. He turned to journalism and eventually became owner-editor of the *Boston Pilot,* in the columns of which he published the work of the Irish literary nationalists mentioned in this chapter.

It is unlikely that Hyde was paid for his contributions to the *Dublin University Review,* the *Gael* or the *Irish Monthly.*

26 There is a story behind this reference to Stockley's song. Long before, when John Kells Ingram was a twenty-year-old student at Trinity College, he had written a ballad that quickly became, and to this day remains, one of the most popular of Irish nationalist songs. Ingram went on to become Professor of Oratory and English Literature, Regius Professor of Greek, Librarian, Senior Fellow and finally Vice-Provost of Trinity College. All this seems incongruous to the soul-stirring sentiments of the lyric which first appeared in the *Nation* on 1 April 1843 (the author had dropped it, anonymously, into the *Nation* letterbox). However, as late as 1900 Ingram included it in a slim volume of his verses entitled *Sonnets and other poems* and in the 'Prefatory Note' to the reader he declared: '. . . " The Memory of the Dead " was my only contribution to the *Nation.* It has already been printed with my name in several collections of Irish verse. I have reproduced it here, though differing in character and date from the other pieces in the volume, because some persons have believed, or affected to believe, that I am ashamed of having written it and would gladly, if I could, disclaim its authorship. Those who know me need not be told that this idea is without foundation. I think the Irish race should be grateful to the men who in other times, however mistaken may have been their policy, gave their lives for their country. But I have no sympathy with those who preach sedition in our own day when all the circumstances are radically altered. In my opinion no real popular interest can be furthered by violence.'

27 John O'Leary was a great collector of books, and very generous with them. See Maud Gonne, *A Servant of the Queen,* p. 87; Yeats, *Autobiographies* (1966) p. 101 etc.

28 The Pan-Celtic Society was founded in Dublin on 1 March 1888. The prime movers were Gerald C. Pelly and Augustine F. Downey, two medical students, and Matthew Daly Wyer, B.L. It was a non-political, non-sectarian literary society, membership of which was restricted to those who had previously published a story, essay, poem or sketch in a recognized Irish magazine or newspaper. John and Ellen O'Leary, Dr Sigerson, Dr Todhunter, Rose Kavanagh and Douglas Hyde himself were among its members. A volume of verse entitled *Lays and Lyrics of the Pan-Celtic Society* was published in 1889, though not officially by the society but as a private venture by one of the members, A. R. Stritch. The Pan-Celtic Society was the forerunner of the National Literary Society established in 1892, into which most of its members were absorbed. (See ' The Pan-Celtic Movement ' in *The Irish Literary Revival* by W. P. Ryan. London, 1894.)

29 ' Go teac Shigerson san trathnóna 'náit a connairc me an bhean budh éblouissante d'á bhfacas ariamh, i. Miss Gonne, a cruinnigh an méad a bhí

fiorann san rúma ann a timchioll, B'ionghantach ard & breagh í. . . . Bhi
suran ann mo cheann le na breághact! !'

30 Miss Ida Jameson, of the famous distillery family, was a close friend of
Maud Gonne, and a nationalist.

31 Miss Sarah Purser (1848-1943), the distinguished portrait painter. Her
portrait of Maud Gonne hangs in the Dublin Municipal Gallery. She was the
first woman member of the Royal Hibernian Academy.

32 William James O'Doherty, by profession a civil engineer, was a keen anti-
quarian and member of the Royal Irish Academy. Among his published
work was *Inis-Owen and Tirconnell, being some account of Antiquities and
Writers of the County of Donegal.* Dublin, 1891 and 1895.

33 'The Signorina' was Hyde's pet name for one of the sisters of his late
friend 'Mackey' Wilson.

34 Hyde later made quite a name for himself as a comic actor in his own
Gaelic plays. W. B. Yeats in *Samhain : 1902* (reprinted in *Explorations,*
London, 1962) p. 86, in reference to a production of his own *Cathleen
ni Houlihan* writes: 'They had Miss Maud Gonne's help, and it was a
fine thing for so beautiful a woman to consent to play my poor old
Cathleen, and she played with nobility and tragic power. She showed herself
as good in tragedy as Dr Hyde is in comedy, and stirred a large audience
very greatly.'

35 Michael Cusack, founder of the Gaelic Athletic Association.

36 Henry A. Hinkson, who married Katherine Tynan in 1893. The 'Royal'
was The Royal University, founded by the Royal University Act of August
1879. It was not a university in the accepted sense of the word but rather
an examining body. It was abolished by the National University Act of 1908.

37 See Maud Gonne MacBride, *A Servant of the Queen* (Dublin, 1950, pp. 93-94):
'Douglas Hyde, a student in Trinity, believed in the language to free
Ireland; to me the method seemed too slow : under his tuition I learned a
sentence or two with which to begin my speeches, because it was almost
a criminal offence to speak Irish and in Gaelic-speaking districts children in
the schools were being beaten for using it and people prosecuted for writing
their names over their shops in Irish, but I could never learn a language
except through hearing it constantly spoken and in Dublin no one spoke it
and I was too constantly travelling from one place to another, trying to
spread revolutionary thoughts and acts, to sit down to the arduous task of
learning a language. So Douglas Hyde never succeeded in making me an
Irish speaker any more than I succeeded in making him a revolutionist.'

38 This song, especially the Irish version, 'Féach tá sinn-ne Clann na
hÉireann', gained wide popularity. See W. B. Yeats, *Autobiographies* (1966)
p. 217: 'He had already—though intellectual Dublin knew nothing of it—
considerable popularity as a Gaelic poet, mowers and reapers singing his
songs from Donegal to Kerry. Years afterwards I was to stand at his side and
listen to Galway mowers singing his Gaelic words without their knowing
whose words they sang.'

39 It is not clear whether it was the Club itself or Hyde's speech that so
affected Mrs Maunsell.

40 See note 32.

41 'The Fate of the Sons of Lir', one of the 'Three Sorrows of Story-telling'
in Irish mythology. Hyde's work on the trilogy will be discussed in the
next chapter.

42 In his *Leabhar Sgéulaigheachta* there are three stories which he took down from 'Eadbhard Loingseach Blácach', (Edward Lynch Blake), whom he describes as 'one of the best shanachies (story-tellers) in Connacht, or in Ireland.' The Stories, 'Cailleacha na Fiacla Fada', 'Colann gan Cheann' and 'Cúirt an Chronnáin' are translated into English in *Beside The Fire*.

43 It was from 'an old woman named Biddy Cussrooee (or Crummey in English), who was living in a hut in the midst of a bog in the County Roscommon' that Hyde got the well-known 'Mo Bhrón Ar An bhFairrge', which he translated so exquisitely as 'My Grief on the Sea'. See *Love Songs of Connacht* (Fifth ed., 1909) p. 29, and note, p. 151. (In another notebook he records that he got the poem from an old woman in Baile 'n Locha in December 1877, having already written down some verses of it from a neighbour, Mrs O'Rourke.)

44 *Tales of the Western Highlands.*

45 Another seanchaí from whom he got several stories.

46 Pousse-café.

It is interesting to note that Hyde's account of the stay in Paris is written in Irish, French and German, in roughly equal proportions. The reason, or perhaps I should say the occasion, for the German is that they lodged with a Miss Puskas, a German, at 22 Avenue Carnot, 'tout près de l'arc de triomphe et pas plus q'un quart d'heure de l'Exposition dans le champ de Mars.' Here he turns to German: 'It was a certain Miss Puskas who, with other Germans, owned the house or the flat. They could not speak English, only French or German. Two other German women also lived with them and only German was spoken during the meals, which F.C. found disagreeable as she did not understand it. All these ladies hated the French and the young ones who were Prussian had to dissimulate this dislike. Otherwise they would have met with insults and incivility. We had three rooms and a salon and were very comfortable.'

As an example of his French I give his account of 26 June: 'Nous avons consacré ce jour-ci à l'Ascension de la tour Eiffel (Effel deirid). Nous l'avons commencé a 10.30 est il a pris cinq heures pour monter et pour descendre. La foule était enorme, le chaleur suffoquant! Nous sommes montés avec l'Ascensoir, et il faut changer d'Ascensoir trois fois. aprés être arrivé au premièr étage il fallait y rester une heure à la queue du monde qui voulait monter, et au deuxième étage nous avons attendu deux heures avant de pouvoir entrer l'ascensoir. Nous avons assez souffert, et j'aimerais pas à le recommencer. Après être descendu, plus morts que vivants, nous avons très peu fait, après avoir diné au bouillon Duval nous sommes rentré, bien fatigués. Ní chuimhnighim cad é an chaoi ar chaitheamar an trathnóna.' (I do not remember how we spent the evening.)

47 'Smaointe Bhróin' (Sad Thoughts) was a poem he published in the *Dublin University Review,* August 1885.

48 The story appears in *Beside The Fire*.

49 Timothy Charles Harrington (1851-1910). As Secretary of the National League he devised the 'Plan of Campaign' for the land war. He was an M.P. from 1883 to 1910, and Lord Mayor of Dublin 1901-1904. John Redmond (1856-1918) was Parnell's chief supporter after the split, and leader of the Parnellites after 1891 when Parnell died.

50 Richard Ashe King (1839-1932), a graduate of TCD, had been vicar of

Low Moor, Bradford. He resigned and took to literary work full-time. He wrote many novels.

51 Fr Edmund Hogan, S.J., a distinguished Irish scholar, professor at the Catholic University College. Hyde acknowledges Fr Hogan's assistance on the history of Irish as a spoken language in his *Literary History of Ireland* (Preface, p. xl).

52 This lecture is among the Hyde papers now in the National Library. It is headed 'Essay on Irish Folklore, written December 1889, Dublin' and consists of forty-two pages of copybook, about 6,000 words.

53 Leading figures in the Pan-Celtic Society.

54 Fr Eugene O'Growney was a colleague of Hyde's in the Gaelic Union. Among other services to the Irish language he prepared a series of simple grammars which were immensely popular. He died in California, whither he had been sent in the hope that the climate would suit his chest condition. His body was brought back for a solemn Requiem Mass in Maynooth College, after which Hyde, as he relates in *Mise agus An Connradh*, kissed the coffin in a last farewell.

55 Hyde dedicated his *Story of Early Gaelic Literature* (1895) to 'the memory of my late dear friends The Rev Euseby D. Cleaver, of Dolgelly, North Wales, and Father James Keegan, of St Louis, U.S.A., whose life-long, far-reaching, persistent and unselfish efforts to stem the ever-increasing Anglicisation of our race, have earned the warm gratitude of all those Irishmen who do not desire to see our ancient Irish nation sink into a West Britain.'

CHAPTER V

1 Quotations are from the preface to *Beside the Fire*, except where otherwise noted.

2 Hyde nevertheless comes very close to such a translation in *Beside the Fire* ('The Tailor and the Three Beasts', p. 11):
> They went to their dinner then, and when they had it eaten, the giant asked the tailor 'would it come with him to swallow as much broth as himself, up out of the boiling.' The tailor said: 'It will come with me to do that, but that you must give me an hour before we begin on it.'

3 W. B. Yeats, *Samhain : 1902*, reprinted in *Explorations*, London, 1962.

4 A shanachie (Irish 'seanchaí') is a traditional storyteller.
Seamus Ó h-Airt (James Hart) was the gamekeeper from whom Hyde gained his first knowledge of Irish (See chapter I).

5 'tráithnín . . . a strong blade of grass, a withered stalk of meadow grass' (Dinneen's *Irish-English Dictionary*).

6 'sídheóg, a fay or fairy' (ibid). Hyde uses the two different spellings 'sheehogues' and 'sheeogues' in this piece.

7 'Guleesh na Guss Dhu', the longest story in *Beside the Fire*. The extract I have given is on page 123.

8 Not to be confused with the journal of the same title published in New York. *The Gael* here referred to was a weekly paper published in Dublin by the Gaelic Athletic Association. The editor was P. T. Hoctor, a prominent member of the Young Ireland Society, while John O'Leary was in charge of a section devoted to literature, to which people such as W. B.

Yeats, T. W. Rolleston, Katherine Tynan, Ellen O'Leary as well as Hyde himself are known to have contributed.

Strange to say, no file of this journal, which should be of such interest to students of the Anglo-Irish literary movement, seems to have survived. Indeed, up to recently all that was known to exist of it were some odd cuttings.

Hyde's diary for 16 January 1888 reads: ' My article on " Unpublished Literature " was printed in *The Gael,* and I sent copies to Miss Hull, Miss Stewart Smith, F.C., Sheehan, Mulrennin, M. Close, Cleaver, Larminie, the two Stockleys, Hewetson, Flannery, and a few other people, O'Neill Russell, Lyster, etc. . . .'

I failed to find any trace of the Dublin *Gael* in either the British Museum or the National Library in Dublin. One day in conversation with Mr James Scully, assistant in charge of newspapers at the National Library, I was lamenting the total disappearance of this interesting little journal when to my surprise he informed me that one single issue had come to light in a recently acquired bundle of old newspapers. I waited, scarcely daring to hope, while he went to fetch his precious find and then, by an extraordinary coincidence he laid before me a copy of the *Gael* for 7 January 1888. There, sure enough, under the Gothic heading ' Literature ', I found an article of eight columns entitled ' Some Words About Unpublished Literature'. The article is unsigned, but at the bottom of the final column, in a rough scrawl which is very likely that of John O'Leary, is pencilled ' D. Hyde '. (The issue is No. 38, Vol. 1, which suggests that the likely date of the first issue is 26 March 1887. It ran for about two years.)

9 *The Spirit of the Nation,* a collection of songs and ballads which had appeared in the *Nation* newspaper, was first published in two parts in 1843. It became one of the most popular collections of verse ever published in Ireland; the fifty-ninth edition appeared in 1934.

10 Thomas Moore of the ' Melodies ' (1779-1852).

James Clarence Mangan (1803-1849).

Thomas Davis (1815-1845), patriot, poet, essayist, journalist (co-founder of the *Nation*), guiding spirit of the Young Ireland movement.

Gerald Griffin (1803-1839). Best known as the author of a novel, *The Collegians,* which was dramatized by Boucicault as *The Colleen Bawn* and on which Benedict's opera *The Lily of Killarney* is based. His most popular poems were ' Aileen Aroon ' and ' Adare '.

While suggesting that Hyde, in his lavish praise of these poets, is trimming his sails to the prevailing winds, mindful of the literary taste of readers of the *Gael,* at the same time Hyde, however he might eschew actual politics, was a practitioner of the art of the possible; if the ideal (a Gaelic literature) was unattainable, he would settle for the best alternative, preferring the work of these poets to the rude verses he had been discussing. Likewise, in his great speech on de-Anglicization which will be examined later, having earnestly urged the preservation of the native language, customs and traditions, he goes on to stress ' the necessity for encouraging the use of Anglo-Irish literature instead of English books, especially of English periodicals. We must set our face sternly against penny dreadfuls, shilling shockers, and still more, the garbage of vulgar English weeklies like *Bow Bells* and the *Police Intelligence.* Every house should have a copy of Moore and Davis.'

11 *Irish Minstrelsy,* an anthology of Irish verse in English compiled by Herbert Halliday Sparling and published by Walter Scott in 'The Canterbury Poets' series in 1887 (second, enlarged edition the following year). (An amusing example of Yeats's notoriously bad handwriting occurs in the *United Irishman,* 12 December 1891, where he refers to a poem of Allingham's being included in what the printer deciphers as 'sparkling Irish minstrelsy'.)

12 The *Irish Monthly* was a popular semi-religious, semi-literary magazine to which many of the young writers mentioned in the preceding chapter contributed. W. B. Yeats, in the course of a letter to a lady who had sent him some poems asking his opinion on them, wrote: 'You should send these poems to the *Irish Monthly,* the editor is the Rev Matthew Russell, St Francis Xavier's, Upper Gardiner Street, Dublin. The *Monthly* is the only literary magazine in Ireland and there is quite a bevy of poets gathered about it. The editor is a Catholic priest of a most courteous kindly and liberal mind . . . . Of course the *Monthly* does not pay for its verse. How few magazines do. But if you send these you will be in good company—all Irish writers of poetry, no matter of what persuasion, sooner or later seem to find their way thither.' The following day he wrote to tell Fr Russell what he had done: 'I dare say you will not thank me for sending another writer of verse to knock at your gate. But then, you know, you keep a kind of college of the bards.'

    (*The Letters of W. B. Yeats,* edited by Allan Wade. London 1954, pp. 104, 105.)

13 Lionel Johnson writes of 'the radiance of his [Mangan's] "Dark Rosaleen", its adoring, flashing, flying, laughing rapture of patriotic passion. It is among the great lyrics of the world, one of the fairest and fiercest in its perfection of imagery and rhythm; it is the chivalry of a nation's faith struck on a sudden into the immortality of music.' (Essay in the Centenary Edition of *The Prose Writings of James Clarence Mangan,* edited by D. J. O'Donoghue. Dublin and London, 1904, pp. xiii, xiv.)

14 'His poetry served magnificently the only purpose which he allotted to it, that of Nationality.' (Padraic Fallon, 'The Poetry of Thomas Davis', in *Thomas Davis and Young Ireland,* Dublin, 1945.)

15 This is almost certainly a passing shot at John O'Leary who, for all his patriotism, saw no value at all in the revival of Irish.

    He believed that the Irish language and literature should be left as a specialist field for scholars. See *Mise agus An Connradh,* p. 29. Ibid, p. 27, Hyde tells how Thomas Davis spent some time in Ballaghadereen, near Hyde's own home, in order to learn Irish, but that in fact he did not make much progress. In the *Nation,* however, Davis urged those of his readers who spoke Irish to value and preserve it. 'The language of a nation's youth is the only easy and full speech for its manhood and for its age. And when the language of the cradle goes, itself craves a tomb . . . . A people without a language of its own is only half a nation. A nation should guard its language more than its territories—'tis a surer barrier and more important frontier than fortress and river . . . .' Quoted in *The Young Irelanders* by T. F. O'Sullivan. Tralee, 1944, p. 451.

16 See Francis Thompson's review of the same anthology in the *Dublin Review,* Vol. XXI, 1889. '. . . We look in vain for Irish singers to companion Wordsworth, Coleridge, Shelley, and Keats . . . . A fact so patent would

seem to argue a racial defect; and on the whole the present volume, we reluctantly confess, impresses us as bearing out such a conclusion.'

17 Although he cannot remember the exact year; it was, he says, 1878 or 1879. It was some years later that he copied his poems into the black leather bound notebooks from which I am copying them.

18 'Tadhg Gaelach' was a Munster poet who composed mainly religious songs; he died in 1800. In his epitaph, written by a fellow Gaelic poet of Munster, Donncha Ruadh Mac Conmara, this feature of his work is emphasized:

> Laudando Dominum praeclara poemata fecit
> Et suaves hymnos angelus ille canet.

See *Religious Songs of Connacht,* Vol. I, p. 226.

19 Sir Samuel Ferguson made a translation from Gaelic that has the same refrain, but otherwise bears no resemblance to Hyde's. It is a surprising fact that Hyde does not seem to have been much influenced by Ferguson who did such similar work immediately before him. None of Ferguson's publications appear in Hyde's booklists.

20 It is interesting to note that in a later version of this song the period is 1867, and O'Donovan Rossa takes the place of Hyde's grandsire: 'And the dungeon flag was Rossa's bed . . .'

21 Apropos of the influence of Edward Walsh, compare his treatment of the same traditional song:

> Have you been at Carrick, and saw you my true-love there,
> And saw you her features, all beautiful, bright and fair?
> Saw you the most fragrant, flowery, sweet apple-tree?
> Oh, saw you my loved one, and pines she in grief like me?
>
> I have been at Carrick, and saw thy own true-love there;
> And saw, too, her features, all beautiful, bright and fair;
> And saw the most fragrant, flowering, sweet apple-tree—
> I saw thy loved one—she pines *not* in grief like thee.

Quoted in *A Treasury of Irish Poetry,* ed. Stopford Brooke and Rolleston, London, 1900. p. 101.

22 *The Three Sorrows of Story-telling and Ballads of St Columcille* by Douglas Hyde, LL.D., M.R.I.A. (An Craoibhín Aoibhinn). London, T. Fisher Unwin, 1895.

23 Hyde's *The Story of Early Gaelic Literature* was published by Fisher Unwin in the 'New Irish Library' series the same year. In it, on page 69, the following interesting footnote occurs, qualifying the statement, 'All the Irish world knows the story of Déirdre': 'Yet when in Trinity College, a few years ago, the subject—the first Irish subject for twenty-seven years—set for the Vice-Chancellor's prize in English verse was "Déirdre", it was found that the students did not know what that word meant, or what Déirdre was, whether animal, vegetable, or mineral. So true it is that, despite all the efforts of Davis and his fellows, there are yet two nations in Ireland. Trinity College might to some extent bridge the gap if she would, but she has not even attempted it.'

24 See diary entry for 17 September 1888 above. For Hyde's subsequent contri-

butions to the *Boston Pilot* and the *Providence Journal* between 1888 and 1893, see Horace Reynold's very interesting article, 'From the Little Branch to the New Island ', in the *Dublin Magazine,* Vol. 13, 1938.

25 For Mangan's translation see pp. 324-325, op. cit., fourth ed. Hyde numbers some of his verses as above; others are unnumbered. It is interesting too to compare Hyde's version with Lady Gregory's prose translation of the poem. This is to be found in *Poets and Dreamers* and also in *The Kiltartan Poetry Book* under the title ' A Blessing on Patrick Sarsfield '.

26 Ferguson's two epic poems, ' Congal ' and ' Conary ', despite their erudition and earnestness, lacked the enlivening spark; besides, the epic was out of fashion. Edmund Dowden remarked sympathetically to their author, ' A poem with epic breadth and thews is not likely to be popular now.'

27 This and the following statement are quoted from Lady Ferguson's biography of her husband, *Sir Samuel Ferguson in the Ireland of his day,* Edinburgh and London, 1896, Vol. II, pp. 291, 292.

28 Katherine Tynan, *The Wild Harp. A selection from Irish Poetry.* London, 1913, Introduction, p. xiv. See also Stephen Gwynn, *Irish Literature and Drama,* London, 1936, p. 121. ' The greatest service that Yeats rendered to Ireland was his persistent refusal to accept as admirable anything that was commended solely by patriotic or virtuous intention '.

29 Austin Clarke, *Poetry in Modern Ireland.* Dublin. First published in 1951. Second edition 1961, p. 16.

30 Irish *cúl,* back, back of the head; hence, head of hair. The Anglicized ' coolun ' is from ' cúil-fhionn ', a fair-haired, handsome person; a fair lady.

31 W. B. Yeats in *Samhain,* 1902, reprinted in *Explorations* (1962), p. 93.

32 *A Servant of the Queen,* Second edition, Dublin 1950, p. 94.

33 It was not his first appearance as an actor in a Gaelic piece, as Lady Gregory humorously recalls (*Poets and Dreamers,* p. 196): ' I hold that the beginning of modern Irish drama was in the winter of 1898, at a school feast at Coole, when Douglas Hyde and Miss Norma Borthwick acted in Irish in a Punch and Judy show and the delighted children went back to tell their parents what grand curses *An Craoibhín* had put on the baby and the policeman.'

34 See Lady Gregory, *Our Irish Theatre,* p. 75: (referring to Douglas Hyde) '. . . while staying here at Coole, as he did from time to time, he wrote *The Twisting of the Rope,* based on one of Mr Yeats's Hanrahan stories.' Of course Hyde was familiar with the story of the poet-suitor who was tricked into putting himself outside the door by twisting a straw rope; he gives it in *Love Songs of Connacht,* pp. 75-77, where he refers to a song of the same name in Hardiman's collection.

Hyde's account fits in with Lady Gregory's, and rules out Elizabeth Coxhead's surmise (*Lady Gregory,* 1966, p. 108), that it was Lady Gregory herself who supplied the scenario.

35 Written by Yeats and George Moore in uneasy collaboration. See Yeats, *Autobiographies* (1966), pp. 434 ff; and Moore, *Ave* (1911), pp. 344 ff.

36 ' na héadaigh ' could perhaps mean scenery, since the actors provided their own costumes.

37 ' báinínídh ' (bawneens): homespun clothes.

38 Lady Gregory, *Our Irish Theatre,* p. 30.

39 Some were first published, with translations by Lady Gregory, in Yeats's *Samhain : Casadh an tSugáin* in October 1901; *An Naomh ar Iarraidh* (The Missing Saint) in October 1902; *Teach na mBocht* (The Poorhouse) in

October 1903. The last mentioned, originally written in collaboration with Lady Gregory, was rewritten by Lady Gregory as *The Workhouse Ward* (1909). *An Tincéar agus an tSidheóg* (The Tinker and the Fairy) first appeared in the *New Ireland Review*, May 1902; *Pléusgadh na Bulgóide* (The Bursting of the Bubble), a skit on TCD, in the same *Review*, May 1903; *An Cleamhnas* (The Match) in *Irisleabhar na Gaedhilge*, the journal of the Gaelic Union, in December 1903. All were afterwards published separately.

40 *Samhain*, 1902, reprinted in *Explorations* (1962), p. 93.

41 *The Trembling of the Veil*, 1922, reprinted in *Autobiographies* (1966) p. 219.

42 Robert Farren, ' Douglas Hyde the Writer ', in the *Irish Press*, 14 July 1949.

CHAPTER VI

1 There is no mention of this elsewhere, but the year 1890 was exceptional in that he neglected his diary from mid-April on. This indicates how dull and unsatisfying he found life at that period. It is the only break of any-think like that length from 1874 to 1912.

2 John Boyle O'Reilly, editor of the *Pilot* who had published a number of Hyde's poems, died in 1890.

3 This ' Fraulein ' is not introduced or explained. She may have been a student at Fredericton.

4 Louise Imogen Guiney (1861-1920), born in Boston, Mass., of Irish parents. She published several volumes of poetry : *A Wayside Harp* (1895), *A Martyr's Idyll and Shorter Poems* (1899), etc., and a number of prose works. Before Hyde's meeting with her in Boston she had visited Ireland and met the young writers in Dublin; she had become a close friend of Katherine Tynan's. Hence the reference later to ' people of her acquaintance '.

5 Thomas O'Neill Russell. ' Patrick ' may be the Patrick Forde mentioned on 13 June 1891.

6 Patrick Forde was editor of the *Irish World*. Hyde mentions in *Mise agus an Connradh* (pp. 44, 45) that Forde was a good Irishman in his own way, but his interest was in politics and not in the language. He says of the meeting recorded above : ' O'Donovan Rossa and I spent most of a day with him and I think we softened him ' (i.e., influenced him in favour of the language movement).

7 The controversy about the O'Shea divorce and Parnell's marriage (at Steyning near Brighton on 25 June 1891) was widely reported in the Irish-American papers. See the *Irish World* (New York) of the period for some of the most bitter anti-Parnell invective.

8 Charlotte Grace O'Brien, the daughter of William Smith O'Brien, leader of the Young Ireland insurrection of 1848. Born in Cahirmoyle, County Limerick, in 1845. She was the author of a novel, *Light and Shade,* which was very well received by literary critics even of such publications as the *Spectator,* the *Athenaeum* and the *Guardian,* and several poems. She deserves to be remembered by the Irish people for the work she did to relieve the material and spiritual misery of poor women and girl emigrants to America after the famine. In middle age she became totally deaf.

Mary Ellen Spring Rice (1880-1924), the heroine of the Howth gun-running, would have been only eleven years old at this time. The lady here referred to may have been an aunt. For the diary of Mary Ellen

Spring Rice see *The Howth Gun-running,* edited by F. X. Martin, O.S.A., Dublin, 1964.

9 Sir Stephen de Vere, second son of Sir Aubrey de Vere. Called to the Irish Bar in 1836; M.P. for Limerick 1854-1859. He published *The Odes of Horace* (London, 1893) and also wrote a good deal of original verse. He succeeded to the baronetcy in 1880.

10 Hyde became very friendly with this Miss Butcher, sister-in-law of Lord Monteagle. It was at her invitation that he visited Cambridge in February 1892, where he spent three days as guest of the Protheros, with whom Miss Butcher was then staying. Among those he met on this occasion were Miss Clough, niece of the poet, at Newnham; Hume Smith, a scientist; and Headlam, a young Greek scholar.

11 W. B. Yeats, *Collected Poems* (1965), p. 107. For interesting examples of Hyde in his role as 'the country squire' see 'Douglas Hyde' by Myles Dillon, in *The Shaping of Modern Ireland,* edited by Conor Cruise O'Brien. London, 1960.

12 For a note on Fr O'Growney see chapter VI.

13 Alan Wade, ed., *The Letters of W. B. Yeats,* p. 201.

14 'i bhfocair Tim O h-Éilidhe bradach acht gan caint leis'. This hostile reference is probably due to Mr Healy's stand against Parnell, whom Hyde admired to the end.

15 The rest of the entry is in English, evidently because Hyde wished to make as exact as possible a record of Sir Charles Gavan Duffy's remarks. The only other occasion—for several years—when Hyde used English is to record a resolution passed at a meeting of the committee of the society on 27 February 1893.

    The Mansion House is the official residence of the Lord Mayor of Dublin. Rooms may be hired for meetings such as this one.

16 'The Library of Ireland' was a series of twenty-two volumes of history and literature written by the Young Irelanders and published, one volume per month, by James Duffy. For a brief account of the series see 'The Library of Ireland' by P. S. O'Hegarty, in *Thomas Davis and Young Ireland.* Dublin, The Stationery Office, 1945.

17 Charles Gavan Duffy, *Young Ireland.* London, 1880, two vols. Dublin, 1884 ('Irish People's Edition'), two vols.

18 The rest of this entry, though not related to the National Literary Society, is of interest: 'Went at about 10.30 to the Contemporary. It was a Ladies Night. Sir Charles too tired to come. Mrs Coffey, Miss Purser, Mrs Hogg, Miss Hayden, etc., there. The most important man was Sydney Webb, Fabian essayist & organiser of the London County Council's Liberal victory. He affirmed Gladstone was the greatest conservative force in England, the only thing that prevented the radicals & socialists from having their way, for nothing could be done while he lived. Thousands & thousands of socialistic working men, he said, had at the last election voted against the Liberals because they wanted to teach them a lesson & had, as they thought, more to get from the Tories who had passed all the remedial legislation of the last few years. Unless they "nobbed the Liberal party" there was great fear of their doing the same again "only more so". Home at 2.30.'

19 Hyde does not state at what meeting he became president, nor does he mention any meeting in the meantime. It would seem, however, that the election took place in late July or early August. In a letter to John O'Leary

written (Alan Wade believes) during the week ending 23 July 1892, Yeats says: ' The meeting on Monday is not our inaugural meeting but the general meeting of members to nominate President, Vice-President, Committee etc and to adopt the rules. You will I believe be elected President while Father Finlay, Dr Sigerson, Count Plunkett, Ashe King, Father Dennis Murphy, Douglas Hyde and Gavan Duffy will be put forward for election as Vice Presidents. There is I admit a certain difficulty in putting up Gavan Duffy as one of several Vice Presidents but it is inevitable. He is coming over in his own words "to consult with our committee " and he can only do this properly by being on that committee. We could hardly put him on in any other way than as Vice President. Finlay and Donovan are afraid of your Presidency and so we put on, as you see, a fair number of Federationists.

The Inaugural meeting will be in the second week in August probably at the Antient Concert Rooms. Sigerson agrees to give the address.'

Yeats would of course have welcomed the election of John O'Leary as President; he would have been sure of O'Leary's backing for his scheme, and his support against Gavan Duffy. In fact, when the row broke out, he was disappointed with O'Leary's attitude. '. . . O'Leary's support was capricious, for, being but a spectator of life, he would desert me if I used a bad argument, and would not return till I found a good one; and our chairman, Dr Hyde, "most popular of men ", sat dreaming of his old white cockatoo in far-away Roscommon.' (*Autobiographies*, p. 227.)

20 Sir Charles Gavan Duffy (1816-1903). Founder and first editor of the *Nation;* Young Ireland leader; several times arrested and tried for treason, released after nine months when successive juries failed to agree. Went to Australia in 1855 and soon became prominent in politics: Prime Minister of Victoria in 1871; knighted in 1873. He was first president of the Irish Literary Society (London), 1892. Finally he retired to Nice, where he died.

21 ' Oisín after the Fianna ', an Irish saying based on the legend of Oisin's return to Ireland after three hundred years in the Land of Youth, to find all his comrades vanished.

22 From a profile of W. B. Yeats in the series ' From a Modern Irish Portrait Gallery ' in the *New Ireland Review* (the anonymous writer is outrageously biassed against Gavan Duffy): ' When Yeats and his young friends were fairly on their forward track, Sir Charles came on the scene, eager to rule, glad to be didactic, proud to play the part of literary potentate, but as the event proved, powerless any longer to inspire . . . . To give Sir Charles his due, he played the part of dictator with great boldness and vigour for a time, and had the satisfaction of seeing that the number of people who were ready to trot to the crack of the Nice whip was surprisingly great. But the end was collapse.' (See also the letter ' Kleinbier, the poet ' in subsequent ' Correspondence '.)

23 ' Diabhal a leithid chonnaic me ariamh acht tháinig mise saor as gan buille ar bith buidheachas le Dia.'

How literally one is interpret this I do not know. The implication is that they came to blows.

24 In effect it was Yeats and O'Leary against Taylor and Sigerson. Yeats's side of the story is given in *Ireland after Parnell (Autobiographies*, 1966, pp. 199-233) and in his *Letters* (ed. Wade, 1954, pp. 199-227). ' When I look back upon my Irish propaganda of those years I can see little but its bitter-

ness,' Yeats writes thirty years later. How deep the bitterness was on his side may be gauged from his petulant description of Dr Sigerson as ' learned, artificial, unscholarly, a typical provincial celebrity, but a friendly man.' John F. Taylor is summed up as ' like a man under a curse, compelled to hide his genius, and compelled to show in conspicuous places his ill-judgement and his temper.'

25 ' Rolleston and D. Hyde.' Rolleston represented the London Society, Hyde the Dublin group.

26 Standish O'Grady, *The Bog of Stars,* a collection of tales set in the Ireland of Elizabethan times, was the second volume of the ' New Irish Library '.

27 This quotation and the brief one preceding it are from *Autobiographies* (1966), p. 200.

28 It is interesting to compare this on-the-spot account of the evening with that which Hyde gives in *Mise agus an Connradh,* pp. 34, 35. There he says he went straight to the Contemporary Club from the lecture hall. In fact, the Club met the following night, Saturday 26 November, and the members were addressed by Blake, a Canadian minister, on Gladstone's new bill.

29 References in diary.

30 ' On the whole, our place names have been treated with about the same respect as if they were the names of a savage tribe which had never before been reduced to writing, and with about the same intelligence and contempt as vulgar English squatters treat the topographical nomenclature of the Red Indians.'

31 See *Mise agus an Connradh,* pp. 34, 35, where Hyde says that the first impressions of some of his listeners, and even of his fellow-members of the Contemporary Club, were that he was talking nonsense.

32 Two speeches of Gavan Duffy to the London Society and Sigerson's inaugural lecture in Dublin. Published by Fisher Unwin, 1893.

33 Denny Lane had been a prominent Young Ireland leader. He spent four months in prison, after which he was released without trial. He was president of the Cork Literary and Scientific Society, chairman of two local railway companies and managing director of the Cork Gas Company. He had a couple of poems published in the *Nation.*

At this meeting his theme was that if Ireland must have a foreign language imposed on her, he would wish for none other than the English language, the precious key that unlocked the treasures of the ages from Chaucer and Shakespeare to their own times. Hyde however repeated his call for the de-Anglicization of Ireland. (See *Mise agus an Connradh,* p. 35.)

34 Miss Jane Barlow was the daughter of the Reverend J. W. Barlow, Vice-Provost of Trinity College, Dublin. She lived almost as a recluse at The Cottage, Raheny, Dublin, but her work in prose and verse all treats of Irish country life. Yeats says of her (*The Bookman,* August 1895): ' She is master over the circumstances of peasant life, and has observed with a delightful care no Irish writer has equalled, the coming and going of hens and chickens on the doorstep, the gossiping of old women over their tea, the hiding of children under the shadow of the thorn trees, the broken and decaying thatch of the cabins, and the great brown stretches of bogland; but seems to know nothing of the exultant and passionate life Carleton celebrated, or to shrink from its roughness and its tumult.' She published *Bogland Studies, Irish Idylls, Kerrigan's Quality, A Creel of Irish Stories,* etc, etc.

35 Alfred Perceval Graves was Secretary of the Irish Literary Society. He was a prolific poet, his most popular poem being ' Fr O'Flynn '. Mrs Sophie Bryant and Sir W. Wilde were prominent members of the society.

36 The Reverend Stopford Augustus Brooke, LL.D., was born at Letterkenny, County Donegal, in 1832. He was a graduate of TCD, was ordained in 1857, but seceded from the Church of England in 1880 and became a Unitarian. He was a noted preacher, and attracted people of various shades of religious opinion to his church, Bedford Chapel, Bloomsbury. With T. W. Rolleston he edited *A Treasury of Irish Poetry* (1900) which in its time was regarded as the standard work in Anglo-Irish anthologies. W. B. Yeats, Lionel Johnson, A. P. Graves, Douglas Hyde and George Sigerson contributed introductory notices to selections from the various poets.

37 Bader was Hyde's consultant oculist in London.

38 Francis A. Fahy, a County Galway man, entered the Civil Service in London in 1873. He was a prominent member of the Southwark Irish Club, forerunner of the Irish Literary Society. He wrote some songs that became very popular: ' The Donovans ', ' Irish Molly O ' and ' The Ould Plaid Shawl '.

39 The National League was one of the many political organizations of the period. It had local branches, which sent delegates to county conventions, which in turn elected thirty-two members of a forty-eight-member Central Council. The sixteen other members were chosen by the nationalist parliamentary group.

40 ' Fraulein Kurtz, cailín do phioc Annette suas i gCiarruidhe '.

41 On 20 June 1892 he has the entry: ' THE FRENCHS LEFT RATRA, and it was a great loss to us.' John French, brother of Lord de Freyne, had been a close friend of Douglas's, and a regular fowling companion. The house had been vacant in the meantime. Hyde lived there for many years; eventually it was bought and presented to him in recognition of his work for the nation. Years later again when Hyde had finished his term as President of Ireland he retired to a lodge in the Phoenix Park which he renamed ' Ratra '.

42 ' Cuir me 5 leabhracha go daoinibh '. These could possibly be presentation copies of his *Love Songs of Connacht*. He doesn't mention the actual date of its publication; it was, of course, 1893.

43 ' Chaith me an oidhche i rumaibh droch-blasta droch-bhalbhacha Mhic Cathmhaoil i Sráid Phádraig. . .' It is interesting that in quoting this entry in *Mise agus an Connradh* Hyde omits the adjectives.

P. J. McCall, born in Dublin in 1861, published two volumes of verse: *Irish Noinins* (daisies), 1894, and *Songs of Erinn*, 1899.

44 At Nice they had lunch with Sir Charles Gavan Duffy and his three daughters. Hyde found Sir Charles looking fit and well, and, in the midst of his Irish narrative, he quotes a statement of the old man on the current political scene in Ireland: ' By God, if this bill passed we'd have a new Tipperary Government.'

45 A folktale which appears in Hyde's literal translation in Yeats's *Fairy and Folk Tales of the Irish Peasantry*.

46 The following year he resigned his presidency of the National Literary Society and was succeeded by his friend George Sigerson who held the office for over twenty years.

47 W. P. Ryan, *The Pope's Green Island*. London, 1912, p. 55.

48 L. Paul-Dubois, *Contemporary Ireland*. Translated with an introduction by
    T. M. Kettle, M.P. Dublin and New York, 1908, pp. 401 ff.
49 There were, of course, exceptions: people such as J. P. Mahaffy of TCD,
    who fumed in the pages of *The Nineteenth Century* about 'the Modern
    Babel', November 1896 (' Is there to be no limit to this absurdity? . . .') and
    'The Recent Fuss about the Irish Language', August 1899, ('. . . we may
    possibly [though not probably] have a serious recrudescence of Irish speak-
    ing, which will have even worse effects than the maintenance and cultiva-
    tion of Welsh in Wales . . .')
50 *Contemporary Ireland*, p. 407. An example of extravagant optimism inspired
    by the Gaelic League is quoted in *The Pope's Green Island*, p. 44. Miss M.
    C. Dobbs, ' a well-known Ulster Protestant worker', writes: ' That the
    Gaelic League is one of the outer signs of an inward rebirth of Ireland
    I have not the slightest doubt. That there is no limit to what Ireland may
    do in the future under the impulse of this inspiration I have not the
    slightest doubt either. . . .But it is my sincere hope that whatever work lies
    before us we Protestants will be found to have played no mean part therein.'
51 From an unpublished letter from Hannay to Hyde (15 April 1907), in the
    possession of Captain MacGlinchey.